HISTORY IN FINANCIAL TIMES

CURRENCIES

New Thinking for Financial Times

Melinda Cooper and Martijn Konings, Editors

History in
Financial Times

AMIN SAMMAN

Stanford University Press
Stanford, California

STANFORD UNIVERSITY PRESS
Stanford, California

© 2019 by the Board of Trustees of the Leland Stanford Junior University.
All rights reserved.

This book has been partially underwritten by the Stanford Authors Fund. We are grateful to the Fund for its support of scholarship by first-time authors. For more information, please see www.sup.org/authorsfund

Printed in the United States of America on acid-free, archival-quality paper

Library of Congress Cataloging-in-Publication Data

Names: Samman, Amin, author.
Title: History in financial times / Amin Samman.
Description: Stanford, California : Stanford University Press, 2019. |
Series: Currencies : new thinking for financial times | Includes bibliographical references and index.
Identifiers: LCCN 2018047675 (print) | LCCN 2018050876 (ebook) | ISBN 9781503609464 | ISBN 9781503608900 (cloth : alk. paper) | ISBN 9781503609457 (pbk. : alk. paper)
Subjects: LCSH: Finance—History. | Financial crises—History. | Global Financial Crisis, 2008-2009. | History—Philosophy. | Economics—Philosophy.
Classification: LCC HG171 (ebook) | LCC HG171 .S26 2019 (print) | DDC 332.09—dc23
LC record available at https://lccn.loc.gov/2018047675

Cover design: Michel Vrana | Black Eye Design

Contents

Preface

Finance is a notoriously abstract business and we all encounter it in different ways. For my part, I have experienced the abstraction of financial crisis three times. The first was the East Asian crisis of 1997–1998. As a fourteen-year-old growing up in Hong Kong, I spent my weekends skateboarding under the shadow of Norman Foster's HSBC building. When the crisis hit it was all over the news, but I went on as if nothing had happened—or at least I did, until a question occurred to me: Is this what they call history? A few years later came the dot-com crash, in 2000. This time I was more clued in, reading books about the Enron and WorldCom scandals, yet my experience of this new episode had the memory of the last one folded into it: Is this what the financial system does? I asked myself. Next came the global financial crisis of 2008. I was about to begin a doctoral thesis on how the meaning of the Asian crisis had changed over time, only now I found that episode taking on yet another shape as a new crisis unfurled around me. But this time, the Asian crisis didn't just return to me; it also returned, along with a parade of other past crises, to those who wrote about it in so many newspapers, books, and academic journals. Finding an echo of my thought process out there in the world brought with it a new question: Might this strange looping of events not tell us something important about the logics of financial history? This book is my attempt at an answer.

The conventional view of economic history, financial or otherwise, is that it moves forward on the back of time's arrow. Joan Robinson was the first to put it in these terms, in one of her many scathing critiques of neoclassical economics. The problem, according to Robinson, was that orthodox economists had no conception whatsoever of structural change. By imagining the market as a kind of perpetual balancing mechanism, they had lost sight of economy's developmental character. Her response was to advance a set of interrelated claims about time and history. First, the economic process was historical. Second, the historical process entailed a particular temporality. And third, historical time was irreversible. The result was an image of history in which the progressive character of time carried economic systems forward through a series of states, stages, or phases—hence time's arrow.

Robinson's position is now so accepted that it is rarely commented on. But when it comes to thinking historically, something important gets lost when we deploy the image of time's arrow. Rather than simply flying forward, time also folds back on itself, taking shape through the cultural memories and imagined pasts that circulate within any one present. This is the reflexive, nonlinear aspect of temporal experience I attempted to illustrate in autobiographical terms. With it comes the suggestion of an altogether different way of theorizing the relation between time and history. If historical time cannot be reduced to chronological time, then the developmental process of history becomes scrambled. The present doesn't slip into the past so that a future might take its place; the past suffuses the present, providing many different routes back to the future. That is the key contention of this book. What we normally think of as 'history' is neither a simple process of linear development nor a neutral means of recording such change over time; it is a nonlinear and reflexive process, in which the presence of the past performs an extraordinarily productive role.

One of the biggest difficulties in writing this book has been finding effective terminology. There is an inescapable ambiguity surrounding the term *history*, but as is so often the case, there are good reasons to stick with the problem rather than go around it. In my case, the book deals with modes of temporal experience that are intimately tied to the discipline of history—time through the lens of historical discourse, rather than time in general. It also seeks to establish a link between this particular coupling of time and history and the referent of historical discourse, typically understood in terms of historical change or development. In other words, this is a book about how the historical process feeds on the discourse of history. There is not yet a satisfactory way of speaking about this broader, recursive process. For better or worse, I am describing it here as a quasi-history that takes shape through strange loops—a strange history.

A loop is a form of feedback in which the outputs of a process are available as inputs back into it; a strange loop is one that crosses boundaries between the imaginary and the real. Douglas Hofstadter develops this idea in his book, *I Am a Strange Loop*, which deals with the question of human consciousness.[1] By employing various analogies and metaphors, Hofstadter attempts to illustrate the role of these cognitive devices in the very constitution of subjectivity, inviting us to understand "the I" as a real abstraction that somehow pulls itself up by its own bootstraps—an impossible and incessant loop that feeds through the physical and symbolic levels of the brain. This book aims to develop an account of contemporary history premised on a similar kind of process. I focus on various aspects of what could be loosely termed the symbolic dimension of financial history, ranging from the use of concepts and narrative archetypes to the circulation of past events and proper names, but my basic argument is that these are all of material significance to the historical process of economy. The result, I hope, is a glimpse into the way we imagine and produce history in financial times.

Acknowledgments

I should begin by thanking my mentors, André Broome and Ronen Palan, who provided valuable advice and support during my time at the University of Birmingham, as well as David Bailey and Bob Jessop, for helping shape my early thoughts on the themes explored in this book. Since joining City, University of London, I have had the pleasure of working alongside a vibrant team of political economy scholars, including Florence Dafe, Jean-Christophe Graz, Sandy Hager, Anush Kapadia, Photis Lysandrou, Richard Murphy, Anastasia Nesvetailova, Stefano Pagliari, Herman Schwartz, Stefano Sgambati, and Nick Srnicek. Each helped in some way to bring this book to fruition, as did a much wider network of colleagues whose names are too numerous to list in full. Having said that, I do want to express my appreciation to Nathan Coombs, Andrew Futter, and Liam Stanley for their camaraderie; to Earl Gammon and Samuel Knafo for their ongoing interest in my work; and to a broader group of fellow travelers for helping expand my notion of what constitutes political economy analysis, including Jacqueline Best, James Brassett, Benjamin Braun, Angus Cameron, Christopher Clarke, Marieke de Goede, Juanita Elias, Penny Griffin, Johnna Montgomerie, and Lena Rethel. I also thank Mark Blum and the late Hayden White for their correspondence on matters relating to the theory and philosophy of history, and Nina Boy for introducing me to the economic sociology scene in

Germany, where I made and consolidated many friendships, including with Oliver Kessler, Kai Koddenbrock, Andreas Langenohl, Ute Tellmann, Timo Walter, Leon Wansleben, and Benjamin Wilhelm. There are others too who deserve mention, whether for good advice or good company, including Ole Bjerg, Michael Bloomfield, Paul Crosthwaite, Daniela Gabor, Joyce Goggin, Peter Knight, Phoebe Moore, Leonard Seabrooke, and Noam Yuran. In addition, I would be remiss not to acknowledge the counsel of Martijn Konings, who has been a reliable source of advice in a personal capacity and through the input he and Melinda Cooper provided in their roles as series editors, as well as Emily-Jane Cohen and Faith Wilson Stein at Stanford University Press, who have been swift and thoughtful in all commentary and correspondence. Finally, I am indebted, as are all writers I imagine, to a support network closer to home. I thank my parents for making this all possible; my two brothers for keeping me on my toes; my bandmates for providing a welcome distraction; and my wife, Elke, for refusing to suffer fools gladly.

HISTORY IN FINANCIAL TIMES

INTRODUCTION

"We Live in Financial Times"

In April 2007, the 'Financial Times' introduced a new format for its printed editions in the United Kingdom, Europe, Asia, and North America. To accompany the redesign, it launched a global branding campaign around three flagship images. One featured a series of great white sharks of different sizes, the smaller being swallowed up by the larger. The caption ran "Mergers and Acquisitions." Another depicted "World Business" in the form of an imaginary island state whose skyline included recognizable business buildings from across the world: the New York Stock Exchange, Commerzbank Tower in Frankfurt, the Gherkin in London, and Hong Kong's IFC 2, among others. The third image, "Business Revolutionaries," featured Virgin Group CEO Richard Branson's face incorporated into the iconic red and black portrait of Che Guevara. All three carried the same slogan: "We live in financial times."

To a certain extent this is unremarkable—just another marketing exercise of the kind we've seen before and will see again. In hindsight, however, the campaign has acquired a different, and deeper, kind of significance. The pithy slogan and surreal images evoke the spirit of the late 2000s, celebrating the ceaseless dynamism and compression of space-time that many thought characterized the era. Yet they now also suggest a later puncturing of these very myths. As one columnist tells it, looking back on their time at the newspaper, "The free-market model engulfing the US and European economies seemed untouchable as the West enjoyed the fruits of global wealth. Then came the collapse of Lehman Brothers in September 2008 and our certainties were rocked."[1] The crisis that followed struck a mortal blow to the manifest destiny of liberal finance, replacing a seemingly self-evident assertion—"we live in financial times"—with a series of searching questions about the evolution of financial markets, their recurring bouts of instability, and the challenges these pose to existing modes of financial governance. For newspapers like the *Financial Times*, which took a reformist turn after 2008, such questions were primarily engaged as technical problems for regulators and policymakers. Elsewhere a more classically liberal focus on the automatic adjustment and regeneration of markets was maintained. But beyond the familiar oppositions between state and market or left and right, these questions also revealed a new and radical uncertainty about the logics of economic and political change, about the kind of present these had produced, and about the possible futures that might be forged through such a moment. In this sense, the questions unleashed by the events of 2008 belong as much to the domain of what used to be called the philosophy of history as they do the field of economics.

The aim of this book is to elaborate and enact a philosophy of history fit for the world of contemporary global finance. In some ways, this is an untimely move. The age of neoliberalism is often thought to correspond with an extinguishing of history by economics, such that everything appears and is administered through the logics of investment, appreciation, and growth.[2] And yet try as we might to banish the big questions, "we remain haunted by history, returning ever and again to the big story" about where we are, how we got here, and what comes next.[3] This is especially so when conventional wisdoms lose their power, as they did for those employed in the financial sector during 2007–2008. Faced with a sudden deterioration of the market for US mortgages and related securities, investors and fund managers were left "reaching for the history books."[4] Politicians, technocrats, and journalists too scrambled around for clues and lessons in the past, while scholars from various disciplines began the slower work of putting the meltdown of 2008 in a longer, explicitly historical perspective. "How," the now familiar question has it, "did the world arrive at the brink of financial collapse?"

One popular response charts a transformation from simple economies of exchange into a globally integrated, abstract, and self-referential economy of financial claims in which more money is produced than can ever be spent. This is the narrative of runaway finance, and it has proved influential across the humanities and social sciences.[5] Another response, which has its roots in anthropology and heterodox economic thought, tells us that economic action is always more than it seems—that economic practices partake in a ritual reproduction of social order, and that this is even so in the futuristic economies of high-tech finance. This is the narrative of finance as a crypto-mythological regime of power.[6] Neither narrative alone can do justice to the mysteries of contemporary finance. Somewhere between the autonomy of financial operations and the deep embeddedness of finance in society is a zone where these two logics commingle—where the endless frontiers of financial capitalism are met by the hopes and fears of *homo historia*, that peculiar creature who thinks and acts through the discourse of history. This is a book about what happens in that zone. It is a book about the historical names, concepts, and archetypes that suffuse the present and the peculiar ways these enroll us into the evolving economies of contemporary finance. In short, it is a book about how we imagine and produce history in financial times.

In this sense, a key premise of the book is that the crisis of 2008 was more than a breakdown in the functioning of financial markets and their regulation. It was also, and perhaps more fundamentally, a breakdown in the language that economics provides, which has proved unable to grasp the crucial functions that history is called on to perform in contemporary life. In particular, the economic imagination remains wedded to simplistic conceptions of time that obscure the reflexive, nonlinear character of history in its developmental aspect. This is evident across a wide range of traditions in economic thought, albeit in different ways. The case of conventional economics is the most straightforward. Building on developments in early physics, classical thinkers like Adam Smith imagined a kind of cosmic mechanics at work behind the earthly activities of production, exchange, and consumption. Modern economists then moved to formalize this idea using the tools of statistical mechanics, ascribing analogous laws of motion, limits, and distributional properties first to commodity markets and then to financial ones.[7] The result has been a set of models in which time figures as a mere medium for processes of market adjustment. This is a purely logical conception of time, derived from the model world rather than world history. It continues to form the basis for neoclassical economics and finance theory in particular.

Unsurprisingly, heterodox theorists have long cast this as the Achilles heel of conventional economics. Karl Marx, for example, was highly critical of Smith and other classical thinkers for mystifying the origins of capitalism, while Thorstein Veblen, Maynard Keynes, and Karl Polanyi sought to push beyond the neoclassical framework, exploring novel aspects of economy as it operated in the late nineteenth and early twentieth centuries. Despite their numerous differences, these critical thinkers all worked with a broadly modern, scientific image of time premised on the worldview of the clock, leading them to theorize not only markets in general but also the way specific market economies evolved over decades and centuries. Today, a chronological conception of time serves as the bedrock principle for any self-consciously historical form of economics. This can be traced back to a set of midcentury debates over the role of time in neoclassical theory, to which Keynes and a number of his contemporaries made decisive contributions. It was Joan Robinson, however, who first explicitly framed the question of economic time in terms of 'history.'[8] According to Robinson, the logical time of equilibrium was at odds with the irreversible character of historical time, which manifested as "an ever-moving break between the irrevocable past and the unknown future."[9] "'Today' is at the front edge of time," she wrote. "It moves continuously forward with an ever lengthening past behind it."[10] Rather than wishing this fact of life away, the task facing the historical economist, as Robinson saw it, was to mediate between a set past and an uncertain future—to sift through the travel logs of history, reconstructing its causal logics and using these to make predictions about where it might lead us next. "History," as Hyman Minsky once put it, "is an input to theory formation."[11] Few others have been so explicit as the post-Keynesians, but Robinson's guidelines for historical research are upheld across a wide range of political economy approaches, including those associated with Marxist and institutional economics.[12]

As far as assumptions go, there are good things to be said about the idea that history flies forward on the back of time's arrow. It is, for example, a perfectly reasonable way of grappling with chains of cause and effect. Did the subprime crisis cause a shift in practices of financial regulation? Are there broader patterns in the relationship between financial crisis and regulatory change that can be inferred from the historical record? Such questions can be answered by equating historical time with chronological time—but at what cost? This book argues that the linear, essentialist conception of time misses something crucial about the dynamics of contemporary capitalism. Time may seem to flow in one direction (when we follow the movements of the stock markets, for example), but often the sequence is scrambled. Sometimes time folds back on itself, such that the present takes shape through a vista of imagined pasts and projected futures (we remember the Great Depression, or we spy another on the horizon). This is the reflexive, nonlinear aspect of temporal experience, and it is central to the character of historical time. Historical time emerges through the historical imagination. That is what makes it historical.

All this has consequences for what we usually think of as history itself, because it opens up a series of strange loops between the historical imagination and the developmental aspects of history as a process. The future can act on the present, for example, through different modes of anticipation. By formatting the expectations held by public and private agents, these can shape the patterns of order that emerge from the economic process. This is fast becoming a key theme for cutting-edge research in economic sociology, cultural economy, and the new field of finance and society studies.[13] Less acknowledged are the strange loops between present and past. These consist of a recursive action of the past on the present. Rather than each present leaving a set past behind it, the past circulates within the present as an evolving repertoire of abstract patterns—names, concepts, archetypes, and so on, all drawn from the recorded past and our efforts to give it order. These patterns are best viewed not as real historical legacies, but instead as vectors of the historical imagination—specifically modern modes of organizing temporal experience that derive their power from the discourse of history and our familiarity with it. The result is a quasi-historical process—a *strange history*—in which the recollected past shapes the way we apprehend and negotiate the present.

The aim of this book is to elaborate such a process in the context of contemporary financial capitalism. By way of introduction, this chapter brings questions of time and history to bear on contemporary finance in three ways. First, it emphasizes how historical discourse has produced an enduring mode of subjectivity distinct to the one associated with economic discourse. Second, it reflects on the way contemporary narratives of financialization bespeak a desire more properly belonging to the domain of history than that of either economy or finance. Finally, it positions my approach within the theory and philosophy of history, distinguishing the logic of the strange loop from contextualist and genealogical approaches to historical study, then briefly outlining the arguments put forward in each of the subsequent chapters.

Homo Economicus and Homo Historia

"The hedonistic conception of man is that of a lightning calculator of pleasures and pains, who oscillates like a homogeneous globule of desire of happiness under the impulse of stimuli that shift him about the area, but leave him intact. He has neither antecedent nor consequence."[14] So wrote Veblen in 1898, putting his finger on the anemic character of the human imagined by economists. His is among the more colorful critiques of this kind, but by no means the first or the last. For as long as there has been a concept of the economic, there has been a conception of the human in keeping with this, and as economists have coalesced around a set of assumptions about human behavior, the name *homo economicus* has become shorthand for these. Proponents of the figure emphasize its status as a theoretical construct, while its detractors have typically underlined how it fails to do justice to the complexity of human motivation. In recent decades, however, critical attention has turned from the theoretical to the practical significance of homo economicus, and in particular, to how the figure works to produce subjects in its own image. With this comes a sense that economic (or indeed financial) considerations are emerging as the governing rationality of contemporary life.

The key reference point in this regard is the work of Michel Foucault, whose late lectures in *The Birth of Biopolitics* provide a reading of neoliberalism premised on a transformation in the figure of homo economicus.[15]

Foucault begins by linking a series of claims about human nature in classical economics to a set of principles associated with the liberal art of government, suggesting that the image of the human as a "partner of exchange" (226) was integral to the rise of commercial society in eighteenth-century Europe. He then identifies a theoretical shift by which the human is instead imagined as an "entrepreneur of himself" (226), linking this figure to an emergent neoliberal form of government in the late twentieth century. The result is a broader argument about the practical effects associated with new forms of economic knowledge: "From being the intangible partner of *laissez-faire*, *homo oeconomicus* now becomes the correlate of a governmentality which will act on the environment and systematically modify its variables" (270–71). We can at this point return to Veblen's "homogeneous globule of desire." The contemporary economic subject, according to Foucault, is a subject based on a desire not for utility but productivity, and the "stimuli that shift him about the area" are not simply given but instead are actively produced through governmental practice. This form of intervention positions government within the market process, establishing "a general regulation of society by the market" (145) that distinguishes neoliberal rule from its classical predecessor.

Foucault's analysis has been influential in recent years for a number of reasons. Among these is the stress he puts on overcoming the dichotomy between state and market—a conceptual move that has been borne out by a broad shift toward interventionist policy across a range of market-friendly institutions.[16] Another is the way he theorizes this shift as an economization of state, civil society, and a host of other domains previously thought to be noneconomic in character.[17] This resonates with contemporary fears about the further privatization of public health, the destruction of the university as a place of learning, and a range of other frontline battles against the march of economic reason. It also intersects with growing concerns over the power of finance in society. Indeed for some, the reemergence of global finance constitutes a new phase in the evolution of neoliberal rule, grounded in a further but now all-powerful iteration of homo economicus. This, for example, is the diagnosis that Wendy Brown offers in her book *Undoing the Demos*.[18]

For Brown, the incipient neoliberalism of Foucault's time has been overtaken by a new formation in which finance has displaced industry as the fulcrum of economic growth, and portfolio rather than capital investment has become its anchoring logic. Subjects within this formation are constituted as "self-investing human capital" (83), "relentlessly committed to appreciating [their] own individual value" (102). But the consequence is more than a refiguring of homo economicus in the image of finance. With this, she argues, comes a triumph of homo economicus over other figures of the human. Brown's primary concern is with politics and the democratic imaginary,[19] but her argument opens out onto questions of history and the historical imagination in interesting ways. In particular, she highlights the constitutive opposition through which homo economicus comes into being. "Every image of man is defined against other possibilities—thus, the idea of man as fundamentally economic is drawn against the idea of him as fundamentally political, loving, religious, ethical, social, moral, tribal, or something else." She continues, "Even when one image becomes hegemonic, it carves itself against a range of other possibilities—tacitly arguing with them, keeping them at bay, or subordinating them" (81). It is on this basis that Brown reads the triumph of homo economicus as a triumph over *homo politicus*, tracing the way the latter has shadowed the former through much of modernity, only to be threatened with extinction by a stealth revolution that would reduce man to "a speck of capital" (94). But as we know from psychoanalysis, the act of repression always brings with it the prospect of return, and in this case the return of a figure of the human conceived through the lens of something other than economy or finance. This is one way to read Brown's story about the death of homo politicus: as a call to bring that figure back to life. Here, however, I want to suggest a different reading, organized around the enduring presence of homo historia.

If homo economicus is shadowed or haunted by its others, then from where do these specters emanate? The answer, more or less explicit in both Foucault and Brown, is that these figures are conjured into being through knowledge practices.[20] But if we accept this analysis, then we must consider the possibility that historical knowledge has a role to play in producing and regulating subjectivities. This is straightforwardly so in the sense that a vast body of knowledge and techniques has been built up around the idea of history, taking shape alongside those associated with the idea of economy.

Just as economic discourse can be understood in terms of its practical effects and functions, so too can historical discourse. Indeed, according to Michel de Certeau, this is precisely how we should understand historical discourse—as a technique for producing "a society capable of managing the space it provides for itself."[21] But the point is not to position historical reason as a substitute for economic reason; the latter continually relies on the former in ways it struggles to acknowledge. In particular, there is a sense in which the narrative logic of historical reason works away at the margins or in the background of other discourses, providing a sense of antecedent, trajectory, and possibility that would otherwise be missing from a purely economic or financial perspective. There is, in other words, a way of being, knowing, and governing associated with history that persists despite the apparent economization of everything. Even at its moment of triumph, homo economicus is haunted by homo historia.

So who is homo historia? In simple terms, homo historia is "historical man," or the human conceived through the lens of history (rather than economy, society, and so on). More pointedly, it is a form of subjectivity associated with the operation of historical discourse. The development of this discourse will be taken up at length in Chapter 2, but the upshot is that the machinery of historiography, as de Certeau calls it, presents the subject with a double bind. On the one hand, the narrativity of historical writing provides a sense of orderly succession around which one can orient oneself in the world. But in order for this effect to obtain, one must go on as if each "new" time is separate from the past through which it is imagined. Speaking to this dynamic, Gilles Deleuze and Félix Guattari use the term *homo historia* to designate the kind of subject that comes into being through a mixing up of past and present, future and past.[22] The example they give is the late Friedrich Nietzsche, whose descent into madness is taken to reveal something of the competing demands placed on life by the discourse of history. Both the past and the future are omnipresent, yet one is reminded at every step not to breach the coordinates of linear succession, not to embody and channel the entanglements on which history is itself based. Nietzsche went too far and ended up sobbing on the neck of a horse (or so they say). Here I want to expand the meaning of the term by using *homo historia* as a name for the subject that must somehow negotiate these competing demands; the

subject that seeks solace in historical discourse yet cannot help but do so
by disobeying its rules; the subject that imagines and produces something
called "history" precisely through a mixing up of past, present, and future.

More concretely, the characteristic condition of homo historia is undergirded by a number of distinct affinities and compulsions. One of these is a
backward orientation, which sees the subject of history respond to present
puzzles or dilemmas by looking to the past for guidance. Paul Valéry called
this "historical-mindedness," a kind of impulse that "presents the imagination with a chart of situations and disasters, a gallery of ancestors, a formu-
lary of acts, expressions, attitudes, and decisions, which offer themselves to
our instability and uncertainty in order to help us *to become*."[23] Related to
this is an affinity for the future, which figures as a site of consequence and
meaning for present events and actions. It is to this that Valéry alludes when
he speaks of "becoming," and there are numerous other inflections of the
idea in modern Western philosophy, especially in the so-called continental tradition. Martin Heidegger, for instance, famously saw this temporal
structure as a quality of Being itself rather than a mere cognitive projection
of homo historia. Nevertheless, he also thought that world history and
historical being would be structured around a "from" and a "towards."[24]
Finally, there is the enduring compulsion to repeat the loop just described,
to return to the past and project into the future, over and again, in order to
make sense of it all—"all" meaning here every situation we find ourselves
in; every disaster that befalls us (or indeed others); and every act or decision that surrounds these, stretching from the present back into the past as
far as memory and record will allow. This amounts to a search for rhyme
or reason in the world, driven by the fear that there may well be no such
order beneath the chaos. Homo historia thus bears an uneasy relationship
to the idea of history, which figures as both its wound and salve. Homo
historia does not experience life as a neatly ordered succession of events,
but precisely as a mounting senselessness to which the discourse of history
offers itself as a solution. In this way, there is something of a spiritual dimension to the discourse of history and the work it performs, and this is so
even in our contemporary financial times. If anything, the hopes and fears
of homo historia have been exacerbated by various changes associated with
the "ascendancy of finance."[25]

Homo Historia in Financial Times

To describe contemporary capitalism as financial is to suggest an epochal shift in the relations between finance and other spheres of economic activity. Over the past few decades, it has become common to think of this shift as an ongoing and global process of financialization. A variety of institutional and technological innovations have contributed to this sensibility, ranging from the normalization of paper money and the collapse of the gold standard to the creation of futures markets, the rise of financial derivatives in particular, and the emergence of low-risk monetary substitutes in the form of government bonds and other so-called safe assets.[26] Collectively these changes reveal how financial markets are more than mere markets for loanable funds, suggesting an increasingly complex entanglement of finance and society. The character of this entanglement, however, is not something that can be put to rest by tales of expansive or intensive financialization. Structural categories of historical analysis like "capital" (or indeed "the financial") are means of periodizing history, and as Peter Osborne points out, all efforts at epochal periodization "bespeak a desire for totalization in the medium of cultural experience."[27] This is none other than a desire for the consolations of history, the desire characteristic of homo historia. What concerns me in this book is the way this desire plays out today. Centuries of innovation may have given us an expanding array of currencies, banking operations, and financial instruments, but how do we, as societies that live under the sign of finance, imagine and negotiate our times in specifically historical terms?

To answer this question, we must eschew the usual starting points for critically theorizing the financial, which would have us begin with the money form, the creditor-debtor relation, the circulation of promissory notes, and so on. These are perfectly sensible starting points if one wants to understand the configuration and inner logic of a financial system, or indeed the relations between finance and other subsystems of society (legal, political, and so on). They are less useful, however, if one wants to grasp the means through which it becomes possible to view society in these terms. As we have seen, to the extent that political economy is historical, it tends to be unreflexively so and cannot see the position from which it orders phenomena into a succession of system states, stages, or phases. Homo historia is a device through which to think such operations, rather than an open window onto the system logics they allege to reveal; it is a means to begin mapping the speculative field of historical society, rather than a concept that promises to reveal the thing itself (universal history, history with a capital H, or what have you). With this concept, then, my aim is to begin theorizing the power of historical imagination in a world whose logics far exceed those of both thought and history. What I have in mind is the world of contemporary finance and, in particular, the changes associated with decades of globalization and financialization. These are slippery terms to say the least, but there are a number of ways in which the discourse associated with them betrays the workings of a distinctly historical form of imagination.

One is through a compulsive recourse to the concept of crisis, which has repeatedly been used to understand the collapse of the Bretton Woods system, the reemergence of global finance, and the increasingly frequent bouts of market volatility over the last thirty or so years, stretching back from the Latin American debt crisis of the early 1980s and the Wall Street crash of 1987 to the Mexican crisis of 1995, the East Asian crisis of 1997–1998, and the Argentinian crisis of 2002, all the way up to the North Atlantic financial crisis of 2008. As Reinhart Koselleck reminds us, the concept of crisis is the historical concept par excellence, transforming uncertainty into a sense of momentous decision over which the subject of history presumes to preside.[28] I take up this point in Chapter 1 through an analysis of the concept's deployment by political economists, in which I argue that the history of crisis thinking provides a repertoire of imagined patterns and signal events that feed back into the constitution of the present as a moment of crisis. The turn to crisis is in this way a turn to history and, in particular, a call for it to provide a ground on which to act.

Another symptomatic attachment is to the figure of the cycle, which pervades longer-term accounts of global capitalism. Here I will give just a few indicative examples, beginning with one from the Marxist tradition. In *The Long Twentieth Century*, Giovanni Arrighi advances a cyclical theory of accumulation in which recurrent phases of financial expansion and collapse underpin broader spatial reconfigurations of the world system.[29] Many have since taken up the idea that the moment of finance is "a sign of autumn," marking the last flourish of capital before its death and rebirth in a new spring.[30] The poetics here tell all, revealing a desire for periodicity in the historical world comparable to the kind found in nature—a desire, it should be noted, that seems to obtain no matter whether one longs for a different cycle of seasons. A similar impulse can be found at work in the liberal tradition. Harold James, for example, has written about a "globalization cycle" in which the world economy oscillates back and forth between periods of integration and disintegration.[31] This too belongs to a broader genre of cyclical world histories, suggesting an alternation between good times and bad that typically goes hand-in-hand with ideas about hegemonic rule and taps into a range of deep-seated myths about golden ages and slain saviors.[32] The recovery of these myths reveals a strange continuity between the historical age and its religious predecessors, which, as Mircea Eliade has shown, sought refuge time and again in the ritual repetition of mythical archetypes.[33] Finally, on a somewhat more prosaic level, there are those cyclical patterns associated with slump and recovery, boom and bust, or the buildup of Ponzi-scheme finance. These are more regular patterns, imagined by many economists to bubble away beneath the broader cycles just described.[34]

Each of these different figures of recurrence bears an important relation to crisis thinking, and I discuss their mobilization in contemporary financial discourse in Chapters 3 and 4. Chapter 4 also distinguishes the figure of recurrence from that of revelation, in which the past is called on to help identify new rather than old patterns in financial history. Here, however, I want to return to the broader idea that our financial times constitute a unique chapter in world history and, in particular, to the narrativity of such a vision. I have already alluded to the narrative logic of historical reason, which I take up throughout the book in connection with the concept of crisis and the various figures associated with it. But an affinity for narrative is also a more fundamental characteristic of what I am trying to foreground with the conceptual persona of homo historia, whose attachment to stories is everywhere accompanied by a creeping awareness of their inadequacy before the world. This is evident in the very terms through which the contemporary moment is imagined. Globalization, for example, is not a simple and unmediated process, entailing the tendential integration of previously national markets for goods, services, or indeed capital; it is a process of spatial reorganization whose contours have been shaped by the stories we tell about it. There is a narrative dimension to globalization, even though globalization cannot be entirely reduced to a story, and this is something that globalization narratives struggle to grasp.[35] The same goes for financialization. Like globalization before it, the term has an explicitly narrative character, yielding so many stories of epochal change in the scale and scope of the financial industry. These stories give voice to a fear that finance is escaping the order of history. But at the same time, they affirm a deeper commitment to historical discourse as a means of negotiating our financial times.

This dynamic is most clearly expressed in narratives that posit a progressive "disembedding" or "detachment" of financial markets from other, allegedly more fundamental spheres of economic activity, such as those associated with the production of material goods.[36] These accounts tell us that finance is emerging as an autonomous realm, governed not by human need or agency, but the abstract and self-referential dynamics of prices themselves. History, or so the story goes, is being hijacked, neutralized, or obliterated by a global process of financialization. Yet these same accounts rely on appeals to a bygone era when the "real" economy ruled the roost, and make promises of a time still to come, in which the tables will be turned and financial market logics put back in their place. In this respect, there is something paradoxical about many critical accounts of financialization, which purport to narrate a world in which things are being increasingly stripped of all narrative sensibility. Fredric Jameson put his finger on this when he argued that the return of "finance capital" had to be seen in terms of its aesthetic consequences, as well as its political and economic ones.

According to Jameson, the unshackling of money from production has been accompanied by a transformation in cultural logics analogous to the one undergone by money itself.[37] If money has become more abstract, fungible, and polyvalent, then so too have our modes of representation, which themselves now circulate as so many modular parts on the social body of capital. "Stories tell themselves," as Lyotard once put it; "they are in motion as a matter of principle, and their narrators are only one of their conductive valences."[38] Jameson was especially concerned with transformations of the image, which he saw as taking on new powers in the era of MTV and twenty-four-hour news, but he also thought this had significant consequences for the narrative operation, which would no longer require the stable home of a fully articulated plot. With the cybernetic revolution in global media systems, he argued, narrative fragments had themselves acquired the price-like capacity to "soak up content and to project it in a kind of instant reflex."[39] This argumentation positions Jameson at the tail end of a boom in postmodern historical theory in which contemporary media systems were taken to mark the arrival of a "windless" or "frozen" present. Jean Baudrillard, for example, wrote at length about the undoing of representation, a process of increasing abstraction he saw as culminating in a transformation of the event—previously thought to be the substance of history—into an appearance that "only survive[s] on an artificial effervescence of signs."[40] As we will see in Chapter 3, for Baudrillard this amounts to an exit from history altogether, and in his own way Jameson says something similar, mourning the loss of "real historical time . . . and a history made by human beings."[41] But there is another way of reading these developments—not as a loss of history so much as a strange excess, in which the components of historical discourse come to acquire a new relationship with that they purport to represent, functioning as so many means through which history itself is produced. It is something of irony, then, that Jameson himself provides a call for the kind of theoretical reorientation such a transformation requires. "What is wanted," he concludes, "is an account . . . in which the new deterritorialized postmodern contents are to an older modernist autonomization as global financial speculation is to an older kind of banking and credit or as the stock market frenzies of the 1980s are to the Great Depression."[42] Jameson wrote these words in 1997, before yet another wave of frenzies and a further series of media technology revolutions, but his call for a new cultural theory of finance capitalism still stands: "What we want to be able to theorize is a modification in the very nature of cultural tokens, and the systems they operate in."[43] In this book, I aim to do something similar, linking the cultural logics of finance to a transformation in the nature of historical tokens and the discursive systems through which they circulate. Historical narratives, or fragments thereof, are one such token that will need to be recast in these terms, but there are others too. The concept of crisis, the figures with which it is associated, event names and dates, even proper names—all of these must be rethought as productive inputs into the process we are accustomed to calling "history." What, I will ask, are the different modes of history production embedded in financial discourse, and how do these enroll us into the evolving economies of contemporary finance?

The Strange Loops of Financial History

At this point, we run up against limits to the conventional lexicon for historical analysis, which would have us use just the one word, *history*, in place of *historical imagination*, *historical discourse*, *historical development*, and a whole host of other related terms. Besides fostering confusion, this vagueness works to maintain "the myth that the term *history* designates something real" rather than something that must be imagined and produced.[44] In this book, I proceed from the premise that history is produced not only through the narrative operations of historical writing, as de Certeau and many others have argued at length,[45] but also through a variety of everyday operations undertaken by homo historia. The first is a more obvious point: historians produce historical narratives. These can be decisive in shaping how readers understand the past, as well how they forge broader claims about the meanings or logics of history as such. In this sense, historical discourse shapes the historical imagination as much as it is shaped by it. The second point is more complex, flowing from the range of historical accounts developed by historians over the ages. Rather than being tied to any one period or sequence of events, these accounts form a pool of abstract, imagined patterns that can reappear in any number of later presents. My argument is that such patterns themselves partake in the process that historical writing purports to merely describe or explain, providing individuals and groups with practical means of navigating temporality in specifically historical terms. In this sense, the historical imagination shapes what we usually think of as the process of historical change or development. I am calling this broader, recursive process a "quasi-history" produced through a series of strange loops between past and present—a strange history.

As I noted in the Preface, the concept of the strange loop is drawn from the work of Douglas Hofstadter, for whom it provides a means of grasping the mystery of human consciousness. "One day . . . it dawned on me," he recalls, "that what we call 'consciousness' was a kind of mirage:

It had to be a very peculiar kind of mirage . . . since it was a mirage that perceived itself, and of course it didn't *believe* that it was perceiving a mirage, but no matter—it still *was* a mirage. It was almost as if this slippery phenomenon called "consciousness" lifted itself up by its own bootstraps, almost as if it made itself out of nothing, and then disintegrated back into nothing whenever one looked at it more closely.[46]

If I want to say something similar about history, then it is because the phenomenon is equally slippery, seeming to belong in one moment to the realm of imagination but then immediately asserting itself as a reality in the next. The concept of the strange loop is a way of giving shape or figure to this process, suggesting a form of feedback that makes every attempt to imagine history a potential input back into it. A strange loop, then, is not just a recursive action of the past on the present, such that the present continually takes shape through the past, but also a loop through the abstract patterns of historical discourse, such that these abstractions themselves acquire real force. What this amounts to is precisely a quasi-historical process, wherein the various components of historical discourse serve as so many inputs into the production of what we usually think of as history's process.

There are a number of precedents for this move in the theory and philosophy of history. It is a cornerstone of the German historicist tradition, for example, that the historian is entangled with the present and pressed on by the past in ways that lead to recurring re-creations of history.[47] With the concept of the strange loop, I extend this logic beyond the narrow domain of historians and their readers, suggesting a similar and equally important process that takes place *between* written histories. Hayden White has alluded to this in his writings on "the practical past," which distinguish between the kind of past we all carry around in our heads and the more formal kind cultivated by historians ("the historical past").[48] I discuss White's late writings at various points throughout the book, but here I want to signpost the methodological implications of thinking history through the figure of the strange loop.

First, the logic of the strange loop can be contrasted with the conventional scientific approach to historical study, which equalizes past and present by seeking out covering laws that apply across time. Needless to say, such an approach is unsuited to the kinds of questions I have raised so far. The logic of the strange loop also differs from the contextualist approach to history, as elaborated by thinkers like John Pocock and Quentin Skinner.[49] The defining operation of this method is a return to the past in order to sift through its specific horizons of meaning. To look to the past in this way is to overlook its possible reappearance and reinvention in a later present, which is precisely the kind of dynamic entailed in the concept of the strange loop. Even the genealogical tradition, popularized by Foucault and exemplified in Brown's approach to neoliberalism, aims at something different, looking to the past as a specific kind of precursor to the present.[50] Thinking history through strange loops therefore requires a different approach, oriented not toward the "laws of history," the "truth of the past," or indeed the "history of the present," but the presence of the past, the entanglements of the present, and the way these underpin the very production of what we usually term "history."

In this book, I develop this idea in relation to economy and finance in particular, providing a quasi-historical account of financial capitalism in the contemporary postcrisis era. Rather than sifting through the various factors and processes that might have contributed to the bursting of the subprime bubble, I instead focus on operations in the speculative field of global finance since that time, tracing out the diverse and peculiar modes of history production at work in contemporary financial discourse. Along the way, I draw on an eclectic set of thinkers, ranging from Koselleck and de Certeau to Baudrillard, White, Eliade, and Deleuze, using their ideas to help navigate the spheres of contemporary theory, journalism, policymaking, and popular culture. Throughout, I argue that in each of these spheres, visions and vestiges of the past circulate in ways that shape what becomes of the present. This occurs through a variety of distinct forms and contexts, ranging from the concept of crisis itself to the figural archetypes embedded in public crisis narratives, from the event names or dates around which these narratives cluster, to the proper names and named persona that travel through film. The result, then, will not be an argument about the sustainability or destiny of today's form of financial capitalism. It will be an experimental, mosaic-like portrait of the role that contemporary means of imagining and representing financial history play in the evolution of finance capitalism. In this sense, I have tried to write a book whose form mimics something of the dynamics I see at work in today's world, where theory and practice, fact and fiction, bureaucratic and popular culture, or indeed any of the other "kinds that should not mix" all serve as so many inputs into the strange history of contemporary finance.

The remainder of the book unfolds over five chapters and three broad phases. The first phase consists of two chapters devoted to the conceptual entanglement of crisis and history. Chapter 1 develops a metahistory of the crisis concept, in which I argue that the development of crisis thinking over time has effectively reconfigured the relation between crisis and history, turning the concept of crisis into a means of imagining and producing history. This analysis hinges on the claim that crisis histories possess an indeterminate temporality, which assumes a particular form only through the recursive narration of both crisis and history. The argument is developed in the register of conceptual history, focusing on the evolution of crisis thinking in modern political economy. Chapter 2 follows this idea through onto the terrain of historical thinking more broadly, analyzing a string of controversies regarding the status of writing, fiction, narrative, and the category of the event. Through these, I argue, historical discourse has gradually written a recursive narration of history into the very category of the event, leading it into a terrain where the lines between history's imagined and developmental aspects are well and truly blurred.

The book's second phase consists of two chapters devoted to the public narration of financial history in terms of crisis. In particular, I focus on how received wisdoms about the lessons of prior crises carry over into the present as figural archetypes for imagining and producing particular kinds of histories. Chapter 3 does so by analyzing the status of the Great Depression within journalistic coverage of the subprime crisis. Here I show how the idea of the Great Depression served as a vector for the production of competing crisis histories, transmitting the figure of historical recurrence through time but doing so in diverse ways, yielding a shifting panorama of history on the cusp of repeating itself. In this way, I argue, past events can be integral to the routine diagnosis and treatment of contemporary crisis, providing a set of patterns on which to place the present within a history of familiar twists and turns. Chapter 4 undertakes a similar analysis, this time focusing on the discursive work of a global cadre of crisis managers in central banks, treasury departments, and international financial organizations. Rather than recurrence alone, past crises here also transmit an archetype of revelation, in which events like the Great Depression and the Asian crisis are taken to uncover new patterns in economic and political history, as well as new practical means through which crises might be better managed in the future. This analysis highlights how appeals to financial history can produce more than the simple threat that it might repeat itself. Through the archetype of revelation, I argue, past events can transform even the most unforeseen of occurrences into a filling out of some long-latent destiny. When this happens, the past functions as a means of reinventing rather than simply reproducing existing modes of crisis management. Who (or what) crisis management is ultimately good for thus emerges as a crucial question for our crisis-riddled times.

The book then moves away from insider discourse on financial history and crisis, focusing on the pop-cultural landscape of the postcrisis era. In particular, Chapter 5 looks at three recent films that take finance as their theme and feature an iconic protagonist. Instead of appraising these films on the basis of their realism, the chapter underlines the performative force of the proper name within financial history. Names like "Gordon Gekko," for example, circulate through time across different media types and genres, taking their place alongside the real names, dates, and events of history. As they do, they bring with them patterns of cause and consequence that serve as diagrams for distinct forms of financial conduct. This analysis points to a different mode of history production, premised less on narrative archetypes than the unique power of names themselves. It also raises a series of speculative, ethico-political questions about possible futures for economy, finance, and society. I take up these questions in a brief Afterword that deals directly with the theme of futurity.

CHAPTER 1

Crisis Thinking

The idea of crisis has a long and complex history in the human sciences. Since at least the eighteenth century, it has been the hallmark of Western thought in a historical key, providing philosophers, political theorists, and especially political economists with a means of elaborating the critical junctures or turning points they see as marking the historical process. The paradigmatic example is Marx, whose vision of capitalist crisis helped establish an entire tradition of crisis theorizing in political economy and to whom many have since returned during bouts of economic turbulence. At the same time, the development of crisis theory is a story of divergent strands of thought, contending philosophies of history, and multiple renderings of the relation among past, present, and future. The concept of crisis is in this way a living concept, taking shape and evolving through the circumstances in which it is deployed. It is also a strange concept, intervening into the very process of history it purports to reveal.

The first thinker to grasp this was Reinhart Koselleck, whose conceptual histories of crisis track how the term's uses have varied across space and time.[1] Koselleck was primarily interested in crisis as a category and condition of European modernity, but in order to establish this, he returned to the etymology of crisis, uncovering two foundational ambiguities that invest the modern concept with its power to not just record but also produce history.

The first of these concerns the referent of the term *crisis*, which is typically used to indicate a mixture of danger, uncertainty, and the compulsion to act. Tracing this back to the Greek term *krisis*, which is derived from the verb *krinō*—meaning "to cut, to select, to decide, to judge; [and] by extension, to measure, to quarrel, to fight"—Koselleck reveals how the word itself brings with it a double meaning.[2] *Crisis* refers not only to the simple or objective need for a decision, but also to the intersubjective measuring or quarreling through which a diagnosis might be made and a decision reached. The second ambiguity he identifies concerns the temporal dimensions of crisis. Deciding or judging requires a diagnosis of time, and so crises can acquire a range of temporalities. On the terrain of historical development, this amounts to a radically open historicity for crisis.

Janet Roitman has taken up many of these points in her book *Anti-Crisis*, which brings Koselleck's account of the relation between crisis and modernity to bear on the contemporary narration of financial crisis.[3] *Anti-Crisis* stands out from most other writing on financial crisis precisely because it begins with the significance of crisis-in-and-of-itself, linking crisis to a diagnosis of time and the diagnosis of time to a judgment of history. In Roitman's words, "Crisis is not a thing to be observed . . . it is an observation that produces meaning" (39). But as the title of her book suggests, Roitman also takes crisis thinking to task, casting it as an unnecessary constraint on the conduct of critique. Crisis is an "enabling blind spot" (13), she maintains; it diagnoses time and judges history but cannot see the position from which it does so. This chapter develops an alternative account of crisis thinking and its metahistorical significance, paying particular attention to the way political economists have used the concept to generate competing figurations of economic and financial history.

My starting point is Koselleck's suggestion that the modern historical concept of crisis emerges through a gradual reworking of the term's original meanings within early legal, medical, and religious discourse. Rather than this culminating in a secular or "post-theological mode"[4] of crisis thinking, I emphasize how the concept has continued to evolve through the elaboration of crisis theories by a diverse range of political economy thinkers. Where political economists once saw crises as the expression of objective historical ruptures or thresholds, they now also see the work of subjective interventions and historical myths, projections, or fictions. With this shift, I argue, the ambiguities of the crisis concept become the very object of crisis theorizing. Crises are imagined as events that *agents themselves* take to be turning points within history. The result is a significant reconfiguration of the relation between crisis and history. Crisis thinking no longer simply functions as a means of producing historical knowledge; it is now also a means by which the discourse of history recursively acts on and produces the historical present. This is less a crisis for critique than a challenge to prevailing modes of historical thought, and specifically those that anchor historical change in a linear, essentialist conception of time. The development of crisis theory scrambles both the sequence and substance of history's process, setting up a series of strange feedback loops that put the history of crisis thinking at the very heart of contemporary struggles over financial history. In what follows, I reconstruct this trajectory, beginning with Koselleck's account of the passage from ancient to modern conceptions of crisis, then extending this to cover later developments in economic thought and the way these intersect with contemporary narratives of financial crisis.

Time and Crisis

Without time, there can be no crisis. The etymology of the term tells us this by underscoring the place of crisis within a process that unfolds through time. To cut, select, decide, and judge is to draw a line between past and future, to perceive a present as belonging to a particular pattern of development, and to intervene in such a way as to change what becomes of that present. From its very beginning, however, the term was used in different contexts and applied to a diverse range of processes. This diversity has yielded a variety of temporalities for crisis, which in turn constitute one of modern crisis thinking's primary ambiguities. What kind of moment is a moment of crisis? The short answer is that there is no limit to the ways in which theory can imagine a relation between time and crisis. This, however, hinges on a prior process of semantic evolution that begins in ancient Greece.

According to Koselleck, *krisis* became a concept as it was put to use in the spheres of law, religion, and medicine. The juridical usage came first, reflecting the centrality of the courts to early Greek democracy. In this context, *krisis* as decision meant trial and judgment by a sovereign third party and was central to prevailing conceptions of justice and political order.[5] Before long, this specific legal meaning was extended to cover "electoral decisions, government resolutions, decisions of war and peace, death sentences and exile, the acceptance of official reports, and, above all, government decisions as such."[6] To the extent that such decisions went on one after the other, the juridico-political idea of *krisis* entailed a temporality of linear succession. Each present slips into the past to make way for the next. By contrast, the time of religious *krisis* was nonlinear and entangled, designating an experience in the present of an event that had yet to actually occur. Koselleck traces this back to the first Greek translation of the Old and New Testaments, in which *judgment* meant the one eventually delivered by God.[7] In Christian theology, the Last Judgment is a prophecy: it will arrive for all but nobody knows when. Salvation therefore demands that one obey God's Word in the present, simultaneously anticipating and experiencing a final crisis for humanity. Koselleck calls this a "cosmic foreshortening of time," emphasizing how each present moment is marked by an eternal return of the future.[8] If religious *krisis* is the end of time, then the end of time waits for no one.

These legal and religious ideas of crisis were soon joined by a medical variant, whose distinguishing features were derived from the practical experience of Greek physicians. In particular, the apparent rhythms of the human body and the doctor-patient relationship were key, providing impetus for the development of a more complex figuration of time and crisis. Most sources point back to the writings of Hippocrates, who used *krisis* to denote a critical point or phase in the progression of an illness.[9] The term was then taken up and used by others to describe not only the condition of an illness, but also the judgment or diagnosis of its future course. This double usage was in keeping with the foundational unity of subject and object in the original Greek meaning of the term. In the physiological context, however, it served to amplify the specifically temporal ambiguity of crisis. As a deciding moment in the "battle between life and death," crisis occupied a linear time marked by definitive thresholds.[10] But as a judgment about the course of an illness that would ultimately determine the outcome of this battle, the temporal possibilities were considerably wider. Hippocrates himself identified a range of options when he described a crisis as occurring "whenever . . .

[diseases] increase in intensity or go away or change into another disease or end altogether."[11] Early medical usage of the word therefore entailed a nonlinear and differentiated temporality. In addition to an overarching and diachronic conception of the relation between sickness and health or life and death, the medical notion of *krisis* suggested the possibility of recoveries, relapses, displacements, and mutations.

Generally, the juridico-political usage of *krisis* was progressively folded into theological discussion, while the medical usage was carried forward through collections and translations of the Hippocratic corpus. But as a Latinized form of the word was translated into national languages during the seventeenth century, classical meanings of *krisis* provided the basis for a further extension of the concept into new semantic spheres.[12] The medical variant, for example, dominated early modern social and political thought, where it was applied to the notion of a "body politic" and used to describe moments of upheaval in the internal or external affairs of state.[13] Meanwhile, the eschatological aspects of its religious variant found voice in later, speculative philosophies of history, in which crisis figured as both an ongoing epoch and coming threshold for humankind.[14] It was also in this context that a distinctly economic meaning of the term began to take shape, doing so at first through a medical language of "convulsions" and "blockages."[15] The crucial point, however, is not that ambiguities already implicit in the crisis idea were simply reproduced via its translation into nascent modern disciplines. Rather, it is that these ambiguities were multiplied as new questions about the condition and fate of Western Europe prompted thinkers of the Enlightenment to combine and redeploy earlier notions of crisis in an explicitly historical register.

History and Crisis

When crisis is historicized, history is temporalized. This is why crisis bears such a crucial relation to modern conceptions of progress and critique. Before its entry into the modern lexicon, crisis consisted in times without history (the time of the polis, the time of the cosmos, the time of the body). But with the application of the concept to event names and dates, "time is constituted as historical through crisis."[16] This turns the time of crisis into a means of recognizing, critiquing, and acting on history. It also, however, opens crisis up to a range of historicities. There is no one diagnosis of time that defines the shape of historical crisis. The different times of *krisis* are layered over one another, interacting to produce multiple crisis histories.

This is best exemplified in Jacob Burckhardt's lectures on "The Crises of History."[17] Burckhardt was a Swiss cultural historian who wrote during the mid-nineteenth century. Most famous for his account of the Italian Renaissance, he is typically read as having provided an alternative to the then dominant Prussian school of political history, trading in causal stories of progressive development for static portraits of past grandeur. But Burckhardt was also interested in the mounting sense of epochal change that characterized Europe at the time, and in "The Crises of History" he drew on the full range of available resources for thinking crisis. For our purposes, what is significant about these lectures is the way they lay bare the productive connections between crisis thinking and the historical imagination. Because of his allergy to systematic thought (he is reputed to have once declared, "I will never establish a school!"), Burckhardt ends up pushing the possibilities of modern crisis thinking to their limit.[18]

This is evident in the way his discussion remixes different phases in crisis thinking, combining classical conceptions of crisis with newer ones characteristic of nineteenth-century historical discourse. By using *crisis* to denote a decisive moment capable of transforming the "political and social foundations of the state" (223), Burckhardt retains the double meaning of the original Greek term. Yet when developing it into an explicitly historical concept, he also draws on its more specific uses within early medical and religious discourse. Consider the medical tradition. While most of his examples are of wars and revolutions, Burckhardt frequently employs the language of physiology, likening the consciousness of crisis to a spreading "infection" (226) or "fever" (248). "Something breaks out" (224), he writes, and "all men are suddenly of one mind. . . . *Things must change*" (226, emphasis in original). He also reproduces the pathological dimension of the term by attempting to identify recurrent patterns in the development of crises. Applied to history, however, this diagnostic exercise serves as the basis for a distinction between different periods in world history—life before and after the Crusades, the Reformation, the discovery of America, and so on. An anthropological pathogenesis of crisis thus transforms the concept into a means of periodizing human history.

Burckhardt also engages creatively with the temporality of religious crisis. This is evident in the epochal character he ascribes to "genuine" (as opposed to "incomplete") crises. The former usher in "an absolutely new form of life . . . founded on the destruction of what has gone before" (247), whereas the latter begin with a "deafening clamour" for change but end up yielding none of the "vital transformations" (223) their onset seems to demand. On this basis, Burckhardt is able to diagnose an ongoing age of crisis, wherein a graveyard of aborted crises bequeaths to the future "a great general crisis" (219) not unlike the Last Judgment. Crucially, though, because this crisis-to-come is rooted in an enduring human desire for "great periodical changes" (226), its resolution is not determined in advance but instead posed in the form of an open question onto humanity itself. Crisis therefore names an entire epoch whose time is defined by the pressure for a different future—a secular prophecy of change, only robbed of the telos that would guarantee a fate for the world.

Rather than clearing matters up, these attempts to think history through crisis lead only to more ambiguity. The medical and religious traditions invest *krisis* with a set of specific temporal parameters, but once the idea moves into the conceptual space of history, these are multiplied, and its meaning as an actual occurrence is opened up to a range of seemingly endless possibilities. Crisis compels a decision and thus marks a threshold, but the kinds of conditions or states it provides a passage between is unclear. A crisis can be unique or recurrent, specific or general, transient or final. It can be ongoing, forthcoming, or both at the same time. And as a condition that must be recognized and experienced as such in order to properly exist, it can in fact be any combination of these things. This mutability also enables the specter of crisis to be met with a range of normative responses (as it was by Burckhardt, for whom the prospect of a "genuine" crisis held both terror and promise).[19] In short, anything is possible.

There has been some debate among historians over Burckhardt's theory of crisis. According to Randolph Starn, it is not so much a theory as "an affirmation of the mysterious vitality, variety, and challenging discontinuities of history."[20] For Koselleck, however, these very qualities are what make

Burckhardt's theory of crisis the historical theory of crisis par excellence. If his account abounds in temporal ambiguity, it is because this ambiguity is what defines the term as a modern concept. "Crisis," Koselleck argues, "becomes a structural signature of modernity" because it gives free scope to the historical imagination—"it takes hold of old experiences and transforms them metaphorically in ways that create altogether new expectations."[21] There may be other ways to perform such an operation, but it is "precisely the exciting possibility of combining so many functions" that makes the concept of crisis such an attractive one.[22] This protean character is also what invests the concept with its strange power to produce history.

Nowhere is this more apparent than in political economy, where crisis theorizing has reached a state of development still uncommon in other fields of study. On the one hand, political economy now operates with an established repertoire of crisis forms, each of which is based on a distinct vision of historical time. The figures of the cycle and the epoch are the most well known in this respect, providing ready-made templates for imagining history through crisis. On the other hand, some theorists have begun to take notice of this, prompting various attempts to incorporate the imaginary dimension of crisis into the theory of history. With this shift, the concept of crisis encounters its own involvement in the historical process, uncovering a metahistorical force based on the recursive narration of crisis events. Before developing this argument in more detail, it is important to distinguish the historical tradition of crisis thinking from a more peculiar, naturalist variety associated with liberal economics.

Natural Crisis

As long as there have been natural disasters, human societies have had to make critical decisions about how to secure their continued survival and prosperity. A flood, for example, may lead a society to question its prevailing set of economic arrangements by taking lives, reducing crop yields, and destroying equipment. Before the invention of economy, however, such disturbances were seen as extrinsic events. This deposited "theological and cosmological questions ... in the field of social ontology,"[23] leading classical theorists to attribute the chaos wrought by later phenomena—such as failing businesses or fluctuations in prices—to an unseen process of adjustment, balancing, or adaptation. The legacy of this approach is a strain of liberal thinking on economy that either externalizes crisis or subsumes it beneath a figure of natural and progressive cycles. The process at work here is not so much a direct line of descent, but rather a recurring motif that appears in all varieties of liberal economic thought, ranging from classical political economy and neoclassical economics to the Austrian school and later new classical frameworks.

Early signs of this motif can be found in the work of the French physiocrats, a group of eighteenth-century thinkers who were among the first to imagine the economy as a natural order. Drawing in equal measure on religious tradition and a growing Enlightenment culture, François Quesnay and his contemporaries saw land as the basis of wealth and God as the giver of this gift.[24] The task of human society, they argued, was simply to administer and harness the divine economy of nature. This normative commitment to laissez-faire, along with the positive conception of an economy divided into factors of production and related classes, would become the hallmark of economic thought during the long nineteenth century. From the perspective of crisis thinking, however, the physiocrats' key legacy was to effect a shift in focus from the sources of instability (in this case scarcity [*la disette*], then a defining political issue in the largely agrarian France) to the system through which such instability might be managed or smoothed out (namely, that of free trade in grain).[25] Despite their numerous points of difference, liberal economists in Scotland and England carried this bearing over into their study of a nascent industrial and financial capitalism. Crucially, though, thinkers like Adam Smith and David Ricardo had yet to situate the mounting instability of industry and finance within their accounts of capitalist growth in the same way that Quesnay had integrated nature into his. Growth and capital accumulation were roundly seen to be the product of market forces, but the market itself was conceived as a self-equilibrating system. This presented classical theory with a choice between one of two roads: either deny the reality of market volatility or "explain disturbances of the system's equilibrium by reference to factors *outside the system*."[26] The former was not a viable option given the rise of stock jobbing in London and spectacular episodes like the South Sea Bubble, and so crisis—to the extent that it figured at all within economic theory—did so as a shock from the outside. This line of thought reached its apotheosis with William Stanley Jevons, who in 1878 attempted to link commercial crises to sunspots.[27] If crises could not belong to either capitalism or history, then perhaps their causes might lie in the stars.

Later revivals of classical theory brought the idea of the cycle back down to earth, but it would always retain an extrinsic quality. Jevons in fact was emblematic in this regard, clinging to the natural cycle because it provided answers where theory could not. He was also something of a harbinger, prefiguring the peculiar way liberal theory would come to depend on business cycle research. This shift has its roots in the formalization of economics at the turn of the century. As marginal utility theory was extended to cover the production process and then the economy as a whole, the framework of static equilibrium effectively displaced earlier theories of value and accumulation. Questions of growth and change were thus excluded from what became known as "pure economics,"[28] leaving the analysis of macroeconomic trends to empirically oriented researchers. Business cycle research developed in a number of directions during the interwar period, but it remained at a distance from theory until the 1970s, when a division of labor emerged between liberal economists across the pure-applied spectrum. Rather than a challenge to the prevailing theoretical models, the cycles found in economic data were now instead taken as proof of periodic adjustment and the tendency toward general equilibrium in market economies.[29] This alliance was formally expressed in real business cycle (RBC) models, which sought to establish a link between volatility and equilibrium using new methods of statistical testing.[30] In order to do this, RBC models assumed that all fluctuations in output were the result of a change in the broader economic environment, typically imagined as a shift in either government policy or technological capacity. The key point is that these changes were theorized as exogenous shocks—exogenous, because they were imagined to emanate from a space outside the market system, and shocks, because this exteriority meant their causal genesis could not be understood using economic science. The result was a new explanation for instability that hewed to the figure of the natural cycle found in earlier liberal thought, providing yet another round of visions in which the historical character of recession was played down to the point of disappearance.

By this time, of course, the place of the market economy within history was already an object of heated dispute. The fact that such questions were missing from economic models should therefore be taken as the expression of a liberal ideology and philosophy of history in the field of economy rather than a sign that no such thing exists. As Fredric Jameson reminds us, "Individual period formulations always secretly imply or project narratives . . . of the historical sequence in which such individual periods take their place."[31] In the case of neoclassical economics, formal proofs of allocative efficiency imbue both the market and its cycles with a progressive character that surreptitiously constitutes a figuration of history. This gesture can in fact already be found in Smith's writings, where wealth creation and its civilizing powers are routinely cast as compensation for the social upheavals wrought by capitalism.[32] With the Austrian school, however, a variant of this theodicy would become the basis for the first and perhaps only liberal conception of economic crisis proper.

The Austrian school emerged alongside neoclassical economics at the turn of the twentieth century, but its leading proponents were far more attuned to questions of time, history, and politics. Thinkers like Joseph Schumpeter and Friedrich Hayek rejected the equilibrium framework in favor of a dynamic evolutionary perspective. Although each would provide a different account of the economic process, both saw periodic slumps as central to the progressive development of economy and society. This was their way of finding reason in the madness of an ever-worsening business cycle. With Schumpeter, for example, capitalist development takes shape through the heroic interventions of entrepreneurs, which push the productive forces of society onto a new plane.[33] But in order for such a leap to occur, production structures must adapt to new possibilities revealed by the entrepreneur, and this will always involve somebody going out of business. The business cycle registers this process of adjustment and is therefore an echo of the vital force that propels both growth and innovation under capitalism.[34] Hayek viewed the discovery process in more inclusive terms, but the upshot was much the same: for some competitive strategies to be rewarded and encouraged, others have to be punished.[35] In macroeconomic terms, this too means that downturns are needed to ensure that industry continues adapting to the changing demands and needs of society.[36] For our purposes, what is significant about these accounts is the way they graft epochal qualities onto the figure of the cycle without fully moving beyond the idea of natural crisis. Slumps and recessions are moments of crisis in the sense that they mark a transition between different stages in the development of capitalism, and in this way, capitalism is delivered over to history. But insofar as capitalism is reduced to the outcome of individuals acting in and through the market, it is now history that assumes the form of a quasi-natural order.

Capitalist Crisis

In order to think capitalism through history and history through crisis, it would take theorists willing to begin with the accumulation process. Marx was among the first and certainly most influential in this regard, developing a vision of capitalist collapse inspired by Ricardo's ideas about the natural limits to growth. Keynes would later pick up on this theme, offering an account of the Great Depression that emphasized its status as a threat to the continuity of capitalism. In theoretical terms, the enduring legacy of these interventions has been to establish the explicitly historical character of capitalist crisis. Marx and Keynes may have had divergent hopes and expectations regarding the outcome of crisis episodes, but both used the concept in epochal as well as cyclical terms. After them, thinking the relation between cycles and epochs became the primary concern of crisis theory.

Marx developed his account in response to the classical notion of secular stagnation.[37] According to Ricardo, a finite supply of fertile land would eventually bring growth to an end by causing rents to rise and profits to fall.[38] In Marx's estimation, Ricardo was right to question the perpetuity of profits but wrong to "seek refuge in organic chemistry."[39] Instead, he argued, the tendency for the rate of profit to fall should be traced back to a contradiction between exchange-value and use-value production, which drives a development of the productive forces to the point where capital can no longer find conditions conducive to its self-valorization. As Koselleck points out, this account contains both "system-immanent and system-exploding elements."[40] The system-immanent elements are represented in periodic industrial crises, which Marx saw not as the consequence of random shocks or disturbances, but as the playing out of contradictions that were specific to the capitalist mode of production. In particular, these periodic crises entail a destruction of the productive forces, such that profitability is temporarily restored to the process of surplus-value production.[41] But because each of these crises serves only to further exhaust the scope for future profits, there is also a singular and final crisis still to come, after which the productive forces of social labor will once and for all be transformed into the basis for a higher mode of production.[42] This is the system-exploding element: crises are the mechanism by which capital undoes itself. By grasping together the cyclical and the epochal in this way, Marx invokes the eschatological dimensions of the crisis concept, demanding a consciousness of crisis in the present that will deliver capitalism over to its inevitable fate.

The subsequent development of Marxist crisis thinking is largely a story of coming to terms with the failure of this final crisis to arrive.[43] Within the orthodox tradition, theorists developed a range of new technical explanations for how internal limits would cause the rate of profit to fall.[44] At the same time, there emerged a revisionist tradition that posited underconsumption (rather than overaccumulation) as the true motor behind capital's tendency toward terminal crisis. This shift in emphasis did nothing to hasten the collapse of capitalism, but it did provide new ways to explain its seemingly constant deferral. Rosa Luxemburg, for example, pioneered an account in which imperial expansion figured as a means of securing the additional demand required to sustain capital accumulation.[45] According to Paul Baran and Paul Sweezy, who combined the orthodox and revisionist views, imperial expansion was but one of three different measures that states could take to prop up demand (they also identify advertising and public expenditure).[46] And in the work of David Harvey, perhaps the leading crisis thinker in contemporary Marxism, capital can negotiate its various limits through not only spatial but also temporal fixes.[47] These are radically different reworkings of Marx's original account, yet they all retain his basic emphasis on the dual role for crisis within history. Recurrent patterns of boom and bust still draw meaning from a later and final breakdown of capitalism. What is truly novel about the historicity of crisis in neo-Marxist accounts is the fear that this final breakdown—the moment of reckoning—may be manipulated and postponed indefinitely, and perhaps even perpetually.

Keynes, by contrast, feared that such a breakdown was indeed a real threat and sought to discover ways in which governments might prevent it from coming to pass. This view was developed in response to the Great Depression, which Keynes saw as revealing the power of finance as a vector for crisis. Consequently, the account he provides in *The General Theory* begins not with overaccumulation or underconsumption but instead with a financial theory of underinvestment.[48] This theory again has both cyclical and epochal elements. Using the analogy of a newspaper beauty contest (in which readers win a prize for identifying the winner of the pageant itself), Keynes suggests that stock market prices are determined by second-order expectations about prospective yields. Prices go up when one expects others to expect they will. The result, he argues, is that financial markets exhibit self-amplifying patterns. This is the cyclical element. But when a stock market boom goes bust, the beauty contest turns ugly and investors seek refuge in liquidity. This flight-to-safety kick starts a downward spiral in the broader economy as consumption levels drop, traders become even more uncertain about the prospects for profitable investment, and attempts by monetary and fiscal authorities to restore investor and consumer confidence become less and less effective. This is the secular or epochal element: a business cycle that is breaking down can breed chronic and even permanent unemployment.

The General Theory had an enormous impact on the subsequent development of crisis thinking, and aspects of its argumentation can be found in both the Marxist and neoclassical traditions. There is something of the early Keynes, for example, in Baran and Sweezy's suggestion that military expenditure can stave off depression, and the same can be said for the faith in a more benign form of demand management that comes with the so-called neoclassical synthesis in macroeconomics.[49] But as Jan Toporowksi points out, Keynes's attempts to refine his theory of crisis were a response to the *failure* of monetary policy to prevent the Great Depression, and the fact that he ended up advocating a socialization of investment reveals just how destabilizing he thought stock markets had become: the problem was not capitalism per se, but rather the fickle financial logics it had spawned.[50] This emphasis on the power of finance has been kept alive on the fringes of the economic establishment in the work of heterodox theorists like Hyman Minsky, whose recent rediscovery is testament to how radically Keynes's ideas about finance were domesticated during the era of actually existing

Keynesianism.[51] From the perspective of crisis thinking, however, the point is that Keynes saw his time as an era of crisis rooted in the twinned cycles of business and finance. Such a moment could not be fully understood with reference to the capitalist mode of production in general, he thought, for it grew out of a historically unprecedented subordination of industrial capital to finance. Keynes therefore imagined crisis in fundamentally different terms to Marx. Rather than any basic laws of capitalist civilization, epochal crises are generated—and ultimately resolved—through the contingent evolution of economic institutions.

Overdetermined Crisis

Though few have commented on it, Keynes's perspective on crisis would end up being fleshed out by heterodox Marxists. This may seem like something of an irony, but it is in keeping with what Thorstein Veblen, an early pioneer of evolutionary economics, often referred to as the blind power of cumulative causation.[52] Ideas, much like practices and institutions, move without predestination and mutate along the way. From the vantage point of evolutionary economics, crisis thinking emerges in the work of Veblen and travels through Keynes into Left Keynesianism and Regulation School Marxism.[53] But from the vantage point of Marxist theory, Keynes's ideas on crisis feed into a longer debate over causality, contingency, and agency in capitalist history. As we will see, this second trajectory turns out to be crucial to the development of crisis thinking in the late twentieth century, opening up a space for the emergence of a strange loop between the idea of crisis and the process of history.

If we start with the evolutionary tradition, then the Regulation School appears as a further development of Keynesian crisis thinking. This is explicit in the pioneering works of figures like Michel Aglietta and Alain Lipietz, who occupied positions of relative influence within the French civil service. Writing against a backdrop of persistent stagflation during the 1970s, Aglietta and Lipietz set out to understand the foundations of capitalist growth and stability. In order to do this, they supplemented the notion of a capitalist mode of production with the concept of historically specific accumulation regimes, arguing in turn that each of these regimes relies on the support of an associated mode of regulation.[54] According to Lipietz, such periods of correspondence between the economic process and social norms or institutions are not a "pre-ordained part of capitalism's destiny" or even a product of conscious design.[55] Nevertheless, their accidental discovery at a particular point in time is integral to the evolution of capitalism, enabling a set of historically specific contradictions to be managed or "mitigated" in new and unexpected ways.[56] Global Fordism is the paradigmatic example of this—a thirty-year period of international growth and stability, the likes of which the world has never since seen.

As Ronen Palan points out, the Regulation School vision of international order and change had a decidedly Marxist-Hegelian character.[57] But by focusing on the question of social reproduction, Regulation theory pushed Marxism beyond Marx, seeking to situate capitalism itself within the contingent evolution of social relations at both the national and international scales.[58] This effort brought with it two new and distinct figurations of crisis. On one hand are crises that have not yet transpired and exist only as tendencies kept in check or mitigated by an effective mode of regulation. These crises are immanent to a social formation and, in particular, to its regime of accumulation. On the other hand are crises that mark the dissolution of an accumulation regime and the beginning of a struggle through which a new one might be found. Rather than a mere playing out of structural logics, these crises are transformative thresholds, marking the point at which such logics themselves undergo change, yielding an entirely new set of institutional arrangements and associated crisis tendencies. It is in this sense that Regulation theory follows Keynes, resuming his attempt to wrest crisis from both nature and necessity.

To do this, however, Aglietta and Lipietz had to relinquish the event of crisis as a site of theory. This was a consequence of their debt not to Keynes but to Louis Althusser, one of Lipietz's teachers and a hugely influential figure in French Marxism at the time. Following Althusser, the early Parisian Regulationists envisioned social formations as complex and overdetermined—there is no "general 'contradiction'" that drives their evolution.[59] Yet Lipietz was also clear that the concept of regulation was meant to moderate some of the more structuralist elements in Althusser's account of social reproduction and, in particular, restore a sense of agency to the process of history.[60] The effect of this double move was to relegate the concrete analysis of crisis events onto either side of their occurrence. On one side, there is the retrospective reconstruction of emergent contradictions within a social formation; on the other, a prospective identification of new and potentially stabilizing complementarities between institutional forms and the classes that struggle on their behalf. In neither instance is the transformative threshold itself opened up to investigation. What happens during a crisis?

One obvious answer is class struggle, which conceivably has a role to play in the constitution of crisis as well as its aftermath. In this respect, Regulation theory lags behind an older tradition of social and political crisis theory in Marxism, which begins with the early Marx and runs from Gramsci through to Poulantzas, Offe, and Habermas. But how exactly do classes struggle through crisis? What happens when the logic of class struggle meets the logic of crisis? This question was not a proper object of Marxist theory until formulated by Régis Debray, a Left Bank philosopher who turned strategic advisor to Latin American revolutionaries in the 1960s.[61] Debray was another of Althusser's students, and this is evident in the way he describes the outbreak of crisis as "objectively overdetermined" (113). A crisis is a knot in history's fabric of contradictory relations. Debray also anticipates the position that Lipietz would eventually adopt, arguing that such events are "epoch-making" (99) and hence cannot be entirely reduced to the logics that either precede or follow them. But rather than stopping here—that is, with the epistemic uncertainty that accompanies the overdetermination of crisis—Debray goes a step further. "In every crisis situation," he writes, "there is an interplay of darkness and clarity":

> The objective conditions provide a background, a containing framework of propositions, which restricts the spectrum of possible initiatives or responses to events, but that background then seems to fade. . . . So much so that the outline, the thing that can be seen by everyone, shifts from the objective to the subjective, the indeterminate, with the individual initiatives of a few characters suddenly thrust into the forefront of the stage. (104–5)

In this visual metaphor, "darkness" is the slipping away of certainty that accompanies the overdetermination of crisis, while "clarity" is the shape given to such an event by those who speak out on it. Crucially, though, this latter process is as much a question of political praxis as it is one of theory. Try as we might to "untangle" the knot of crisis, what it demands is instead to be "cut" (111). He continues: "We must try to untangle it in theory . . . but only so as to be able to make practical decisions . . . [based on] resolutely simple, even simplistic-seeming, formulae for action" (111). In other words, it is only through the strategic reductionism of social agents that crises can ever be envisioned and resolved in one way rather than another.

Debray may be a marginal figure in conventional histories of crisis thinking, but within political economy, he marks the confluence of two key trajectories. Following the lead of Marx and Keynes, he affirms both the historical novelty and path-shaping power of crises. Yet he also explicitly recovers the unity of subject and object inherent in the Greek notion of *krisis*, enabling him to ask how accounts of crisis feed into the very processes they purport to explain. By making both these moves at once, Debray profoundly refigures the relation between crisis and history. History doesn't objectively determine crisis; crisis episodes find their place in history through the subjective interventions they elicit. As we will soon see, these interventions themselves entail a recursive deployment of the crisis concept and its prior applications to history.

Imagined Crisis

Since the 1980s, there has been a range of further developments in crisis theory. The most recent among these is a return to heterodox theories of money and finance, be these in the Marxist, Keynesian, or post-Keynesian traditions. There has also been a steady stream of further advances in the Regulation approach, both within and beyond the original Parisian school. Here is not the place to provide an overview of this literature; interested readers have a wealth of other sources to consult.[62] Instead I want to emphasize the legacy of Debray's ideas, particularly in relation to Roitman's critique of crisis thinking. To the extent that Marxist and even Keynesian accounts operate on the basis of a distinction between productive and financial capital, there is some truth to Roitman's characterization of contemporary crisis narratives. "Crisis," she writes, "signifies a purportedly observable chasm between 'the real,' on the one hand, and what is variously portrayed . . . as fictitious, erroneous, or an illogical departure from the real, on the other."[63] But it does not follow from this that all crisis theories are blind to the imaginary character of crisis or to the constitution of crisis through narrative discourse. After and with Debray, crisis becomes the name for an event that *agents themselves* imagine to be a turning point within history. This is the hallmark of what I call the new crisis theory, which attempts to fold the narrative grammar of crisis into the task of crisis theorizing.

The new crisis theory is not a unified school; it comes in a variety of flavors, emerging over the past twenty years through the institutional and cultural turns in comparative and international political economy. Colin Hay, for example, is a British political scientist whose early work was developed in direct response to the Althusserian moment in crisis theory. For Hay, the theoretical question posed by crisis is that of how structural change might emerge from a situation characterized by subjective indeterminacy.[64] Following Debray, he conceives of crises as both overdetermined and indeterminate—overdetermined, because there are always too many contradictions behind the breakdown of an accumulation regime, indeterminate because there is never any certainty about which diagnosis will prove to be path shaping. Hay's response is to posit narrative as a device that bridges these two registers. Before a crisis can be said to exist, contradictions must be discursively recruited as "symptoms" and incorporated into a "meta-narrative of crisis."[65] But once such a meta-narrative does emerge, it opens up a space of struggle between itself and other competing narratives, mapping out a "discursively selective terrain" that privileges some narratives of crisis over others.[66] Crucially, though, this process of discursive struggle is itself indeterminate, for just as contradictions can be recruited as symptoms of systemic failure, so too can they be negotiated in ways that absolve that same system from blame. Structural change—or historical change, if you prefer—is thus a nonnecessary response to systemic failure, and its eventuation is contingent on the public narration of that failure as a crisis of preexisting structures.

A similar line of analysis can be found across the pond, in US political science departments, where it has become increasingly common to argue that agents need simplifying ideas in order to overcome the uncertainty that comes with crisis.[67] There are echoes of Debray in this formulation, but here the nature of uncertainty is somewhat different. Rather than a corollary of overdetermination, uncertainty instead specifies the inability of agents to derive their interests from existing economic structures. One of the first to develop this argument is Mark Blyth, who does so via the concept of Knightian uncertainty.[68] During periods of economic instability, Blyth argues, agents become "unsure as to what their interests are, let alone how to realize them."[69] But because purposive action requires both means and ends, agents need some kind of mechanism for overcoming uncertainty if they are to ever respond to it. For Blyth, it is the "ideas that agents themselves have about the causes of uncertainty" that enable them to identify goals and formulate strategies.[70] Moreover, it is through the attempts agents make to impose their ideas on others that collective or institutional responses to crisis take shape. Business and policy elites might wage wars in the name of their various "crisis-defining ideas," and these inter-elite debates may themselves be held to account by "everyday discourses constructed by mass public agents."[71] In both instances, processes of interpretation and persuasion are integral to the dynamics of crisis. This vision of the crisis event yields a double function for the concept of crisis. Crisis designates an event that agents "interpret as necessitating change," but at the same time, it also entails the "processes of persuasion" that such events ignite and which ultimately determine the very nature of the change they produce.[72]

Most recently, Bob Jessop has sought to incorporate Hay's notion of discursive selectivity into a more avowedly Gramscian theory of crisis.[73] Jessop's framework defies simple summary, but within the context of this discussion, three points are worth emphasizing. The first is that Gramsci's account of hegemonic leadership provides a class basis for the subjective interventions that crises elicit.[74] This is implicit in Debray, increasingly less visible in Hay, and more or less absent in Blyth. The second is that the subjective indeterminacy of crisis is understood through the lens of complexity and systems theory. Specifically, Jessop argues that the reproduction of an accumulation regime is always dependent on complexity-reducing imaginaries, which are what enable a subset of economic activities to be identified as an object of intervention or management.[75] Once the contradictions that these and other activities produce are construed as symptoms of systemic crisis, efforts at complexity reduction lose their unity and competing imaginaries proliferate. The indeterminacy of crisis therefore stems not from overdetermination or complexity itself, but from the multiplicity of ways in which complexity might be reduced. Finally, the eventual diagnosis and resolution of a crisis episode are seen to hinge on the emergence of a "master economic imaginary,"[76] whose role is to coordinate and lend structural coherence to the visions and strategies of key economic agents. Crises are therefore periods of hegemonic struggle. During such periods, agents vie to remake social relations from within, and imagined economies serve in equal parts as weapons and bridges in this process.

So what, then, is the upshot of all this theorizing? What does it mean to think crisis in connection with ideas, narratives, and imaginaries? Although there are significant differences among its various branches, what the new crisis theory underlines is the deep intersubjectivity of crisis. Crises do not simply exist; they must be collectively imagined into existence. To be sure, things happen—asset prices fall, people lose their jobs, their pensions, their homes—but these occurrences constitute a crisis only when publicly imagined as belonging to a crisis history. This is a fundamentally new chapter in the conceptual history of crisis, wherein the narrative quality of crisis interacts with the narrative dimension of history's process.

Reimagining Crisis

We are now in a position to grasp the strange loops that ground the relation between contemporary history and crisis. The intersubjectivity of the crisis event opens out onto and empowers what Koselleck calls "the historical imagination." For a crisis to even exist, let alone be managed or resolved, present-day agents must imagine a relation between their time and prior events or processes. They must articulate a crisis history. This is the narrative quality of crisis, and it is this quality that the new crisis theory emphasizes. Crisis episodes are constituted and traversed through causal stories that connect past, present, and future, identifying failures, apportioning blame, and mapping out a path forward through the wreckage. But in order for a crisis to be properly historical (rather than legal, medical, or religious), these stories have to be routed through the historical record. In this way, the temporal dimension of narrative lends crisis histories a doubly recursive character. The first recursion is a loop through the figures of crisis theory, yielding so many narrative templates for cyclical and epochal crisis. The second, however, is a loop through the archives of history, such that accounts of past crises feed back into the contemporary narration of crisis.

This is clearly evident in the recent history of capitalism, which has been marked by a persistent reappearance of crises past. The imagined crises of neoliberalism, for example, have been decisively shaped by the crisis of the 1970s. In the British context, the crisis of Keynesianism and the postwar welfare state has served as a touchstone for much subsequent discussion of economic and political disorder, "seemingly appealed to, and conjured, in each wave of industrial unrest, in each hint of political turmoil and, until recently, whenever the election of a Labour government looked credible."[77] But as Hay rightly points out, the crisis of British Keynesianism was an imagined crisis to begin with, emerging through a bitterly fought struggle over who and what was to blame for the breakdown of postwar growth and stability. Contemporary crisis discourse thus builds narratives up from narratives.

The fact that the 1970s have been conjured as a crisis of Keynesianism reveals the extent to which a prior crisis narrative can haunt the historical imagination, shaping the way later events are narrated and responded to as crises. But past events can live on in more than one narrative construction, and there is no a priori reason why any of these must be conjured in the service of extant visions of historical development. In recent years, for example, many Marxist commentators have returned to the period of the 1970s, using the classic lens of profitability crisis to generate new narratives about the reemergence of global finance and the rise of debt-based accumulation.[78] Some have even recast the crisis of the 1970s as the beginning of a long-wave transition from wage labor to a fully automated, postcapitalist economy.[79] This latter process, in which past crises are returned to and refigured in the practice of contemporary crisis narration, is most obvious with respect to the Great Depression.

The meaning and significance of the Great Depression has been the subject of sustained controversy and revision, both in its own time and the eighty or so years since. As financial historians Michael Bordo and Harold

James have observed, "The Great Depression analogy refuses to go away."[80] The result has been a proliferation of possible relations between the 1930s and the contemporary period as signal chapters in the history of financial capitalism. Was the subprime crisis of 2008 a replay of the Great Depression? Did it mark a continuation or reversal of processes that began back in the 1930s? Or was the subprime crisis the fulfillment of some long-latent destiny, already present but only intimated by the advent of the Great Depression? The short answer is that it was all of these things, albeit at different times and to different people. I return to these questions at length in Chapters 3 and 4. The broader point, however, is that crises are always and everywhere metahistorical. Crisis episodes take shape through a return not only to inherited figurations of crisis but also to other past crises that appear to be somehow similar or affiliated. Returning to the historical record in this way is a structural necessity; it is what the time of crisis demands in the register of history. But moving from the historical record to a contemporary crisis narrative entails a leap beyond the domain of concepts. This is an open and fundamentally practical operation, oriented toward the task of diagnosing and intervening on the historical process itself. In this way, the concept of crisis is at once both a vector of the historical imagination and a mode of history production. Crisis obtains through the recursive narration of crisis and history, a strange looping back through past figurations and accounts of crisis. The next chapter develops this argument by delving into the history of historical writing, showing in greater detail how the narrative operation sets up a feedback loop between history's imagined and developmental aspects.

CHAPTER 2

Historical Imagination

Much like crisis, the idea of history brings with it a foundational and productive ambiguity: Is it a retelling or the thing itself? This is clearly registered in the French and German languages, where there is only one word with which to say both "story" and "history" (*histoire*/*geschichte*). But even in the English language, where separate terms provide a means of distinguishing one idea from the other, common use still suggests a certain degree of mutual implication. When we want to designate something as belonging to the past, we describe it as being history (as in the phrase, "You're history!") And yet we use the same term when alluding to the stories we tell about the past. In theoretical discourse too, the double meaning persists. In his own attempt to define the term, Dutch historian Johan Huizinga began by observing how *history* can refer to either "something that has happened" or "the narration of something that has happened."[1] This ambiguity is significant because it reveals the simultaneously enabling and destabilizing power of the imagination vis-à-vis the historical. There are numerous ways of narrating history—both in terms of *how* historians tell stories and *which* stories they end up telling. The result is a multiplication of the possible relations between historical discourse and our image of history as a developmental process. Different modes of discourse are capable of producing different visions of history.

In the twentieth century, historians and philosophers of history have dealt with this quandary in one of two ways. The first involves scrutinizing, codifying, and policing the conduct of historical inquiry. This was the preferred approach among Anglo-American historians, whose affinity with positivist-empiricist philosophy led them to stress the importance of "getting the facts right." In this tradition, narrative discourse figures as a neutral device used to make the facts of history speak. The second route instead treats narrative as a linguistic and cultural form integral to the production of historical meaning. This has been the preferred approach among philosophers and new theorists of history since around the 1960s, and from the 1980s onward, it has influenced the practice of historians as well. By now, much has already been written on the question of history and narrative. For our purposes, what matters most is the way these debates are part of a longer and indeed ongoing series of encounters with the reliance of history on imagination. In this chapter, I reconstruct this series, following it into a terrain where the lines between history's imagined and developmental aspects are well and truly blurred.

My starting point is the notion of epistemological crisis developed in the writings of Michel de Certeau. De Certeau was one of many French thinkers who helped revolutionize the philosophy of history in the 1960s, but he was unique in doing so by elaborating a metahistory of historical writing (or historiography). Crisis is central to this history. His account begins, however, with an observation on periodization and chronology. "Historiography separates its present time from a past," writes de Certeau, "But everywhere it repeats the initial act of division."[2] The result is a peculiar relationship between historical discourse and the various temporal breakages or ruptures it institutes. "Each 'new' time provides the place for a discourse considering what preceded it to be 'dead,'" yet every new discourse must confront and navigate a past "already . . . specified by former ruptures."[3] There is, in other words, a recurring drive to separate past from present within all modes of historiography, but this is fundamentally an impossible drive. As a result, what really distinguishes one mode from another is how each negotiates its relation to the chronological divisions that precede it.

This is straightforwardly so in the sense that any form of historiography must navigate the historical record according to its own truth procedures. It is at a metalevel, though, that the figure of epistemological crisis operates.

On this level, philosophical controversies regarding truth and meaning in the writing of history tell us something about the evolving character of the historical imaginary. With the recurring controversies that separate one mode of historiography from another, we find a means through which to situate these modes of writing within a metahistory of historical thinking. In what follows, I use the work of de Certeau and others to diagnose a series of crises regarding the status of writing, fiction, narrative, and the category of the event within historical discourse. In one sense, these crises express the way historians have tarried with the productive role of the imagination within history. But at the same time, they also reveal how this process has led to a reflexive incorporation of the imagination into historical discourse. This is especially evident in contemporary discussions of memory and trauma, which write a recursive narration of history into the very category of the event. The result, I argue, is a historical terrain traversed by strange loops.

History and Writing

History entails writing, but what drives one to write? To answer this question, I begin not with historical literature but literary fiction, in particular the prose of German language poet Rainer Maria Rilke. Writing at the dawn of the twentieth century, Rilke produced what many consider to be one of the first great modernist novels, *The Notebooks of Malte Laurids Brigge*. In its opening, the eponymous protagonist passes a series of hospitals and is struck by the strangeness of death. Different deaths are there for the dying, he observes, but die we all will. In the face of this realization, Malte finds himself impelled to act: "I have done something against the fear. I have sat up all night and written."[4] Rilke too felt this urge, and in the novel that resulted, both he and his character find recourse to a range of childhood memories and historical sources, all of which figure as part of their attempts to learn how to live in a new and uncertain age. In so doing, Rilke and Malte indicate precisely the relation between past and present that de Certeau sees as haunting the history of historiography.

For de Certeau, our relation to the past is born of an obsession with death. Because everyone knows they are going to die, they are forced to remember how life goes on in order to continue living. But because the past is forever gone, our attempts to recall and represent it are charged with an undercurrent of impossibility that ceaselessly threatens to throw us into meaninglessness.[5] In *The Writing of History*, de Certeau develops this idea into an elaborate account of the relations between history as discourse, history as writing, and history as generative process. For de Certeau, historical discourse should be understood in terms of its essentially practical function—to produce "a society capable of managing the space it provides for itself" (6). Historical writing is the means through which this occurs. But this is a paradoxical operation, for the task of writing is to represent that which cannot be represented (what de Certeau calls the real [*réel*] of history), while at the same time appearing to do nothing of the sort. Moreover, and this is the crucial point, it is through this very operation that history as such is produced. What we usually think of as history's process emerges through an ongoing interplay between the representations of history that discourse provides and the hidden, sublime "underside" (4) that accompanies each and every one of these. De Certeau's critique of historiography therefore consists in an attempt to reveal not just the production of histories by historians, but also the production of history itself by historiography.

In methodological terms, this approach entails a focus on three distinct but related dimensions of the historiographic operation. First, there are the institutional arrangements that enable historical writing to occur, which de Certeau describes as a "combinatoire" (57) of place, labor, and discourse. From where and within what does the historian do his or her work? Second, there are the acts of selection and exclusion that determine historical study's fundamental "postulates of analysis" (68). These are the rules of the historian's workplace, and they function as a means of regulating the kinds of histories that historians are able to produce. Finally, there are the crises— "encounters with the real," as de Certeau would have it—which make history seem like a succession of different times or eras. These are the raw materials with which the historian works, providing a sense of discontinuity needed for forming chains of events through narrative. Each of these three dimensions is important in its own right, but together they enable de Certeau to advance a radical vision of history premised precisely on the power of writing and discourse. History, according to de Certeau, is an institutionally determinate and strangely productive kind of recording process, wherein specific modes of historiography endeavor to shore up their functional value and historicity figures within this as both subject and object.

As Ian Buchanan points out, the corollary of this insight is not only that a culture is best understood through its response to epistemological crisis, but also that the very nature of this response will set the parameters for its subsequent struggle against the "real" of history.[6] For our purposes, this is significant in that it provides the starting point for a metahistory of historiography. If we invert Buchanan's formulation, then de Certeau's wager can be expressed as follows. First, each mode of historiography will possess an underside that its discourse works to keep hidden. This is a structuralist claim: there are things that cannot be said. Second, the precise form this "other" takes will reflect an epistemological movement that was undertaken in response to an earlier crisis. This, for want of a better word, is a historical claim; there is a secret genealogy of what can and cannot be said. But if we dive into specific moments of epistemological crisis, these can provide an opening through which to glimpse the mode of relation between a discourse and its own historicity. This is a deductive claim, and it forms the basis of de Certeau's distinctive approach to understanding historiography. If we want to account for the changing appearance of historical discourse over time, then it is to the disavowals and displacements of epistemological crisis that we must turn.

One such crisis that de Certeau identified was the undoing of God's Word, which he saw as providing a place for the initial emergence of historical discourse.[7] With the transition from an oral to a scriptural economy, he argues, the sacred text is no longer heard as voice, but instead produced through the work of criticism. Yet in their attempts to "redefine themselves without that voice" (137), modern societies become unmoored and are left to float in the "vast sea of a progressively disseminated language" (138). This new situation drives the subject to "set himself up as a producer of writing" (138), transforming the subject of writing into a master and the mastery of language into a new power: "that of making history and fabricating languages" (139). The discipline of history thus emerges at a time when the fiction of truth is revealed, and this is precisely why it establishes the idea of facticity. Facticity, or the colligation of individual truth statements, is what enables historical discourse to take the place of God's Word. But in order to continue performing this function, modern historians must disavow the origins of their craft. To remain authorized to speak in the name of the real, they must bury the story of how they came to do so in the first place. The art of fiction is in this way the "repressed other of history"; it is the underside against which historiography struggles.[8]

History and Fiction

If we begin our story with fiction, it is not because fiction and imagination are identical, but because they are affiliated in ways that illuminate what has been an enduring problem for historiography. Similarities between fictional and historical writing, for example, were central to the debates over objectivity that engulfed academic history in the 1960s, evolving into what was widely construed as a crisis of the discipline during the 1980s.[9] De Certeau's emphasis on the narrative dimension of historiography helped contribute to this sense of crisis, an issue we return to in the next section. What I want to stress here, though, is how he interprets this 'crisis' as an abreaction to the discipline's entry into science.

According to de Certeau, panics over objectivity emerge within historical science due to its inaugural denial of the letters. In the earliest examples of historical writing, namely those associated with ancient Greece and the Roman Empire, the very form was inseparable from its literarity, its dependence on narrative and rhetoric. But as attempts to codify the study of history gathered pace during the early nineteenth century, the tools of fiction were relegated to the status of a "shameful and illegitimate" component in the writing of history.[10] The result was a kind of disavowal that couldn't help but return in the form of a later, seemingly affiliated controversy over the status of narrative within historical writing. The story of fiction in this way maintains a unique relationship with history, providing a vantage point on the evolution of historical discourse that a scientific perspective is unable to offer. If "fiction is the repressed other of history," then it is also a way of reading the repressed history of historical science.[11] Take literary modernism. From the perspective of literary history, the novel is typically seen as responding to a world wracked by intellectual and industrial change. Its emergence is therefore taken to signify a crisis of form and its possible content rather than a full-blown epistemological crisis. But as Hayden White has shown, the birth and legacy of the novel bear a crucial relation to the professionalization of historical study that so intrigued de Certeau.[12]

According to White, the entry of history into science sends ripples through literary fiction because it robs historical study of its ability to speak to the present. To develop this argument, he deploys a distinction the English conservative philosopher Michael Oakeshott once made between two different kinds of past and their related uses or functions.[13] The first of these is "the historical past," which is a past authenticated by the truth procedures of the historian. For Oakeshott, this past is an end in itself, and its discovery is properly motivated by nothing more than a desire to provide as full and objective a portrait of the past as possible.[14] In contrast, the function of what Oakeshott calls "the practical past" is to enable and inform the decisions of individuals as they confront the dilemmas of an ever-changing present. This past consists of the loose or unexamined memory that people carry around with them. It includes elements of the historical past, but these are filtered through idiosyncratic mnemonic practices, yielding potentially divergent visions of history. Although Oakeshott originally drew this distinction in order to protect historical research from the degenerative effects of an instrumental attitude toward the past, White turns it against him. Specifically, White suggests that a new quest to uncover the historical past, which promises to tell us "what people in other times, places and circumstances have done," effectively prevents historians from sustaining an earlier concern with the practical past, which might tell us "what we, in our situation, in our time and our place, *should* do."[15] This, for example, was how the great Roman historians conceived of their enterprise: as an exercise in instruction, in keeping with the classical Greek notion of preparatory education (*propaídeusis*).[16] According to White, the loss of this dimension worked to undermine the ability of historians to see the present as belonging to history, effectively pushing the question of how to negotiate new social realities beyond the boundaries of mainstream historical discourse. It is for this reason, he argues, that radical new literary forms emerged during the nineteenth and twentieth centuries: the historical novel, the modernist novel, the postmodern historical novel—all of these were so many attempts to question or supplement "the kind of knowledge about the past produced by the new cadres of professional historians."[17] Thus, with the entry of history into science, we also find the genesis of a displaced crisis in literature, wherein a new generation of novelists set out to explore how the past might once again serve "as a resource for social and cultural renewal" in the present.[18]

At this point it is worth returning to the story of Rilke's Malte. Malte's fear of death drove him to write, and it was an appeal to the past that furnished him with much of his subject matter. While Malte is usually seen to have failed in his attempt to become an artist, Rilke is not, and this is because he imagined a rich and gripping nexus of memory, facticity, and historicity. With Rilke we find a 'now' that cannot be divorced from the 'then,' a recollection that cannot be reduced to the mere recovery of facts, and a discourse whose form must somehow mediate between the registers of fiction and history. This is not to say that the site of literature is privileged in relation to that of history, but rather that the literarity of historical writing is integral to its efficacy in ways that modern historians have struggled to acknowledge. As a contemporary of Rilke, Wilhelm Dilthey, once put it, "The tale of the novelist or the narrative of the historian . . . produces an act of re-experiencing in us," an act whose triumph is to render "the fragments of a course of events in such a way that we believe them to possess a continuity."[19] In this respect, the narrative form provides a key to understanding not only the relation between history and fiction but also the recursive, imaginary institution of historicity. The following sections elaborate on this claim by connecting the story of history and narrative to a series of debates within the theory and philosophy of history.

History and Narrative

Before Huizinga offered his definition of history, Hegel had already asked what it might mean to use the term to connote both objective events and their subjective apprehension. For Hegel, the double meaning was more than a "mere outward accident" and had to be grasped as an expression of how events can *only* be historical when a subject of history is there to record and interpret them.[20] Putting his philosophical system to one side, Hegel's basic point was that a will and capacity to imagine something like history is part of what provides historians with their subject matter. But as modern historians have become more aware of their own reliance on narrative (which is how Hegel imagined historical consciousness to perceive itself), the ideal of objectivity has emerged as a focal point for debates over the nature of historical study. As I have already suggested, these debates reveal an underlying preoccupation among historians with the relation between imagination and truth or meaning in history. This plays out in various ways throughout the history of historical writing, but almost all histories of historiography afford the category of narrative a central position.[21] Among those that focus on the Western tradition, it has become customary to begin with Herodotus and Thucydides, whose works on the wars of ancient Greece and Rome are seen as marking the birth of a distinctly historical form of writing. In *A History of Histories*, for example, John Burrow credits both with an emphasis on inquiry that was lacking in the epic verse of Homer's *Illiad*, as well as a purposive use of narrative that would set them apart from the later annalists and chroniclers of the Middle Ages.[22] Burrow's account quite clearly works to produce a sense of progression or modernization in the development of historical study; yet in his emphasis on "truthful narrativity" as a distinguishing feature of proper histories, he raises precisely the question that has haunted historical writing throughout the modern era: What exactly is truthful in historical narrative?

In order to appreciate the productive force of this question, nominally discrete debates over the status of narrative must be grasped together and read through the enduring fact of their recurrence. Such a reading does demand an attention to the various controversies that have surrounded the relation of narrative to history, but more important than this, it requires that these be approached as entangled intimations of an underlying reliance of history on the imagination. In other words, it requires an extension of the story that de Certeau began with the emergence of a scriptural economy and that White supplemented through his focus on a later crisis in literary fiction. Because both writers emphasize an affiliation between these crises and the entry of history into science, there is no better place to start than with the alleged father of modern historical science, Leopold von Ranke.

Ranke was a leading Prussian historian, famous not only for his detailed accounts of the papacy, the Reformation, and the royal houses of Europe but also his influence on the conduct of historical inquiry during the nineteenth century. In 1825 he was offered a professorship at the University of Berlin, and from this position he trained what many consider to be the first generation of professional historians, placing particular emphasis on the use of primary source material.[23] In the preface to his breakthrough study, he describes himself as consulting a wide range of "memoirs, diaries, personal and formal missives, government documents, diplomatic dispatches and first-hand accounts of eye-witnesses."[24] The purpose of going through such material, he would later argue, was "to show what actually happened [*wie es eigentlich gewesen*]."[25] Within the contemporary context, Ranke's dictum is routinely used as shorthand for a naive objectivism in historical study. There has been much debate over the translation of the phrase, as well as whether it is indicative of Ranke's method.[26] Nevertheless, his emphasis on the privileged status of primary sources is in keeping with a positivist view of the past. Moreover, insofar as Ranke labored to undermine the speculative or transcendentalist philosophies of history that dominated Germany during the 1830s, he can also be credited with advocating an empiricist approach to history. The more important point, however, is that Ranke's aphorism is widely taken to have helped establish the idea that facts can somehow speak for themselves.[27]

It is something of an irony then, that Ranke's own use of narrative would open him up to the charge of affording too much scope to the influence of literary artifice. In a now famous polemic, "The Situation of History in 1950," Fernand Braudel criticized Ranke for having encouraged unduly "dramatic" representations of the past.[28] For Braudel and his peers in the French Annales school, narrative was not simply a device unsuited to the science of history; it was also one whose deployment threatened to turn the study of the past into too narrow and superficial an exercise in storytelling, whereby key political figures and the events that punctuate their lives are treated as the sole determinants of historical change.[29] In this way, Braudel's Ranke restages the tension between fiction and history identified by de Certeau. Though Ranke sought to put history on objective grounds, he could do so only by employing a mode of literarity that defined the kind of historical writing he wished to leave behind.

Moving into Braudel's present, it is important to note that his critique formed part of yet another attempt to put history on firm ground. Unlike

Ranke, who wanted to distinguish history from other scientific disciplines, Braudel envisioned a form of "total history" in which not only the new social sciences, but also disciplines like geology, biology, and climatology, would be integrated into a comprehensive science of change and development.[30] By the early 1960s, this broad movement was bearing enough fruit for some to feel confident announcing the "eclipse of narrative." It wasn't long, though, before others were celebrating its revival.[31] The strands of thought responsible for this turnaround are various, but they all stem from a new and more explicit concern with the function of narrative in historical discourse. Some of the first to voice this were a group of Anglo-American philosophers of history, including W. B. Gallie, Arthur Danto, and Louis Mink.[32] Critical of the so-called speculative approach (which followed Hegel in seeking to identify an overarching pattern and meaning in history), these thinkers set out to instead "make clear the nature of the historian's own inquiry."[33] This led them to carve out a specifically epistemological function for narrativity within historical study. Histories, they argued, take the form of narratives because these provide for a kind of knowledge that scientific method cannot. Or, as Mink would later have it, the narrative form is a "cognitive instrument" that enables truth to be claimed for a configuration of events rather than a mere succession of them.[34] According to this view, narrative is neither the specious influence that Braudel rallied against nor simply one among many possible and legitimate stylistic options facing historians. Rather, it is a necessary component in generating explanations befitting of distinctly historical events and processes.

Outside of the analytic tradition, a rather different reappraisal was underway in postwar France and Germany. The new varieties of continental philosophy can be subdivided into two camps. First, there were those who took what White describes as a "semiologically oriented" approach to narrative.[35] Drawing on the ideas of Friedrich Nietzsche and Roland Barthes, these predominantly French thinkers—such as Michel Foucault, Julia Kristeva, and Jean-François Lyotard—joined the Annales school in questioning the neutrality of narrative histories, but then took a further step by linking the narrative form to a broader ideological function associated with historical discourse. This kind of argument exerted a significant influence over historical theory during the 1980s, leading many to view narrative as a means of obscuring the true formlessness of history—a kind of screen that made history appear as if it possessed an internal logic.[36] In contrast, there were those who instead took what White calls an "existentialist-phenomenological" approach to narrative.[37] This second approach—typically associated with the hermeneutics of Hans-Georg Gadamer and Paul Ricoeur—begins with the human experience of time and arrives at history by treating narrative as a mode of understanding uniquely suited to the structure of temporality.[38] In so doing, it effectively asserts an ontological reliance of history on narrative. This is a stronger claim than the epistemological one made by analytic philosophers. It is also an inversion of the idea that historical narrative should be understood as an ideological mask or screen. So which one is it: Does narrative reveal, obscure, or express the substance of history? The diversity of positions here itself tells us something important. Returning to narrative does more than simply reflect the contradictions inherent in Ranke's project, or indeed historical science more generally; it actually multiplies these, producing a proliferation of new perspectives on the nature of meaning and truth in history. As we will soon see, this is a moment in which the quasi-historical powers of narrative as such begin to emerge within theoretical discourse.

Narrative Powers

The debate over history and narrative moved away from analytic philosophy during the 1970s, coming to draw more heavily from the so-called continental tradition. Among other things, this brought with it a greater interest in issues relating to temporal experience and historical consciousness.[39] These themes would transform the status of historical narrative in significant ways, shifting questions about the power of narrative from the domain of cognition into that of mediation, and eventually uncovering a recursive narrative logic on the plane of history itself. In what follows, I reconstruct this shift by focusing on the trajectories of two key thinkers: Hayden White and Paul Ricoeur. Although typically associated with the semiological and hermeneutic traditions, respectively, both also engaged with the earlier analytic philosophers of history. This makes each a useful lens through which to track the pull of narrative in contemporary historical thought.

If we begin with White, it is because for nearly fifty years, his name has been associated with the seam between literature and history. His first book, *Metahistory*, was a unique attempt to write a structuralist history. Using the tools of literary criticism, White analyzed the major texts of nineteenth-century historians and philosophers such as Burckhardt, Hegel, Nietzsche, and Ranke.[40] His argument was that these and other writers enacted a "poetics of history," wherein their use of narrative was a means of both using and stretching the existing coordinates of historical imagination. Marx, for example, combined the ancient archetype of tragedy with contemporary mechanistic argumentation, producing a simple yet radical ideology that would alter history forever.[41] According to White, narrative is the glue that binds these rhetorical maneuvers together. The historical work is thus a work in which narrative acquires and creates unique powers. "A historical narrative," he explains, "is not only a *reproduction* of the events reported in it, but also a *complex of symbols* which gives us directions for finding an *icon* of the structure of those events in our literary tradition."[42]

The impact of White's work in Anglo-America was enormous. *Metahistory* devastated the idea that historical writing could ever just be about facts plain and simple. But even before its publication in 1973, White had gone a step further by underlining the necessarily fictional representation of reality implicit in all narrative histories.[43] In *The Content of the Form*, he takes this up at length, repeatedly arguing that there is no such thing as a "true story." Past events, structures, and processes may indeed have really existed in one present or another, but a story order is something that can only be imposed on them through the kinds of techniques that characterize the labor of the poet or the novelist.[44] The historian must select, sequence, and configure. Here White endorses Mink's suggestion that to narrate is to extract a configuration from a succession. But to "narrativize," as White would come to call it, is also to extract a sense of order from what would otherwise be sublime chaos. Here, he reveals his own debt to Nietzsche and de Certeau: the apparent coherence of history hinges on the stories told by historians.[45] To this he adds that in telling such stories, the past is something historians must invent rather than simply uncover. By invention, however, White means not fabrication but the kind of production at work when a story transforms the minds of those who read it. Written histories are not invented so much as they are part of a broader invention process, a process by which the historical past is collectively imagined into existence through the enterprise of historiography.[46]

Ricoeur comes to narrative from a different angle. Rather than beginning with historical discourse, Ricoeur's narrative theory was developed as part of his attempt to understand the conditions of possibility for selfhood. The parameters of this project are too complex to fully elaborate here, but for our purposes, it is worth noting how it involved combining phenomenological thought (in which questions of temporal experience were paramount) with a religious sensibility that saw a quest for meaning as characteristic of human subjectivity. Narrative, for Ricoeur, figured as one of the linguistic or textual models through which this quest played out, lending structure and providing scope to our efforts to imagine how the world hangs together. From this perspective, he argued, there was less that distinguished fictional from historical narrative than commonly thought: both observe a certain unity in the sense that they rely on the same textual model or structure. This is a point on which he would concur with White. For Ricoeur, however, this structural unity reveals a deeper phenomenological condition, which is our being 'within time.'

He develops this point in the first volume of *Time and Narrative*, using the ideas of Aristotle and Saint Augustine to show how both experiential and historical time emerge through a process of "emplotment."[47] According to Ricoeur, plot structure has a consoling effect on lives lived in a world of constant flux. But where White sees narrative as a kind of metacode that covers over this chaos, Ricoeur instead discovers a "healthy circle" between time and narrative that is properly constitutive of history.[48] In one respect, plot is something that allows us to experience time as something other than a series of unrelated instants; it "provides a transition from within-timeness to historicality."[49] And yet by virtue of this very function, it is also something that is already written into the fabric of reality. "Historicity . . . comes to language only so far as we tell stories or tell history," but at the same time, "We belong to history before telling stories or writing history."[50] What Ricoeur calls "emplotment" is therefore not only a means of giving shape to time in general, but also an act that refigures the time within which human action occurs.[51] In this way, the coherence of life itself hinges on our ability to view the present through the lens of narrative time, and if the narrative operation pervades attempts at self-understanding, then it should come as no surprise to find it at work in attempts at historical understanding too. Each is in essence a response to the same condition—the aporetic experience of temporality. And so we arrive at Ricoeur's key argument about written histories, which is that they can't help but take the narrative form. Even allegedly nonnarrative histories, such as those of the Annales school, can be shown to rely on operations of quasi-emplotment, and this is because there is no better means of moving one's self from the register of time to that of history.[52]

Much more could be said about either White or Ricoeur, but the theme I pick up on here is how they push the logic of narrativity beyond the space of writing. In particular, as they theorize the unique properties and powers of narrative, the narrative form gradually escapes the confines of historical literature, breaking out onto the very terrain of this literature's ultimate or figurative referent. To start at the level of the historical text, both White and Ricoeur begin with the same assertion: that the significance of any one event emerges through a web of affiliations with those that precede or follow it. This is a correlative of their respective claims that narrative works to invest either history with meaning or time with history. Because narrativity entails the grasping together of more than one event, all events contained within a narrative find their meaning in relation to one another. As a result, no one event can fully determine its own place within a narrative history. This is what the episodic character of narrative entails even when dealing with a single narrative. But with the intrinsic discordance of time or history, this instability extends to cover *all* narrative understanding. So long as things keep happening, what happens next can always shed new light on what went before. Arthur Danto once called this a "retroactive re-alignment of the Past," and if we consider the formulation more closely, we may find in it the seeds of a radically constructivist view of history.[53] Historical episodes will accumulate new kinds of meaning and significance as they are reconfigured into ever-longer event sequences. But because the narrative operation opens out onto a potentially endless series of such realignments, there will be no end to the histories it produces, only an infinite vista spread out behind and in front of us. And here is the crucial point: these histories need not be confined to the pages of history books.

White and Ricoeur suggest as much when they acknowledge the diverse genres and domains through which narrative can produce history. This, however, eventually leads both of them away from the formalist approach that characterizes their early work. For example, in Ricoeur's *Time and Narrative*, it sometimes seems as though the content of the narrative form can explain its own emergence. But according to Ricoeur, no narrative powers are that strong; someone must do the emplotment. This is what he means when he says that emplotment is enmeshed with the practical world of human action.[54] The proper critique to be leveled at the early Ricoeur, then, is that a focus on written works of history ends up pushing to one side the question of how, exactly, we move from narrative time to historical time. It is one thing to analyze the story-like qualities buried in a work like Braudel's magnum opus, *The Mediterranean*; to map their intersection with lived experience is another altogether. What goes on in the space between temporal perception, on the one hand, and the production of historical narrative, on the other? With this question, I argue, we begin to glimpse how the looping logic of narrativity participates in the very process that written histories purport to explain or reveal.

Memory and Event

The site from which this deeper entanglement of history and narrative emerges is that of *the event*. In recent decades, a concern with the status of the event has become a signal feature of Left philosophy, most notably through the influence of thinkers like Alain Badiou.[55] For Badiou, the category of the event holds the secret to understanding and unlocking change in the world, and is thus tied to a longer Marxist tradition of revolutionary thinking. What sets contemporary evental thought apart from this tradition, however, is a more explicit aspiration to move beyond classical notions of linear, progressive historical development.[56] The concept of the event in this way wants to designate a moment of disjuncture not unlike that of crisis, in which the future is somehow freed from the shackles of the past. But as we have seen, the concept of crisis cannot escape the strange looping of crisis histories, and insofar as this rests on the intrinsic narrativity of crisis, then neither can the concept of the event simply shed its episodic attributes. The event is the category through which the narrativity of history as such obtains and the work that figures of crisis perform is in fact a conceptually delimited instance of this broader process. We can see this if we further follow the trajectories of White and Ricoeur, each of whom eventually opens up the category of the event in interesting ways.

With Ricoeur, this takes place through a turn to the concept of *memory*.[57] Rather than developing a theory of social, cultural, or collective memory in which memory somehow takes the place of narrative, Ricoeur instead locates memory in the space between temporal experience and historical writing. There is the narrative operation (which delivers time over to history), but now there is also a mnemonic operation that feeds into this. For our purposes, what matters is the way this new formulation fundamentally transforms the status of the historical event. In *Time and Narrative*, "historical events do not differ radically from the events framed by a plot," and all that marks them out from fictional ones is that their status as "real" is verified by the documentary truth procedures of the historian.[58] This is a formal proposition. With the pragmatics of memory, however, things become more complicated. For an event to be enshrined in the record as historical, we know that the historian must recall or recollect a string of seemingly affiliated prior events. But this same mnemonic operation must be deployed in order to experience life through the lens of history, and so the historical record also feeds back into practical, everyday efforts to make sense of world history. Historical events are therefore the object of a perceptual process that entails an interface between social practices of memorization on the one hand and those of historical writing on the other.[59]

The substance of Ricoeur's reevaluation of the event, then, is to foreground the relation between memory and narrative. From this perspective, the representation of past events—and indeed the very belonging of such events to history—comes to hinge on a complex dialectic of remembering and forgetting.[60] Where before, the production of historical narrative was coterminous with the labor of the historian and his or her configurational acts, it is now a broader process that brings together the making and recalling of histories by historian and nonhistorian alike. Returning to Oakeshott's distinction, we can think of this as a feedback loop between the historical and the practical past, in which the practical past (which serves to tell us "what we, in our situation, in our time and our place, *should* do") not only draws on the existing, authenticated histories of historians, but also shapes the future production of such histories. Moreover, as Ricoeur himself eventually concludes, such a process can only ever end in one thing: "Incompletion."[61] The link between memory and narrative thus transforms the historical event into the product of an endless looping back through the archives of history.

White reaches a similar verdict in his later writing, albeit via a somewhat different path. During the 1990s, White was invited to comment on whether his account of historical writing implied that the Holocaust might legitimately be given a comedic meaning, as opposed to the tragic one with which it is typically associated.[62] His response was to underline the inescapable contingency of both the historical imagination and the forms through which it makes meaning.[63] An event such as the Holocaust, he argued, is not exceptional in the sense that it intrinsically possesses a particular kind of plot meaning or that it somehow presents an absolute limit to representation as such. Instead, it is unique because it partakes of a new and distinctly "modernist" kind of historical reality, wherein the very nature of the event undergoes a decisive transformation.[64] In a certain sense, this is a conventional historical claim: times have changed. But what matters here is where this argument leads White, which is beyond the space of conventional historical discourse.

According to White, social modernization and its attendant upheavals breed an order of event whose "nature, scope, and implications" are all of a kind that "no prior age could even have imagined."[65] With the Holocaust, for example, mechanization, automation, and the weaponization of biological and communicational sciences were integral to the very substance of the event in question. This, for White, is an order of event that fundamentally belongs to the twentieth century. Something similar could be said of the assassination of John F. Kennedy, which he also interprets as a signal modernist event. And yet at the same time, the very upheavals that provide the conditions of possibility for such events work to rob them of any determinate place within the discourse of history. With the advent of mass media in particular, occurrence itself is exploded into a kaleidoscope of images—endless replays of JFK's head snapping back on the evening news, to the point where no one, as Andy Warhol once observed, knows the difference between the footage and the event itself. Jean Baudrillard would later say something similar about the oil crisis of the 1970s, the Wall Street crash of 1987, the Gulf War of 1991, and just about every other major media spectacle until he died in 2007; these events may as well have never happened, such is the strange emptiness of their appearance.[66] White essentially strips this argument of its black humor, simply asserting that events have been divested of any immediate belonging to either chronology or the real.[67] This leads him to conclude that the elusive truth of the modernist event might best be approached through its experience or perception, and that this in turn might call for a departure from those realist modes of representation that prevailed during the nineteenth century. His logic here is difficult to fault. Any kind of historical writing that would privilege the perception of contemporary events requires a substantive revision of "the event" as a category within historical theory. Events must become more than atomic facts.

White's own attempt at such a revision is organized not around memory but instead the related notion of trauma. In historical discourse, the terms *trauma* and *traumatic* typically function in a similar way to *crisis*, naming "something like a massive blow to a social or political system that requires the kind of adjustment, adaptation, or reaction that any organism must make if it is to survive it."[68] But in the theory of psychoanalysis, and in particular Freud's later writings, trauma entails an element of afterwardness or apperception such that the meaning of a shock or wound to the psyche is fully revealed only under the press of a later, seemingly affiliated shock or wound. For White, this is a distinctly historical form of recognition that warrants more than a simple analogy between the psychic event and its historical counterpart:

> Is it possible that the specifically historical event is a happening that occurs in some present (or in the experience of a living group), the nature of which cannot be discerned . . . because it manifests itself only as an 'eruption' of a force or energy that disrupts the ongoing system and forces a change . . . the end, aim, or purpose of which can only be discerned, grasped, or responded to at a later time? But not just any old 'later time.' Rather, that later time when the eruption of what seems to be in some way affiliated with an earlier event reveals or seems to reveal in the fact of that

affiliation the 'meaning,' significance, gist, even foretelling, though in a masked and obscure way, both of the original event and the later one. Such that the later event can be plausibly represented in a narrative in which it is the fulfillment (or derealization) of the meaning having lain latent and now made manifest retrospectively in the earlier one. (30)

This is an elaborate formulation, to the say the least, but a provocative one too. By suggesting that a properly historical event might be defined by its apparent return in some later present, White implies that its place within history depends less on the choices of the historian than it does a psychosocial process, whereby an affiliation between two events is transformed into a retroactive foretelling of one by the other. In so doing, he hints at a kind of deep narrativity intrinsic to the historical event. This is the narrativity of the trauma concept in its "historiotheticized" form (26), and it is this narrativity that gives substance to the modernist or contemporary event. It is not simply the case that an event like the Great Depression, for example, lacks determinate meaning; it is that the meaning of such an event emerges through the webs of affiliation in which it is entangled, acquiring a historical character only through the onset of a later event with which it may seem to bear a relation. But from where do these affiliations emerge, and what transforms a mere affiliation into an apparent return or "double occurrence"? How is it that an event like the subprime crisis, for example, can transform the meaning or significance of the Great Depression, and how is that this very process can equally determine the meaning or significance of the later event? These questions take us past the limits of narratology, staging a return of history's primordial moment of epistemological crisis.

Reimagining History

When history enters into science, it disavows its prior basis in fiction. The return of this past is a return of the repressed knowledge that there can be no such thing as a purely factual or objective history. The idea of narrative is a vector for both of these tendencies, registering a desire to establish the measure of truthfulness in historical discourse, while at the same revealing how this "truthfulness" can only ever be a product of the imagination. Over the course of this chapter, we have seen this dynamic play out through various phases, from Ranke's mission to construct a narrative science of history, to Braudel's Ranke, who was charged with leaning too much on literary artifice; from the Anglo-American philosophers like Mink and Danto, for whom narrative discourse was in fact the proper form of historical knowledge, to Ricoeur's Braudel, whose dependence on quasi-plots was seen to reveal the impossibility of ever fully severing the link between history and a form of imagination characteristic of literature. This is precisely what de Certeau meant when he said that "Western historiography struggles against fiction."[69]

But beyond this struggle, we have also seen the narrative form escape the confines of historical literature, breaking out onto the very terrain of this literature's ultimate or figurative referent. This occurs through a reflexive incorporation of the imagination into historical discourse, such that the category of the event comes to acquire properties previously ascribed only to the narrativization of events. With White's Freud, for example, the substance of the historical event is a kind of recursive narrativity, such that the meaning or significance of any one event is brought into being through the quasi-historical powers of narrative itself. The result, I argue, is a situation in which the narrative operation and the written histories it has helped produce *themselves* serve as inputs into the production of historical events. In such a situation, there is no easy way of distinguishing between history's imagined and developmental aspects. If we want to insist on the distinction, then these are levels traversed by strange loops.

With "strange loops," I mean to designate something more than a simple form of feedback. Even linear, cause-and-effect accounts of history entail a process by which one round of effects becomes a next round of causes. What marks out a strange loop is a recursive action of the past on the present, such that the present continually takes shape through the past, as well as a form of "level-crossing" by which the imagination itself acquires real force.[70] On the terrain of history, what this entails is precisely a quasi-historical process, whereby historical concepts and figures, as well as established event names and historical narratives, all serve as inputs into the production of what we usually think of as history's process. The following chapters develop this idea in the context of economic and financial history. Building on the arguments about crisis thinking and the historical imagination put forward in this chapter and the previous one, they trace out a series of strange loops characteristic of contemporary financial capitalism.

Each chapter does this in a slightly different way, but all focus on the aftermath of the 2008 crisis. Chapter 3 focuses on print journalism and the specter of another Great Depression. Routing White's comments on the modernist event via Baudrillard and other theorists of mediation, it finds in the Great Depression a signal event that produces the present through oscillating figurations of recurrence, such that crisis obtains through the recursive application of narrative archetypes to the substance of financial history. Chapter 4 looks instead at the domain of policymaking, and specifically the real-time efforts of bureaucrats to manage a moment of apparent crisis in the global financial system. Here the narrativity of the event is explored through the themes of memory and trauma. With the repetition of traumatic episodes in the historical record, an archetype of revelation is mobilized in such a way that contemporary efforts at crisis management appear as the filling out or fulfillment of an earlier, originary crisis of global finance. In this case, both the Great Depression and the Asian crisis emerge as signal events of this kind. Finally, Chapter 5 takes a sideways step into the domain of popular culture, analyzing a series of recent films about finance. Rather than a unique mode of representation, it finds in these a transmission belt for the circulation of named personae (Gordon Gekko, Jordan Belfort, Eric Packer). Much like event names, these proper names carry with them their own set of strange, quasi-historical powers.

CHAPTER 3

Return and Recurrence

"History feeds upon history," wrote Paul Valéry, looking back on World War II and the way European elites had organized their attempts to negotiate a radically uncertain present. Rather than confronting the novelty of their situation, he thought, they instead allowed their deliberations to be shaped by "imaginary memories" of what had gone before.[1] With the breakdown of global finance that began in mid-2007, the world's elites once again succumbed to the kind of historical-mindedness that concerned Valéry, invoking a string of past crises stretching from the dot-com crash in 2000 all the way back to the Dutch tulip mania of the 1630s. Among these, however, it was the Great Depression that emerged as the key reference point, figuring repeatedly in the pronouncements of central banks, finance ministries, and international organizations.[2] With the benefit of hindsight, this phenomenon can be grasped as a crucial dimension of what we now refer to as the subprime crisis. Beyond an alphabet soup of ABSs, MBSs, and CDOs, the events of 2008 brought with them a return of the Great Depression.[3]

At the time, this was registered in a number of ways. In the economics profession, there was a scramble to draw the correct policy lessons from the 1930s.[4] Popular nonfiction was equally affected, with best-selling titles on *The Bankers Who Broke The World* during the interwar years, the coming *Return of Depression Economics*, and the need for policymakers to resurrect

Keynesian methods of crisis management.[5] In the trade presses, analogy emerged as the tool of choice for journalists, such that every new development came to be measured against a different phase of the Great Depression. By now the practice is such a cliché that anyone writing on the subprime episode must begin by noting how everyone else compared it to the 1930s. And yet so far, few have addressed the broader questions to which Valéry alludes. What, exactly, is the function of the past during times of apparent crisis? If this function depends less on the past itself than our recollections of it, then from where do these recollections come? If "history feeds on history," how does this process play out? All of these questions directly pertain to the return of the Great Depression. On which versions of that episode did financial history feed, and what kind of histories did this feeding produce?

In this chapter, I argue that the day-to-day coverage of financial newspapers and magazines was integral to the way the subprime event was understood and responded to as a recurrent form of crisis. "Journalism," as *Financial Times* editor Lionel Barber wrote in 2009, "is the first draft of history."[6] But because the ink of history never dries, every draft is always a work of redrafting. The past therefore functions within financial commentary not as a fixed and distant record (as in Oakeshott's notion of "the historical past"), but instead as a shifting stream of recollections, parallels, and imputed affiliations, the purpose of which is to deal with a set of fundamentally pragmatic concerns (as in White's take on "the practical past"). Under the press of "urgent and perplexing circumstances," journalists sift through a reservoir of imagined histories, hoping to find in these something that might shed light on a muddled present.[7] There is no guarantee, though, that the past will reveal the present in a new light. "Even when it is a question of dealing with an entirely new problem," the imagination "casts around for precedents and yields to historical-mindedness," such that the present can always appear as the return of a familiar event or pattern.[8] This was very much the case during the late 2000s, when the pages of the financial press were littered not only with appeals to the Great Depression, but also with visions of financial history on the cusp of repeating itself. These visions reveal something strange about the place and power of the Great Depression within financial history. If the Depression was everywhere during the subprime crisis, it was because it seemed to possess a capacity to put the events of 2008 into historical perspective. Rather than simply presenting itself, the subprime crisis appeared through the lens of the Great Depression, and the result was an image of history's process based on the perspectives associated with that earlier episode.

If I use the language of visuality here, it is to emphasize how elements of historical discourse, such as the idea of the Great Depression, actually mediate between appearance and essence in financial history, revealing a quasi-historical process that neither category is able to fully grasp. Art history provides an illuminating metaphor in this regard. During the height of landscape painting, it was common practice to use a convex tinted lens to help bring a view into perspective and reveal, as it were, the essence or truth of nature.[9] In much the same way, droves of financial journalists turned to the 1930s, hoping that this uniquely structured event would enable them to unlock the mystery of the present and reveal the essential truth of history's process. Yet as with the painter's black mirror, the images produced were ones shaped by the observers' positioning and choice of lens. Building on this metaphor, I argue that while the Great Depression acted as a privileged mediator between the historical present and visions of financial history as such, this mediation took place through different versions of the 1930s, resulting in various, and sometimes contradictory, visions of historical recurrence. During the height of systemic fear in 2008 and 2009, these visions seemed to help save financial capitalism from itself, securing the conditions needed for its ongoing reproduction. But at the same time, the contradictions between them opened up a fissure in elite discourse, specifically on the question of the state's proper role regarding the financial industry. In this way, the idea of the Great Depression has functioned as a paradoxical force, holding out a promise of ordering events into cycles and phases reminiscent of nature, while simultaneously unleashing into the world all the patternings of financial history we can possibly imagine.

Mediations

In order to develop this argument, it is necessary to first address the significance of mass media in relation to economic and financial history. Chapter 2 touched on the question of media in connection with Hayden White's account of the historical event, but here I situate the mediated status of the event within the Marxist tradition of theorizing culture. This tradition is an important precursor to White's diagnosis of "modernist reality," presenting a series of grand visions in which the historical development of media transforms the historicity of life under capitalism. Beyond their own projected end points and horizons, these visions provide a means of beginning to grapple with the productive power of the Great Depression. Uncovering this involves a move from the histories of media and capitalism, through the concept of mediation, to an account of history premised on the mediations of contemporary financial society.

If there is one thing that defines Western Marxism, it is a conviction that media and capitalism must be conceived in terms of their intertwinement. This can be seen by way of a simple contrast with Marx's spatial metaphor of base and superstructure.[10] Though Marx meant to distinguish a primary domain of economic production from a secondary or reflective space of culture, media, and the like, each side of his equation contaminates the other. Information and communication technologies are clearly implicated in the development of different modes of production. The printing press, for example, was as integral to the birth of a market for news commentary and fiction as it was to the growth of mass culture qua culture, and many have argued that mass-market novels were themselves integral to the rise of capitalist finance.[11] Electronic communication technologies were also a key spur to the Third Industrial Revolution, which ushered in a new era of global finance, along with a range of new markets for informational and cultural products.[12] And yet print and broadcast media have been implicated in the *re*-production of corporate and state power since at least the turn of the century, whether through advertising and salesmanship or news and propaganda.[13] The Ford Motor Company, for example, began taking out color lifestyle ads in 1924, while Gabriele D'Annunzio, Italy's flamboyant poet-at-arms, was dropping pamphlets over disputed lands from as early as 1915.[14] In this way, the opposition between base and superstructure breaks down. Media technologies defy the classical model not simply by belonging to both domains at once, but also by revealing the cultural character of economy.

This is precisely why Western Marxists turned to the concept of "mediation."[15] György Lukács was one of the first to do so, using it to theorize the organizing powers of culture as such. Everything, he argued, was mediated by bourgeois culture, and the mediations performed by specific technologies were to be understood as constituent parts in a broader process of ideological mystification.[16] Lukács was famously paranoid but influential nonetheless. As John Guillory points out, some of the key divisions within Western Marxism can be traced back to the uptake of the mediation concept, and in particular to the way it influenced the project of ideology-critique.[17] For Frankfurt school theorists such as Theodor Adorno, *mediation* became the name for a theoretical task that sought to wrest a possibility of change from the culture industry and its reified image of the world.[18] But for those on the French New Left, such as Guy Debord and Jean Baudrillard, the modern apparatus of cultural mediation had to be understood as the basis for an entirely new kind of reality—the real unreality of the spectacle or the hyperrealism of simulation. Standing Marx on his head, they maintained that the realm of appearance had effectively replaced that of production, giving rise to a "base-less" regime of representation in which the order of signs and images functioned as both an anchor and a horizon for capitalist society. "The spectacle is capital accumulated to the point where it becomes image," and yet it is "in the sphere of the simulacra . . . that the global process of capital is founded."[19] With the advent of mass media, then, capitalism had been transformed into a grand tautology.

The discovery of this tautology was accompanied by a significant reappraisal of history. For Debord, the spectacle was the beginning of a "paralyzed history," devoid of historical consciousness and thus condemned to an "eternal present."[20] His stance on the matter was clear: this was not a good development. Yet he would frequently voice a desire to find tactical sites and levers that might somehow bring history back to life. Baudrillard expressed no such hope. Having relinquished any sense of nostalgia, he saw the progressive logic of representation as having produced an exit from history altogether. The prevailing regime of appearance, he argued, was one in which events have been divested of all belonging to chronology and the real, and there is simply no way of going back: we are stuck in a system that simulates history rather than obeys it.[21] This is what separates Baudrillard from Debord, the question of whether history has a future. But there are important commonalities in terms of the steps in their analysis. Both were in agreement, for example, that the dynamism of early capitalist history had given way to a strangely fluid stasis. Each also saw this as the product of a systematic logic of representation, grounded in the irresistible power of new mass media. The result is a diagnosis that does more than reposition media within capitalist history. With Debord and Baudrillard, mediated capitalism threatens the very consistency of history.

In the context of contemporary finance, this threat has played out in decidedly ambiguous terms. At first glance, the age of derivatives and securitization has in many ways been an age without history. Finance in general has become a timeless media spectacle, figuring forth as "a never-ending series of daily stories" and a "cacophony of voices, images and events."[22] Meanwhile, new interactive media have exacerbated an already mimetic market rationality, turning financialized accumulation into a hyper-real loop of reflexive performance.[23] Finally, there is the truly peculiar case of option-pricing models (which were integral to the creation of a market for subprime mortgage-backed securities). These models envisage their own end to history in the form of a market-completion fantasy, which imagines that derivatives might one day create "fungible prices for all times, places and things."[24] We are still far from such a day, but as financial models have been embedded in market practice through successive waves of new media (beginning with printed tables and culminating in the computerized platforms of contemporary securities trading), market dynamics have come to increasingly reflect or register the workings of numerical formulas—perhaps not an implosive absorption of the real by the code, but at the very least a form of bricolage that replaces history with a succession of equations.[25]

On a second look, however, history refuses to disappear. If it had ever been neutralized, obliterated, or concealed, then the crisis of 2008 marked its reincorporation into the financial imaginary. The web-like markets for risk, the cascading automatism of their undoing, the constant news bulletins about this very process: none of these were able to repress what *Financial Times* journalist Gillian Tett referred to as a sudden and "violent thirst for historical knowledge."[26] Names and dates from the past burst into the present, circulating as so many omens and lodestars of what lay ahead. But more than any other episode, it was the Great Depression that captured the financial imagination, emerging not simply as one among many but *the* signal event, as if the name itself promised to deliver the present over to a time before models and screens had vanquished history.[27] Nowhere was this more evident than in the pages of the financial press.

During the subprime episode, financial newspapers and periodicals were awash with different versions of the 1930s. Well-known and widely circulated specialist publications, such as the *Economist*, the *Financial Times, Forbes*, and the *Wall Street Journal*, repeatedly published editorials and opinion pieces drawing comparisons to the Great Depression.[28] These appeals were varied in nature, touching on and in some cases speaking directly to a range of specific policy debates. A significant proportion of them, however, entailed the suggestion of a recurring set of conditions or dynamics, such that the idea of the Great Depression carried within it that of history repeating itself. The return of the Great Depression should be understood in terms of this doubled character. In addition to the literal return of the Great Depression to financial language and discourse, there was also a second, figurative return, in which the 1930s were invoked in ways that envisioned their recurrence in either the present or some near future. The significance of this double return consists in the way it turns visions of recurrent crisis, long prominent in economic and financial discourse, into a means of mediating between the Great Depression and the subprime event. In empirical terms, at least three such visions emerge alongside the broader imaginaries of crisis and recovery. The first rests on the figure of the *cycle*, the second on that of the *epoch*, and the third on a related figure of *reversal*. In each case, the Great Depression allows journalists to see in the present a replay of some familiar pattern, but when these instances are taken together, they reveal the power of the press to produce financial history in diverse and ultimately contradictory ways. The following sections trace out this process in real time.

Visions of Cyclical Recurrence

Cyclical thinking has long dominated liberal economics and financial theory in particular. It should come as little surprise, then, that the figure of the cycle would be the first that journalists reached for during the subprime years. From as early as mid-2007, references to the 1930s as a cyclical event begin to emerge across the financial press, effectively relaying markets as reaching a natural inflection point. The *Economist*, for example, does this by citing the response of American banker Leon Fraser to the 1929 crash: "Better to have loaned and lost than never to have loaned at all."[29] Fraser's quip is well known within investment circles for capturing an appropriate answer to the enduring reality of the business cycle. Its quotation by the *Economist* therefore casts developments in the housing market as yet another inevitable correction, simply the latest installment in a long series of booms and busts.

Numerous variations on this theme appear throughout 2007, when a certain denial about the gravity of the situation still holds sway. One of the more interesting examples comes from Gillian Tett, who observes that although "few pundits have attempted to suggest . . . a replay of the best-known drama of all—1929," a certain return of the past is nevertheless underway as investors "reacquaint themselves with the unpalatable truth that almost every bubble is accompanied by a belief that innovation has changed the rules"—"a belief," she adds, that "typically proves to be false."[30] In this formulation, the Great Depression figures as a kind of limit event against which the normal course of boom and bust can be ascertained. Tett acknowledges the specificity of the 1929 crash, but she does so only in order to assert the same psychology of boom and bust expressed in Fraser's aphorism—a psychology that is itself integral to the idea of natural cycles in finance.[31] And so the crash of 1929 again serves to emphasize the familiar and unavoidable aspects of the subprime meltdown and not its historical specificity. This logic even applies to recurrence itself, which is not so much a unique development as something that just happens over and over again.

Things begin to change as the sense of crisis deepens in early 2008. Following the rescue of Bear Stearns in March, some publications start drawing parallels with the 1930s as an epochal moment in financial history. First and foremost among these is the *Economist*, which identifies a string of similarities between the two episodes, focusing in particular on the scale of the asset bubble collapse, the extension of emergency support to an investment bank, and the rate of decline in US house prices.[32] It later goes on to read this last factor as symptomatic of a failing American capitalism.[33] Meanwhile, the *Financial Times* takes the International Monetary Fund's description of events—"the largest financial shock since the Great Depression"—and situates this alongside emerging threats of geo-monetary disorder, announcing the arrival of a decisive turning point in the management of the world economy.[34] This transition reflects a move beyond the historical data sets associated with financial economics, such that efforts to interpret the present come to draw not only on price comparisons but also a broader set of political and economic histories. In particular, journalists begin to retrieve and reinstitute earlier historical accounts in which the Great Depression features as a pivotal event in the story of global capitalism. The result is a vision of recurrence quite distinct from the one associated with the figure of the cycle. Rather than another in a long line of market corrections, the subprime meltdown now appears as the potential return of a more virulent strain of historical crisis. Certainty slides into speculation, and recurrence starts to take the form of an open question: Can it happen again? Will it happen again?

Interestingly, this vision of recurrence does not immediately take off, and for some months, it remains latent or at least counterbalanced by the commentary provided in the pages of *Forbes* and the *Wall Street Journal*. In early 2008, for example, *Forbes* repeatedly rejects comparisons to the 1930s as overblown: "Gloomy people are saying that we are in the midst of the worst financial crisis since the 1930s. They said the same thing in 1998. Bullish!" It goes on to expand the point, putting it in more general terms: "You can't find a time in the 20th century when, less than five months into a real global bear market, people were talking bear market and recession in any visible numbers. But they always talk disaster during corrections."[35] The message, of course, is that such comparisons with the 1930s are themselves a product of cycles in investor sentiment, of the kind we've seen before and will see again.

Both US publications also begin to address fears of epochal crisis through the use of direct counteranalogy. For the *Wall Street Journal*, another 1930s-style depression would require a return to the "major policy blunders" of that era, which it suggests have yet to prove forthcoming.[36] Meanwhile, for *Forbes*, the lack of protectionism and use of expansionary monetary policy already signal the existence of a different policy landscape to that of the 1930s.[37] The *Wall Street Journal* also focuses on key economic indicators, pointing out how US mortgage delinquency rates are not nearly as high as they were in the 1930s, and both growth and employment figures not nearly as low.[38] This line of argument culminates in an article published at the peak of crisis fever, entitled "We're Not Headed For a Depression." In it, author and Chicago economist Gary Becker explicitly dismisses suggestions of an epochal crisis, observing how "the crisis that kills capitalism has been said to happen during every major recession and financial crisis ever since Karl Marx."[39] In none of these instances, he argues, did it ever arrive, and so people would do well to start recognizing the ongoing crisis for what it is: a natural phase within the cyclical process of business and finance. In this rather extreme view, history is in no danger of repeating itself because history is itself nothing more than a recurrence of cyclical ups and downs. Indeed, the only real danger is that governments might fail to recognize this and respond to these cycles in misguided ways.

Visions of Epochal Recurrence

Although they do not disappear entirely, visions of benign recurrence give way in late 2008 to fears that capitalism is entering into another epochal crisis. Rather than supporting cyclical readings of the subprime event, appeals to the Great Depression increasingly emphasize its status as a specific and properly historical episode, bringing the weight of its received consequences to bear on the present in the form of various imagined futures. As I have already suggested, this shift entails a transition from the kind of knowledge associated with financial markets (in which the past consists of so many data points from which to extract patterns) to the kind of knowledge cultivated by historical discourse (in which the past acquires the form of a story or plot). The Great Depression figures within the latter as an event already enshrined in the story of capitalism, affiliated through various historical narratives with a whole host of political and economic trajectories. During 2008 and 2009, these affiliations are taken up and put to work by journalists as a means of situating the present within a history marked by epochal crises. This occurs through a number of distinct rhetorical maneuvers.

As Vico long ago argued, the work of rhetoric is not simply to persuade but rather to conjure up a persuasive reality. In the present context, two key maneuvers are involved in conjuring up visions of epochal recurrence. First, there are analogies with the scale and scope of the Great Depression. The *Economist* begins drawing these in mid-2008 following the bailout of Bear Stearns, but after the bankruptcy of Lehman Brothers in early September, the other publications join in, and all begin making numerous and frequent comparisons with the 1930s. *Forbes*, for instance, considers a massive consumer retrenchment in the United States on a par with that of the 1930s, while the *Wall Street Journal* focuses on the scale and persistence of US stock market losses, which it suggests are comparable only to those of December 1931.[40] For their part, both the *Financial Times* and the *Economist* emphasize the spread of financial market panic beyond the confines of the United States,[41] and in a similar vein, the *Wall Street Journal* identifies a threat of "global stag-deflation" that would see the macroeconomic dynamics of the Depression replayed on the world stage.[42]

In these examples, analogical reasoning works to attach different attributes of the Great Depression to the present, such that the latter begins to accumulate a set of affiliations with the former as an episode of epochal crisis. In this way, analogy establishes the figure of epochal recurrence as a question in the public mind. But in order for this question to be posed both *in* and *to* the present, the idea of epochal recurrence must be invested with some kind of determinate content. What, exactly, might happen again? Analogies of scale and scope alone cannot achieve this. This is where a second rhetorical maneuver comes into play, by which various appeals to the causes and consequences of the Great Depression work to fill out the figure of epochal recurrence in more concrete terms. Again there is considerable variety in this regard, but two themes do emerge as dominant motifs. The first relates to questions of international trade, the second to those of political instability and war.

References to trade first appear in mid-2007, when *Forbes* uses the Smoot-Hawley Tariff Act of 1930 to illustrate the self-defeating effects of protectionism.[43] These remain relatively isolated instances until mid-2008, when both *Forbes* and the *Economist* start applying this kind of lesson to contemporary developments in trade policy. It is not until late 2008, though, that journalists begin bringing trade-focused accounts of the 1930s to bear on the fallout of financial market instability. The earliest and most basic references of this sort simply assert the importance of keeping world markets open. *Forbes*, for example, reiterates its claim that "the Depression was actually triggered by the Smoot-Hawley Tariff," and the *Wall Street Journal* uses this same claim to underline the need to address stalled multilateral negotiations.[44] Meanwhile, the *Economist* links the question of trade to resurgent debates over the future of Anglo-Saxon capitalism, insisting that "the free movement of non-financial goods and services should not be dragged into the argument—as they were, to disastrous effect, in the 1930s."[45]

These lessons are all derived from a liberal account of the interwar years that has dominated academic economics for some time now, and so at this point, the practical past is more or less indistinguishable from the historical past. The contemporary lesson, as it were, is essentially the same as the one encoded into established accounts of the Depression. But as the fear of a collapse in trade is hooked up to novel aspects of the contemporary economic and political landscape, the old lesson begins to take on new urgency and significance. The *Financial Times*, for example, identifies global imbalances as a potential driver of protectionism, arguing that "if the surplus countries do not expand domestic demand relative to potential output, the open world economy may even break down," adding, "As in the 1930s, this is now a real danger."[46] The *Economist* focuses instead on possible transmission mechanisms, pointing out that global supply chains "could be disrupted by policies much less dramatic than the Smoot-Hawley Act."[47] Finally, both the *Economist* and *Forbes* counsel against any complacency regarding a repeat of Smoot-Hawley, identifying proposed "Buy American" provisions in the US stimulus package as an ominous harbinger of futures to come.[48] In each of these instances, lessons drawn from conventional accounts of the 1930s reveal history to be heading down a familiar and dangerous path. Epochal recurrence becomes imminent threat.

An exaggerated version of this process can be identified in references to political instability and war. Once again *Forbes* takes the lead, arguing that "the Great Depression made possible the rise of Nazism and the Second World War."[49] This, again, is a rather conventional narrative of the Depression, but as the sense of crisis deepens in late 2008, other publications begin to echo this account in slightly different ways. For example, while *Forbes* continues to restate its case, using the legacy of Nazism to warn against a turn away from free and open markets in the United States, the *Financial Times* instead invokes "Hitler's rise" and "the horrors a depression might bring" in order to urge Congress to rethink its rejection of Treasury Secretary Hank Paulson's rescue plan for the financial sector.[50] Convergence does emerge, however, around a related trope in which the figure of epochal recurrence is rendered in geopolitical terms. This first to do this is the *Wall Street Journal*, which maps a threat of instability onto the present by comparing the leaders of contemporary "rogue states" to the "remorseless fanatics who rose up on the crest of economic disaster" during the Great Depression.[51] The *Financial Times* performs a similar maneuver in early 2009 when it locates in the present another "grave threat to world stability and democracy," pointing out that "revolutions often start as bread riots."[52] Finally *Forbes* joins in too, emphasizing the importance of an engaged and free-trading United States by casting Latin American populism as the latest threat to liberal democratic capitalism:

> At that time [the 1930s] there was a region in play: Europe. A self-involved U.S. turned inward, allowing Mussolini and Hitler free rein. Today Latin America is in play, and Venezuela's Hugo Chávez is waiting in the wings, ready to fill the post-Castro vacuum.[53]

In each of these instances, the specter of another Great Depression takes the form of a potential slide into political instability and war. But as this last example illustrates, this particular fear of epochal recurrence is in no way incompatible with that of another collapse in trade. Rather, because trade functions within these visions as a cause and war as an effect, the one figure of recurrence in many cases already entails the other. That is, while not every vision of another Great Depression emphasizes trade-related dynamics, those that do draw their force from an implicit link between protectionism and some set of outcomes deemed worthy of averting, here fleshed out in extreme form by the figure of another Hitler on the horizon. Comparing someone to Hitler is by most accounts a pretty cheap rhetorical trick. And yet the logic is entirely in keeping with the way fears of epochal recurrence acquire their force, whether they relate to international trade, to war, or both. By transposing a chain of causal claims from the past into the present, cause and effect become scrambled, allowing the projected effect to undo the cause before it manifests. This is one of the ways "history feeds upon history": as an injunction to keep the mistakes *of* the past *in* the past. "Never again," as the saying goes.

Recurrence Averted, Recurrence Resumed

Epochal recurrence is not invoked with quite the same energy once the sense of crisis begins to abate in mid-2009. But rather than disappearing altogether, visions of recurrence continue to produce affiliations between ongoing events and those of the 1930s. Three specific developments contribute to this process.

First is a shift away from visions of imminent epochal recurrence. This can be traced as far back as late 2008, when all four publications start incorporating crisis-response measures into counteranalogies with the 1930s, but it is not really until early 2009 that these take off. The London Group of 20 (G20) Summit in April is pivotal here, providing some sections of the press with new faith in the powers of liberal internationalism. Soon after the landmark meeting, both the *Economist* and the *Financial Times* begin to regularly emphasize the scale and scope of various measures enacted by policymakers, suggesting that these have reduced the likelihood of another Great Depression. The *Economist*, for example, speaks of "the biggest and most synchronized macroeconomic stimulus since the Second World War," while the *Financial Times* adds to this "the most far-reaching socialization of market risk in history."[54] Both also use these same measures to express concerns about the need for exit strategies, but the basic point is still reiterated throughout the latter half of 2009. The *Economist* puts it succinctly: "It has become known as the Great Recession. . . . But an equally apt name would be the Great Stabilisation."[55] "It," of course, is 'the crisis,' which through sheer force of policy support is now seen as no longer worthy of its old epithet: "the next Great Depression."

Second is the emergence of a new variation on the figure of epochal recurrence. This can be observed in references to protectionism, which begin to take on a different form as fears of another Depression subside. There is still the occasional reference to trade collapse as a "really existing" threat, but on the whole, these are pushed into the past tense, where they instead name a threat that "really existed" but has since been overcome. The *Economist*, for example, argues that although "trade has contracted by more in this crisis than it had at a comparable stage of the Depression ... [there is] little doubt that the decline in trade has bottomed out."[56] Meanwhile, even *Forbes*, the publication most critical of US trade policy, backs away from its earlier predictions of a return to the 1930s, claiming that "[al]though Barack Obama is the most protectionist President since Herbert Hoover, we are not likely to pass another Depression-creating Smoot-Hawley-like tariff bill."[57]

This same change is also evident in references to political instability and war. These become far less common in late 2009, but when *Forbes* and the *Financial Times* do revisit the theme, their discussion is inflected with a palpable sense of relief. For *Forbes*, this rests primarily on what it sees as a lack of "credible alternatives to traditional democratic liberal values," which it suggests has kept the "ghastly ideologies" of the 1930s at bay.[58] However, in the case of the *Financial Times*, this argument is incorporated into a much broader counteranalogy with the early 1900s:

> The good news is that the world has not made mistakes as big as those that followed the noughties a century ago: thanks, partly to nuclear weapons, direct conflicts among great powers have been avoided; a liberal world economy has survived, so far; the lessons of the 1930s were applied to the financial crisis of the 2000s, with at least short-run success ... [and] while the movement towards democracy of the early 1990s has slowed, the number of grossly malign totalitarian regimes is now small, at least by the standards of the 20th century.[59]

Here, against a similar geopolitical and ideological backdrop to the one depicted by *Forbes*, two specific explanations are offered for why the subprime crisis was not as deep as the Great Depression. First, "the open liberal world economy has survived," and second, "the lessons of the 1930s were applied." In both instances, the 1930s are used to illustrate how a threat to political stability was overcome rather than to indicate the existence of any such threat in the present. Visions of imminent epochal recurrence are in this way gradually neutralized via broad counteranalogies, as well as more specific references to both trade and war.

It is important to note, however, that what takes their place remains a vision of recurrence and that this new vision rests on a largely unchanged reading of the 1930s. With references to war, for example, there is agreement on *what* it is that might happen again—gulags, concentration camps, the end of the world, and so on. Meanwhile, with references to trade, there appears to be agreement on *how* this might happen again, for a link between tariffs and the Great Depression is affirmed not only at the height of the perceived protectionist threat but also in its aftermath. The key difference, then, concerns *when* all of this might happen again. Is history threatening to repeat itself tomorrow, or are we just reminding ourselves that it might at some point in the future? With this in mind, early references to trade and war can be understood as the beginning of a process through which latent visions of epochal recurrence, based on hegemonic historical narratives, were called on by actors in the global financial press and transformed into visions of imminent epochal recurrence. Conversely, the shift that occurs in late 2009 can be read as a kind of becoming latent, whereby fears of epochal recurrence were returned to the storehouse of history via counteranalogy and the use of past participles.

Finally, there is a reemergence of references to the 1930s that underpin a vision of cyclical recurrence. The figure of the cycle was crowded out in late 2008 when publications began drawing instead on that of epochal recurrence, but it was never abandoned entirely. In fact, during the months following the Lehman bankruptcy, all four publications incorporate the 1930s into a contrarian and opportunistic reading of the business cycle on at least one occasion.[60] In late 2009, however, both *Forbes* and the *Wall Street Journal* return to this figure, retroactively rejecting the prospect of another Great Depression and announcing instead the arrival of a new bull market. In August, for example, *Forbes* dismisses recent stock market dips by identifying 1935 as the only bull market that did not encounter "some material indigestion within its first twelve months."[61] Meanwhile, the *Wall Street Journal* recalls the bear market trough of 1932, pointing out how "investors who had the courage to invest realized handsome long-term gains."[62] In each instance, references to the Great Depression once again serve to emphasize the familiar and cyclical aspects of the now receding crisis event. Thus, at the same time as there is a shift away from fears of imminent epochal recurrence, there is also a parallel shift back toward the figure of the natural cycle and the kind of recurrence this entails. The only difference is that this is now achieved by retrospectively identifying an inevitable upswing rather than assessing the immediate prospect of another downturn.

Reversals

While the figure of cyclical recurrence is rooted in a particular understanding of investor sentiment, the figure of epochal recurrence is based instead on a reading of how trade policy once threw democratic capitalism into crisis. In this sense, these two figures relate to the domains of the market and the state, respectively. But as various emergency measures are enacted in response to the prospect of another Great Depression, a third set of visions emerges in which the present appears as a recurring moment of pendulum-like reversal in the relation between state and market. Unlike the cycle or the epoch, the figure of reversal produces a division within the financial press as individual publications come to take rather different views on the political legacy of the subprime episode.

This process can be traced back to January 2008, when *Forbes* portrays the initial provision of relief to subprime borrowers as a turn for the worse in terms of policy orientation. Comparing this move to Hoover's attempts to secure a voluntary freeze on redundancies and wage cuts in 1929, it suggests that the Treasury-backed plan "follows bad precedents made during the Great Depression."[63] It continues in this vein as further crisis-response measures are enacted, casting both Hoover and Roosevelt as symbols of a more generic and recurrent form of misguided interventionism. In June, for example, it argues that the "myth" of a passive Hoover and an activist Roosevelt is skewing US electoral debates and that Obama's proposed policies risk repeating their respective mistakes not only on trade but also on tax and bailouts.[64] It also reiterates this same point in early September, describing Obama as a dangerous "Hoover-FDR hybrid" whose activism would leave "the punitive power of natural economic forces . . . deadened and restrained."[65] Thus, as fears of epochal recurrence mount, *Forbes* suggests that a cyclical downturn might indeed be transformed into another Great Depression, but only with a reversion to 1930s-style interventionism. The *Wall Street Journal* adopts a similar position in response to the bailout of insurance giant AIG, arguing that the risks of "socialized finance" are clearly illustrated by "the record of the Depression-era Reconstruction Finance Corp."[66] On this view, the only true route to recovery lies in a new bear market.

It is not long, however, before this nascent vision is inverted by both UK publications, which cast the initiatives of the US Treasury and Federal Reserve in a decidedly different light. The *Economist*, for example, explicitly rejects "predictions of a sea change towards more invasive government," arguing that the deployment of public money should be seen as *reducing* the likelihood of a 1930s-style reversal: "If Mr. Paulson and Mr. Bernanke have prevented a Depression-like collapse in output with their actions," it reasons, "then they may also have prevented a Depression-like backlash against the free market."[67] Meanwhile, the *Financial Times* directly counters the position taken by *Forbes* on Hoover and Roosevelt, characterizing the US legislators who blocked Paulson's Troubled Asset Relief Program as irresponsible liquidationists who "should realize that now is not a time for Hoovernomics."[68] Of course, neither the *Financial Times* nor the *Economist* denies that a "redrawing [of] the boundaries between government and markets" is underway, and both acknowledge that precisely such a redrawing followed the Depression.[69] The point, however, is that they do not interpret state rescues as another turn away from markets. Instead, they see them as the proper response to a recurring paradox: sometimes bank failure means that government has no choice but to "Nationalise [in order] to save the free market."[70]

At the peak of market turmoil, both US publications somewhat soften their views on the dangers of governmental intervention. *Forbes*, for example, concedes that "emergency measures may have been necessary," but still worries that these could create Washington's "biggest power expansion since the New Deal."[71] Similarly, the *Wall Street Journal* accepts that in exceptional circumstances, "radical government policies should be considered," but it continues to argue that "many . . . including several pursued by Franklin Roosevelt during the Great Depression . . . can make things worse."[72] However, once fears of epochal recurrence give way to extensive international cooperation, both return to a more unambiguous stance. Following the London meeting of the G20, for example, the *Wall Street Journal* uses the 1930s to diagnose and decry an ongoing, global process of historical reversal:

The Depression put in motion an historic tension between public and private sectors. ... After 50 years of public dominance, Reagan's presidency
tipped the scales back toward private enterprise ... [but for] every waking
hour of this economically liberal era, the losing side has wanted to tip the
balance back. ... The opportunity to achieve that goal finally arrived—with
the Great Recession of 2009.[73]

Here the Great Depression is portrayed not simply as an event that might
repeat itself, but also as the origin of a tug-of-war between statist and pro-
market forces. Moreover, within this particular patterning of history, the
subprime crisis is revealed as an event through which statists are seeking
to repeat the reversal they achieved in the 1930s. *Forbes* performs a similar
move in late 2009, when it once again compares existing US policy to the
New Deal, and then describes the latter as having kicked off "a decade of
contest between an ambitious public sector and a dazed private sector."[74]
With both *Forbes* and the *Wall Street Journal*, then, visions of epochal
recurrence mutate into explicit fears about another reversal in the relation between states and markets, such that business would once again be
hampered by the doings of government.

Elsewhere, visions of reversal continue evolving along different lines.
Although both the *Economist* and the *Financial Times* do start to identify some
risks associated with new state powers and responsibilities, neither comes
to question the necessity of their introduction in relation to the subprime
episode.[75] The figure of reversal thus continues to reveal a recurrent danger
that accompanies state inaction; in addition, it also serves to designate an
outcome that has been averted by timely intervention. For the UK-based
publications, then, there is consensus that governments helped save financial
capitalism from itself. This stands in stark contrast to the pronouncements
of the US-based publications, which essentially suggest that if capitalism
survived the crisis, this was in spite of misguided public actions. The process
at work here is one in which the same basic of figure of reversal is fleshed out
using different narrativizations of the 1930s, such that the present assumes
a place within two diametrically opposed historical trajectories. The result
is a significant split within the financial press over the future of the capitalist state. Such is the peculiar power of the Great Depression, whose status

within the discourse of financial history seems just as capable of undermining order as producing it. It is to this broader process that I now turn.

Making History Dis-appear

How should we grasp the historical function of the Great Depression? The most common way to approach this question is through visual metaphor. Financial journalists have employed this trick on numerous occasions. During 2008, for example, the *Economist* began one of its article sections by inviting readers to view "Smoot-Hawley in the rear mirror."[76] As we all know, the purpose of a rear mirror is to keep a receding horizon in view, specifically so as to better comprehend the situations one is entering. In historical terms, the equivalent would be a process by which past events like the Depression help provide a fuller picture of the present. But as I have shown, the subprime episode brought with it numerous versions of the Great Depression, suggesting that the Depression cannot function as the simple mirror point that journalists and others may want it to. Financial historians have acknowledged as much, devoting considerable attention to the different kinds of analogies with the 1930s drawn by pundits and scholars alike.[77] And yet here too, a metaphor of the mirror persists, continuing to obscure as much as it reveals. Renowned historian of the Depression Barry Eichengreen, for example, has written about a "hall of mirrors" in which distorted reflections of the 1930s keep the truth of financial history from view.[78] But how exactly is anyone to tell a distorted reflection from an accurate one, a correct image of history from a false one?

History itself provides no such means. Past events, structures, or processes become histories only through narrative operations, and there is always more than one way of narrativizing the past. This means not only that historical discourse can provide different accounts of the same episodes, but also that the lessons of the past must change with the histories from which they are drawn. An apparently signal event like the Great Depression thus acquires this status through the very institutions of historiography, which position the Depression within the story of capitalism in such a way that it seems able to reveal the hidden patterns of history. Moreover, the signal event produces the very patterns it purports to reveal, which are none other than the figures inscribed into its various narrativizations. Rather than a hall of mirrors, then, the Great Depression functions as a different kind of object—one that enables the historical present to emerge through recollected histories of finance. If we still want to think of this in terms of imaging and reflection, a better template can be found in the object known to art historians as the black mirror.

During the age of the picturesque in the late eighteenth century, landscape painters across Europe used small tinted convex mirrors to reduce and unify the objects under their gaze. On their walks, they would stop, turn their back on the scene that interested them, and look instead into their mirror, adjusting their position until they were confronted with an image they deemed beautiful enough to paint (beauty, of course, being synonymous with truth in the romantic imagination).[79] In a similar fashion, few financial journalists have seemed willing to wander far without a history of the Great Depression at the ready, as if only these would enable them to bring the whole of the present into view and locate the subprime event within history. The metaphor of the black mirror in this way speaks to a desire for order in history of the kind that landscape painters looked for in nature. Just as these painters believed that a black mirror could reveal to them the unity of the natural world, journalists want to believe that the Great Depression can somehow reveal the recurring patterns that organize financial history.

Of course, at different times, journalists invoke and deploy different Great Depressions. Different mirrors, as it were, render financial history in different ways. Again, the appeal of the landscape provides an interesting perspective, specifically through what are known as Claude glasses. Rather than a single mirror, these were a portable set of convex tinted lenses that tourists often carried with them on walks through the countryside. Upon encountering a compelling scene, walkers would experiment by looking at it through any one of their different colored lenses, allowing them to "modify the weather and the luminosity of a day or a season in the space of a few seconds."[80] With Claude glasses, one's physical position and lens interact to reveal the "truth" of nature, but this truth is filtered through the color of one's chosen lens. Claude glasses were in this way less tied to the romantic ideal of beauty's truth and more attuned to a bourgeois sensibility in which the organizing truths of nature could be modified or perfected to suit one's tastes. This is an illuminating way of grasping the variety of patterns that journalists have seemed able to find in financial history. As before, the Great Depression is believed to be an event uniquely capable of revealing history's patterns, but the fact that the Depression arrives to us through so many figures of recurrence means that in any one present, visions of history are easy to produce yet difficult to unify. The 1930s were repeatedly invoked in ways that purported to reveal the historicity of the subprime crisis, but these figurations of the 1930s interacted with the present to produce different images of its historicity—different lenses, different vistas.

In this sense, there is no simple unveiling of financial history to be had, but neither is there a simple concealment or occlusion. By acting as a historical black mirror, the idea of the Great Depression has simultaneously performed both these functions. Competing portrayals of the 1930s served to bring specific histories into view, but in so doing, they also worked to obscure other possible figurations, which would have revealed different truths about the present. In theoretical terms, this process implies a feedback loop between the events we narrate as crises and the inventory of crisis narratives associated with financial history. In the context of contemporary mass media, a financial event can be transformed into a moment of apparent crisis by bringing past events and imagined histories back into the orbit of the present. And yet during such a moment, it is these self-same events and histories that we draw on in order to put history back together again. As Valéry put it, "History feeds upon history."

This strange loop is fundamentally different to the kinds of oppressive tautology theorized by the French New Left. For Debord, the real of history somehow feeds on bad or corrupted historical imagery, leaving itself bloated, sick, and unable to go on. For Baudrillard, history enters into a carnival of metaphysical cannibalism, eating so much of itself that auto-referentiality is all that remains. But within the logic of the historical black mirror, it is the historicity of the present that feeds on figurations of the past, and it does this precisely in order to recognize itself. Moreover, it seeks this recognition so that it may remain within history and will rewrite the very logic of history's process if this is the price it must pay. It is not simply the self-image of the historical present, then, that is entangled with its own regime of representation, but also the actual historicity of said present, which is indistinguishable from its appearance as a figuration. By acting as a privileged mediator between the historical present and visions of historical recurrence, the idea of the Great Depression has revealed the fundamentally constitutive relation of historical imagination to historical process. Hence, in place of Debord's "false consciousness of time," we should speak instead of the necessary fictions of historical process, and within Baudrillard's destruction of history by virtualization, we should identify the preconditions for a new mode of its very production.[81]

The results of this process, however, are decidedly indeterminate. Over the course of the subprime episode, this was forcefully illustrated not only in the way the Great Depression gave rise to different visions of historical recurrence, but also in the impact of these visions on the discursive production of crisis. In the coverage of the financial press, we saw denial slip into a state of emergency as visions of cyclical recurrence gave way to fears of epochal recurrence; we saw the notion of historical reversal emerge and take shape alongside state initiatives that were expressly intended to prevent cyclical recurrence from sliding into epochal recurrence; and we saw visions of cyclical recurrence reemerge and support a return to business as usual. In all of these ways, the Great Depression would appear to have helped save financial capitalism from itself, securing the conditions for its ongoing reproduction both during and in the wake of its apparent crisis. On the flip side, the Great Depression also produced a significant point of divergence within the global financial press. Through the figure of historical reversal, British and North American publications came to adopt diametrically opposed positions on the necessity and desirability of emergency crisis response measures. For the former, these measures were precisely what prevented a return to the 1930s, whereas for the latter, they were the only remaining threat of any such return. Insofar as this disagreement concerns both the historicity of the crisis and the future of the capitalist state, it constitutes an important new fissure within financial capitalism: no longer is there agreement on what kind of crisis it experienced, and no longer is there agreement on the proper role of the state within financialized accumulation. This kind of discord remains an enduring feature of the postcrisis landscape, suggesting that while visions of the 1930s may have helped weather a financial storm in 2008, they also worked to rob finance capital of a coherent self-image. The outcome of this new precarity is still uncertain, but one thing is clear: it will depend on whether the commentariat of global finance can once again establish a shared vision of world history.

CHAPTER 4

Repetition and Revelation

On October 7, 2008, at the inaugural World Policy Conference in Evian, Jean-Claude Trichet, president of the European Central Bank, addressed an audience of finance ministers, heads of state, policy experts, and senior officials from international organizations. "We are all, together, writing the history of crisis management as we speak," he declared.[1] Only a day before, chancellor Angela Merkel had announced the rescue of one of Germany's biggest banks, and a mere day later, Prime Minister Gordon Brown would announce his plan for the recapitalization of British and UK-based financial institutions. Trichet therefore spoke amid a frantic search for policy solutions, and his words were a way of underlining just how novel a situation he and his colleagues found themselves in. Every day brought new emergency measures. But in his commentary on these initiatives, Trichet—along with the full cast of his fellow crisis managers—repeatedly returned to a range of prior crisis episodes, as if their shared past might contain within it a vital clue as to what the world needed from them next.

Rather than asking what is at stake in such a scramble to the past, scholars of world politics have tended instead to write their own crisis histories through similar means. Thomas Oatley, for example, has characterized the subprime episode as the latest in a cycle of global crises generated by the expansion of American military and financial power.[2] Daniel Drezner offers a somewhat different account, celebrating the way global elites pulled together to prevent the world from sliding into another Great Depression.[3] These opposing views reflect a broader trend within political economy thinking on crisis, which is to oscillate between optimism and pessimism about the likely recurrence of prior crises, as well as our ability to effectively deal with them when they do.[4] Yet if figures such as Trichet underscore the novelty of the present at the same time as they call on the familiarities of the past, then their appeal to history must amount to more than the simple threat that it might repeat itself.

In this chapter, I suggest that statements such as Trichet's provide a window onto the scrambled nature of financial history and the strange loops through which efforts to govern or manage it take shape. More specifically, I argue that the diagnosis and treatment of contemporary financial crisis hinges on the recollection of prior crisis episodes, whose imputed affiliations enable the present to assume a place within familiar narrative templates. The previous chapter examined this process in connection with figures of recurrence, identifying how these emerged within the financial press as a means of mediating between the Great Depression and the subprime event. This chapter turns instead to the figure of linear progression, arguing that it too is central to the way history is produced in financial times. Rather than simply configuring a succession of events into a causal story, narratives of linear development entail a looping logic whereby the past is repeatedly called on to reveal the present anew. This process recalls the temporal dimensions of trauma, wherein the traumatizing event continually reappears as an awareness or presence of the past. Here, however, I stress a distinctly metahistorical form of trauma in which history itself appears as both wound and salve. The reappearance of the past is a symptom of historical malaise: it registers a profound confusion about what has become of our financialized present. Yet it is also a means of shoring up the historical mode of experience, a kind of defense mechanism against the fear that life on earth might be little more than "one damned thing after another."

Mircea Eliade, a historian of religion, thought this fear so important he gave it a name: "the terror of history."[5] Eliade had in mind the peoples of ancient societies, for whom the return to mythical events was a means of keeping the terror of history at bay, but in much the same fashion, the managers of global finance have returned to the events of recent financial history, using these to restore their sense of agency and purpose during a time experienced as traumatic. The result, however, has been more than a reiteration of familiar historical insights. Under the press of the subprime event, global elites like Trichet repeatedly called on the past to reveal new histories, uncover new truths and lessons, and identify new sites and modes of financial governance. In particular, prior episodes like the Great Depression and the Asian crisis were retroactively transformed into prophetic events, such that ongoing efforts at crisis management appeared as the filling out or fulfillment of a destiny already inscribed into the story of global finance. This is a truly strange and uneasy deliverance from the terror of history. In one sense, the return to the past provides a vital anchor for global projects of crisis management, effectively reestablishing financial history as a terrain on which to act. At the same time, though, it lays open how such projects themselves depend on a kind of magic trick. While efforts at crisis management appear to have the truth of history on their side, this truth can emerge only through a ritual practice in which both history and crisis are conjured into being through their self-reference. The return to the past in this way functions as a secular form of revelation, repeated in the face of trauma to sustain history as a mode of power.

Memory and Trauma

In order to develop this argument, it is necessary to further clarify the relations among history, crisis, memory, and trauma. We already know that history and crisis are entwined through their reliance on the narrative form: crisis obtains through the recursive narration of history, and one of the ways events become historical is through narratives of crisis. We also know that the content of this narrative form is its ultimate or figurative referent: every crisis narrative invokes a thing called "history," and every history of crisis invokes the reality of a "crisis" event. But these figurative referents cannot produce or reveal themselves; something must be narrativized and someone must do the narrativizing. In particular, a series of past events must be recalled before they can be narrativized, and recollecting the past can occur only through institutions that are specific to a particular present. This is where memory enters the picture.

In recent decades, memory has emerged as a powerful "counter-concept" to history, reorienting the focus of historical studies in new ways and producing a remarkable boom in scholarly output.[6] For many, the promise of memory is to push historical theory beyond the confines of the historian's workshop, such that national holidays, commemoration ceremonies, historical museums, and a range of other institutions might be brought to bear on the question of what constitutes a public awareness of the past. Social and collective memory studies in particular have gone down this route.[7] For others, though, the concept of collective memory reveals a whole host of problems when it comes to theorizing the productive role of historical discourse. Jeffrey Barash, for example, has argued that new technologies of mass communication, and particularly those associated with the image, have unmoored the symbolic configurations of collective memory from the historical past.[8] As with White or indeed Baudrillard before him, mass media here threaten both past and present with a form of historical unreality or irrealism. This is a significant development, but one that transforms rather than extinguishes the power of historical discourse. In the context of my argument, what matters is precisely the hook-up between memory and this power, and so I return here to some of Ricoeur's thoughts on the matter.

In his final book, *Memory, History, Forgetting*, Ricoeur issues two important reminders regarding the history-memory nexus. The first is that there are both cognitive and pragmatic dimensions to memory.[9] The cognitive dimension consists of a simple capacity to recall, such that things like names, events, and dates can be brought to the forefront of one's mind. The pragmatic dimension, however, entails an active searching and finding. This is an operation that elevates memory beyond pure recall, such that particular names, events, and dates can be brought to mind. Ricoeur's second key point is that anything beyond individual memory—such as social, cultural, or collective memory—cannot be understood without reference to the conventions and practices of historians.[10] It is through such conventions and practices that a repertoire of historical events is produced, and it is precisely these kinds of events that must be recalled and narrativized in order to transform the passage of time into history. Conjuring history or historical crisis therefore entails sifting through a past produced and preserved by historiography, no matter how complex the broader ecology of contemporary media. In other words, memory becomes historical through the discourse of history and crisis.

Ricoeur had much to say about what this meant for historians, but it has equally significant implications for the politics of public speech. To speak out on events in the register of history, one must engage in processes that are neither objective nor neutral. To announce a crisis, one must remember or recall past events; for this crisis to be properly historical, one must route their recollections through those events already enshrined in the historical record; and to do this, one must submit—if not entirely, then at least in part—to the writing practices that enabled prior events to be recorded as historical in the first place. This, according to de Certeau, is how the machinery of historical discourse "produces a sense of reliability."[11] Yet because agents occupy different positions in relation to this machinery, the power to produce historical crises is not evenly distributed; there are history makers and there are history takers. This is the political import of crisis mnemonics: to remember crisis is to produce history in a way that reflects the power relations inscribed into historical discourse itself.

Since 2008, this entanglement of crisis and memory has emerged as a focal point for critical studies of global finance. James Brassett, for example, has written at length on financial crisis and trauma. Linking trauma to crisis immediately opens out onto the politics of historical memory because, as we have seen, the traumatizing event not only demands a response, but does so in a way that reflects the recovery of a forgotten past. According to Brassett, it was precisely such an operation that gave shape to the subprime crisis.[12] One example he gives in passing is the way the Great Depression resurfaces within public discourse. By serving as "the historical mirror point for the sub-prime crisis," he argues, the Great Depression worked to radically curtail the ways in which that later present was experienced and responded to, relaying the subprime event as extrinsic, as natural, and, above all, as demanding a familiar kind of therapeutic response.[13] This formulation overlaps with the argument put forward in the previous chapter, registering something of the urgency with which visions of recurrent crisis typically present themselves. Here, however, what the traumatic experience of crisis fundamentally exposes is the connection between crisis and governance. Indeed, for Brassett, crisis *is* governance.[14] Simply experiencing the present as a moment of crisis, he argues, can work to reproduce the subject positions on which existing configurations of power depend, such that those charged with crisis management are able reassert their authority through the very discourse that affords them such a position in the first place. The basis of this power, however, is the deep narrativity of trauma and crisis. The present becomes a moment of traumatic crisis through "a stringing together of multiple occurrences," and it is precisely by relaying the present as a replay of the past that familiar diagnoses and treatments can appear as self-evident.[15] Trauma and crisis discourse are thus a means of narrowing down the political possibilities of a present.

Unlike other discursive accounts of crisis, Brassett goes a long way toward denaturalizing the category of the event.[16] He does, however, continue to ascribe a univocal character to the traumatic or traumatizing event. In particular, he seems to suggest that experiencing a financial event as traumatic hinges on the narration of that event as a recurrent form of crisis. Yet crisis histories can take many forms, and there is no reason they need always take shape through the figure of recurrence. The figure of linear progression has an equally prominent place in the history of crisis thinking, providing a template for an altogether different variety of crisis narratives. With these, I argue, the logic of trauma takes on a revelatory character. When narratives of linear progression relay events as novel forms of crisis, they do so through a retroactive structure in which the past itself undergoes transformation— not so much history repeating itself as a ritual return to the past, repeated so as to grasp the deeper, more distant origins of an apparent shock to the financial system. In political terms, this shifts the locus of trauma from the subjects of crisis discourse to the agents of crisis management, highlighting how crisis histories can reinvent rather than simply reproduce old modes of governing through history and crisis.

Trauma and Terror

So far the term *trauma* has been used quite loosely, reflecting the way it features within critical finance studies.[17] But like memory, the concept of trauma has become increasingly prominent within historical theory. In particular, trauma thinking has proved influential in the analysis of the Holocaust and other genocides, as well as plagues, wars, famines, and terrorist attacks.[18] Common across these diverse case studies is a concern with the way certain events resist being confined to the past, lingering instead at the margins or below the surface of the historical imagination, ready to burst back into the present at some unknown point in the future. Trauma is thus typically seen as possessing a nonlinear temporality, naming a shock or wound that refuses to go away—a rip in the fabric of experiential time. In this respect, trauma theory remains indebted to Freud's landmark account, in which trauma figures as a psychic event characterized by repression, then return. This, however, is a formulation that leaves open both the nature of the shock and the ways in which it later returns or is repeated. There are good reasons to think of both these questions in explicitly historical terms.

The rationale for this can be found in debates over the limits of historical representation. During the 1990s, Saul Friedlander posed this question in relation to the Holocaust, and ever since, the concept of trauma has been used to designate "limit events" that defy or pose acute challenges to traditional modes of historical writing.[19] But how exactly does an event become a trauma beyond the level of the individual psyche, and why do collective traumas return when they do? As Ricoeur said of social or cultural memory, the institutions of historiography are integral to such a process of "level-crossing," providing in this instance the mechanisms of both repression and return—which is to say that the ground of historical trauma is precisely the one produced through historical discourse. It is not the case that there are traumatic events that themselves resist representation, but rather that there is a certain kind of invasive occurrence that disrupts or throws into question prevailing modes of historical representation, such that these feel inadequate, troubled, or somehow disturbed from within. But at the same time, the traumatic event cannot return all on its own, somehow unfolding itself in a way that "corresponds with the unfolding of history."[20] Rather, it is *we* who must return to the past and interpret it as somehow affiliated with the present in order for a trauma to be constituted. This is precisely why Hayden White reads Freud's account of trauma as a window onto the nature of the historical event itself. "There is no such thing as an inherently traumatic *event*," White maintains, for just as crises must be narrated into existence, so too must traumas.[21] Trauma, then, "names only a particular response to crisis," which entails a crisis being "apperceived rather than perceived" as the rupture it will later be taken for.[22] It is in this apperception that the therapeutics of repeating history resides. Episodes of historical trauma register a deep fear about the consistency of history as such, and the returns to the past that invariably accompany these express nothing less than the transformation of historical discourse into a form of homeopathic therapy. Repeating history can in this way be grasped as a ritual practice for the historical age.

In *The Myth of the Eternal Return*, Eliade develops a detailed analysis of the rites and rituals practiced in various archaic religious societies. Throughout, his focus is on how the repetition of such rituals provides the people of these societies with a defense against the terror of history. By "terror," Eliade means the senseless onslaught of suffering and catastrophe, whose arbitrary appearance threatens to make life itself intolerable. In the face of this terror, he argues, archaic man rejects or takes flight from history, finding solace instead in rituals that generate and reaffirm his place in the cosmos. Eliade's terminology is unlikely to sit well with contemporary readers, but what he means to designate with terms like *archaic* are societies without historical discourse. This category covers a broad range of what are usually thought of as premodern or traditional societies, as well as the ancient cultures of Asia, Europe, and America. More importantly, for Eliade, the ontologies of such societies register a response to uncertainty that persists into the age of modernity and historicism. Indeed, rather than seeing a progressive transition from the religious to the historical imagination, he anticipates the opposite: that "as the terror of history grows worse . . . the positions of historicism will increasingly lose in prestige," providing their religious precursors with a new foothold in the secular world.[23]

A similar diagnosis can be found in the writing of Constantin Fasolt. According to Fasolt, historical discourse has gradually morphed into a set of technologies charged with doing the work gods once did, not so much offering an alternative to the religious imagination as subsuming it beneath a range of expressly modern, secular rituals.[24] With this in mind, the idea of ritual repetition provides a useful lens through which to view recent appeals to past crises among financial elites. As ritual repetition, these returns appear as part of a response to the terror of postmodern capitalism—a kind of reflex reaction to the pervasive fear that there is neither rhyme nor reason to our terminal economies of crisis. But rather than providing an escape from history altogether, this ritual serves instead as a means of reinstituting history as a space through which to govern. The ritual is thus a return to the historical record, and it is repeated in order to shore up the discourse of history at the very same time as its limits are revealed through the terror and chaos of pure occurrence. Somewhat paradoxically, the rites of this return display a striking continuity with earlier, antihistorical imaginaries.

One way that early religious societies dealt with the terror of history was through an archetype of *recurrence*. This mythical figure, which was transmitted between generations through various rituals and ceremonies, enabled ancient civilizations to refuse history and identify instead with the eternal periodicity of the cosmos.[25] We have already encountered this figure in a number of guises throughout this book, from the natural cycles of liberal economic theory to the visions of epochal return in the pages of the financial press. In both instances, the figure of historical recurrence draws on a much older archetype whose function is precisely to banish any sense of uncertainty or contingency from the world. When in the previous chapter, for example, the events of 2008 appeared as a replay of those that threw the world into turmoil during the 1930s, they appeared first and foremost as something that had already happened before. The archetype of recurrence thus serves to give recognizable shape and figure to the historical process, but in so doing, history is invested with the kind of regularity whose absence otherwise makes the cosmos such an attractive refuge. Visions of recurrence in this way perform a work of reiteration and reassurance, enabling an ongoing crisis to affirm old truths about the logics of political and economic history.

Enduring or eternal truths are all well and good, but they are not the only way to strip the world of contingency. There is another, equally long tradition associated with the archetype of *revelation*, which as Eliade points out, works to tame history's terror by transforming every misfortune into a theophany.[26] "Theophany" designates the kind of epiphany brought on through an appearance or manifestation of God in the world. Once the sufferings and catastrophes of human existence are cast in this light, they are no longer senseless—everything acquires providential meaning and justification. The way this occurs is again through a return to the past, only this time the past acquires the character of an enabling step in the development of some later, divinely sanctioned state of affairs. Speaking of Hebrew and Christian theodicies, White describes this as the "figure-fulfillment model": "the substitution of the ram for Isaac in Abraham's intended sacrifice of his son is an anticipation of the Law of Moses that fulfills it, the Fall of Adam that is fulfilled in the Resurrection of Christ, and so on."[27] The structure of revelation is in this sense one of belatedness or apperception. Rather than uncovering a preexisting telos, revelation consists in the retroactive constitution of a higher-order meaning for past events. A secularized equivalent of this gesture can be found in the way financial policymakers have reengaged the past as an expression of the multilateral spirit. When in 2008, Dominique Strauss-Kahn explains how the International Monetary Fund was created in the wake of the Great Depression, he apperceives that earlier episode as a point of origin for changes now culminating in the vigorous multilateralism of his time. Similarly, when Trichet recalls the Asian crisis of the late 1990s, this too becomes a harbinger after the fact for the rise of new multilateral forums, such as the G20 and the Financial Stability Board. In both cases, there is a form of *historiophany* at work, wherein an ongoing crisis enables the past to reveal a new apparent truth about the logics of political and economic history.[28] This novelty-bearing capacity is what distinguishes the archetype of revelation from that of recurrence.

In what follows, I show how the archetypes of recurrence and revelation were mobilized in ways that worked to both *sustain* and *reinvent* contemporary modes of crisis management. In order to do this, I analyze public discourse on financial crisis during the subprime years, focusing on speeches and press statements delivered by representatives of the European Central Bank (ECB), the International Monetary Fund (IMF), the US Federal Reserve Bank (Federal Reserve), and the US Treasury.[29] This combination of governmental ministries, independent technocratic bodies, and international organizations provides a way into the "tangle of local spaces and times" through which global finance is governed.[30] Moreover, by virtue of their direct involvement in crisis management efforts, these organizations provide another concrete entry point into the modes of history production that characterize contemporary financial capitalism.

The Birth of Multilateralism

The 1930s are typically construed as a time of crisis for the world economy. Whether it is the expiration of British hegemony and the undoing of laissez-faire, or the rise of Keynesianism and the emergence of a new "embedded liberalism," most historians identify some kind of transformation that has had lasting structural impact.[31] This is in keeping with the prominence of crisis thinking in political economy, as well as a related tendency to imagine change and continuity in capitalism through the figure of historical reversal. It also reflects the unique status ascribed to the Great Depression by the operations of twentieth-century historiography. But in much the same way as these histories reappear within the pages of the financial press, they also resurface within the public discourse of those charged with managing the subprime crisis.[32]

As before, rhetorical tropes and maneuvers are crucial to grasping the productive powers of this return, and analogy in particular comes to play a pivotal role in shaping the apparent world historical character of ongoing events. This is evident in a long and evolving series of comparisons with the scale and scope of disruption wrought by the Great Depression. Analogies of this sort begin to appear in mid-2008 and are initially posed in tentative terms. In June, for example, the IMF characterizes the preceding months as "one of the most trying times for financial markets in several decades, perhaps since the 1930's Great Depression."[33] A month later, the Federal Reserve describes the events of the previous year as "one of the worst financial shocks that the United States has confronted since the Great Depression."[34] But once financial market dynamics begin to affect growth rates, the qualifying clauses are gone and officials from all four organizations are opening their speeches by alluding to "the most severe and synchronized economic downturn since the 1930s."[35] While these analogies might seem to serve as a mere preface to technical policy discussion, they do more than work to convey the magnitude of the challenge facing policymakers. By relaying the present as a familiar, albeit undesirable state of affairs, they recuperate and put to work the archetype of recurrence, contributing to the construction of a narrative understanding in which there is no real place for radical uncertainty. In so doing, they also serve to decisively frame and shape each organization's pronouncements on crisis prevention, crisis management, and crisis resolution.

This process can be seen across a range of different policy areas, but it is most evident in discussions of international cooperation. As early as July 2007, the IMF cautions against a repeat of the "narrow nationalism that characterized the Depression era."[36] Some seven months later, the US Treasury also invokes the "insular policies of the 1930s," describing these as "ill-fated efforts to gain an edge in world trade."[37] Given their timing, such warnings probably speak more to the stalled negotiations of the Doha Round than financial or economic instability per se. But by mid-2008, lessons of this sort begin to be drawn in explicit relation to destabilizing financial sector dynamics. The first to do this is the ECB, which uses the Smoot-Hawley Tariff Act of 1930 to illustrate the self-defeating effects of a protectionist response to financial crisis. According to its then executive board member Lorenzo Smaghi, "Experience shows that such measures damage economic growth and tend to worsen crises," meaning that to even think about "curbing international trade would be a mistake in the same way as in 1929."[38] The IMF makes more or less the same move in late 2008 when it argues that "an upsurge of nationalism" was not just "one of the worst consequences of the Great Depression" but also "one of its causes."[39] Here again US tariff policy serves as a case in point. The US Treasury and ECB soon follow suit, focusing on the role of exchange rate policy and trade protectionism more generally, and by mid-2009, appeals of this sort are commonplace.[40] Crucially, though, while various dimensions of economic nationalism are highlighted, in each instance, the Great Depression is put to work in the service of free-trade principles. This is in keeping with classic narrative accounts of the 1930s, wherein a slide toward protectionism and a subsequent drying up of world trade are cast as the primary drivers of economic collapse.[41] But here such accounts are transposed into the present as a narrated threat of recurrence, and because this threat brings with it the specter of unemployment, fascism, and war, the idea of the Depression works to ensure a liberal response to ongoing financial and economic uncertainties.[42] This is precisely the kind of disciplining effect that Brassett foregrounds in his analysis of trauma narratives and the performance of crisis as governance. It is also the force at work in those visions of epochal recurrence we saw emerge in the coverage of the financial press.

Elsewhere, though, analogical reasoning begins to produce quite different effects. This occurs through a further sequence of rhetorical maneuvers associated with analogy, beginning with an equation of trade with finance. At the same time as they speak of direct barriers to trade, both the ECB and US Treasury also highlight the role of competitive currency devaluations during the 1930s.[43] These measures remain linked to conventional lessons about the errors of economic nationalism, but they also feed into a broader set of narratives and lessons about international cooperation. In December 2008, for example, both the IMF and ECB interpret recent financial sector developments through the lens of the 1930s. For its part, the IMF depicts the rush to provide deposit guarantees for financial institutions as a 1930s-style "beggar-thy-neighbor" policy,[44] while the ECB instead stresses how "a lack of trust within and between financial systems" is impairing trade financing.[45] What both end up doing, however, is engineering a kind of short circuit between the trade protectionism of the past and a nascent form of financial protectionism in the present. If the former did not work, then why should the latter? In one respect, this short circuit reinforces and supplements the disciplining effects performed by narratives of traumatic recurrence. The image of the Great Depression as a recurrent or recurring form of crisis remains fundamentally unchallenged, and because its lessons for trade policy are transposed into the domain of finance, this same image now enables fundamentally novel developments—such as the uneven provision of deposit guarantees—to be apprehended through a preexisting paradigm for crisis management. It is through this process that old lessons find new applications. But at the same time, this short-circuiting is also implicated in another process whereby the Great Depression starts to emit a new message to those charged with managing crisis. This occurs through the archetype of revelation, which produces an awareness of crisis in which the historical mission of global elites undergoes an expansion in both scope and depth. By enabling new emergency measures to be recruited as symptoms of a step-change in policy collaboration, the archetype of revelation works to rediscover, augment, and transform the task of multilateralism as a mode of governing global capitalism. Rather than simply a question of tariffs and exchange rates, collaboration now becomes more explicitly linked to the domains of monetary, fiscal, and even financial sector policy, and rather than simply a task for the established clubs and Bretton Woods institutions, the coordination of these measures is now also entrusted to new forums such as the G20. There are two key steps in this process.

The first involves incorporating novel policy responses into a counteranalogy with those enacted during the 1930s. This process begins in October 2008 when Strauss-Kahn, then managing director of the IMF, addresses the board of governors at the annual joint meeting of the IMF and World Bank. In his speech, Strauss-Kahn reiterates the need to keep nationalist reflexes at bay, but here the "mistakes of the past"—and in particular, those of the 1930s—are contrasted with the sheer range of unorthodox measures being enacted by central banks and finance ministries in the Western world.[46] But in order for such measures to be truly effective, he argues, "action should be coordinated, at the global level, and at the regional level where appropriate."[47] Strauss-Kahn and his colleagues at the IMF repeat this demand on a number of occasions over the following months, and as crisis response efforts continue to evolve, more and more of their references to the 1930s contrast that period with the comprehensive cooperation of the present.[48] Coordinated interest rate cuts, central bank liquidity swaps, simultaneous fiscal stimulus packages, and a range of other unprecedented initiatives are in this way taken to signify an important change in the form and content of international cooperation.

The second key step involves using these new cooperative measures to rewrite the story of multilateralism. The US Treasury is first to revisit this story, but its accounts remain more or less in keeping with precrisis orthodoxy (that is, while its narratives consistently portray the Great Depression as a motivating force behind the creation of the Bretton Woods system, these hinge only on lessons-learned regarding tariff wars and competitive devaluations).[49] By mid-2009, however, signs of recovery prompt a search for the origins of what is increasingly seen to be a novel and effective paradigm for crisis management. Here it is the IMF that takes the lead, finding new clues about the present in its own organizational history:

> One of the key lessons of the Great Depression was that a lack of cooperation and a retreat to isolationism can make things dramatically worse. . . . The IMF was born in Bretton Woods, forged in the furnace of this multi-

lateral idealism, and endowed with a mandate to oversee the global financial system and to act as a lender of last resort to members with balance
of payments needs. . . . Over sixty years later, although the contours of
the world financial system would be unrecognizable to the Bretton Woods
delegates, the IMF remains as central as ever. *But it took the worst financial
crisis since the Great Depression for this to be made manifest.*[50]

In this passage, Strauss-Kahn returns to the Bretton Woods conference
and the creation of the IMF, presenting the latter as a direct response to
the mistakes of the 1930s. But rather than faithfully reproducing this familiar narrative, Strauss-Kahn instead rereads the 1930s as the moment in
which the IMF's present-day purpose first emerged. Although the world
of finance has been transformed beyond recognition, its need for the IMF
has been "made manifest" through an emergent affiliation between then
and now. The Great Depression and the subprime crisis therefore reveal
something new not simply about each other, but also about the place of
the IMF within the governance of global finance.

This self-celebrating narrative is repeated on numerous occasions, and
it is typically accompanied by an emphasis on the unprecedented degree of
policy collaboration undertaken in the face of crisis. But beyond this, the
IMF also goes on to link this process to the rise of the G20, which it now
depicts as central to the success of global governance going forward:

In the face of crisis, countries came together to face common challenges
with common solutions, focusing on the global common good. . . . This
collaboration encompassed more countries than ever before in history—
showing us that in our modern globalized world, responsibility for the economic policy agenda can no longer rest with a small club of countries. The
crisis heralded the ascent of the G20—a group that includes the dynamic
emerging economies—as the leading vehicle of multilateral cooperation.[51]

Here Strauss-Kahn again conjures up the spirit of multilateralism, but
where before, it was to the birth of this spirit that he spoke, he now focuses instead on the "ascent of the G20," which suddenly appears as its
latest and most comprehensive manifestation. Taken together, these narrative operations produce a sense of historical crisis that does not conform

to the figure of recurrence. Neither the Great Depression nor the global downturn that began in 2008 makes sense without the other, yet the relatedness of the two episodes does not emerge through their apparent similarities alone. There are new affiliations that transform the very character of the Great Depression, turning it into the beginning of a grand drama in which the spirit of multilateralism struggles against and ultimately overcomes the materiality of crisis. On one level, this simply reflects the way twentieth-century historiography has given pride of place to both the Great Depression and the story of multilateralism. But it is also and perhaps more fundamentally an expression of what happens to the present when these features of historical discourse are engaged through the archetype of revelation. The next section develops this point by showing how the looping logic of revelation was extended forward to encompass another, more recent crisis of global finance.

The Rebirth of Multilateralism

The Asian crisis is usually identified as the first truly global financial crisis of the post–Cold War world. After the collapse of the Soviet Union and the apparent failure of state-led models of development, globalist ideology acquired a more strident character, with Wall Street, the US Treasury, and the IMF all lining up behind a push for capital account liberalization. Questions about national development quickly became questions about how states should best tap into global reserves of capital, and the fate of North and South East Asian countries emerged as a kind of testing ground for the hopes and dreams of the developing world. Opinion was already sharply divided on the origins of the so-called East Asian miracle, and so when currencies collapsed and a wave of capital flight spread across the region in 1997, scholars tended to interpret this reversal in one of two ways. In the first, it was seen as an expression of the dangers that global capital flows could pose to developing nations, suggesting a need to rethink the rush toward financial integration.[52] In the second, it was taken instead as a sign that the developing world needed to be "made safe" for capital flows.[53] Both interpretations went on to shape policy debate in the years that followed, prompting broader arguments about the end of the Washington Consensus and cementing Asia's place at the heart of a story called neoliberalism.[54] But as global markets tumbled again a decade later, the cement came unstuck, allowing the Asian crisis to take on an entirely new set of meanings.

Generally the return of the Asian crisis is a less acute phenomenon than the return of the Great Depression.[55] It is also a more varied affair, with the Asian crisis assuming different forms from month to month. Early on, it tends to appear as just one more example of how financial cycles unfold. The Federal Reserve, for example, uses it to illustrate how uncertainty can reduce market liquidity, while the IMF invokes it in the context of a discussion about how banking sector panic can adversely affect growth rates.[56] But beyond these kinds of passing analogies and lessons (which leave prior accounts of the Asian crisis largely intact), the events of the late 1990s are also subject to a set of narrative operations that retroactively reconfigure the history of financial globalization. For example, while initial discussions of the Asian crisis still focus on the interaction between domestic institutions and international capital flows, the Federal Reserve pioneers an "oversaving" narrative that is gradually taken up by the US Treasury, IMF, and ECB. In this account, the Asian crisis figures as a point of origin for global payments imbalances, which in turn are linked to a destabilizing search for yield in the West.[57] This is a significant revision in that it overturns and reappraises the apparent "demolition" of the Asian developmental state.[58] Here, however, I focus on how the events of the late 1990s take on a new and central position in narratives of multilateral progress.

If the Asian crisis is inextricably linked to the question of global governance, then it is because the IMF worked closely with many of the countries involved over a period of not months but years. From the IMF's perspective, this partnership was in keeping with its mission to provide the world with global public goods, and on the ten-year anniversary of the Asian crisis, it is quite explicit about this, recalling how it successfully fulfilled its function as international lender of last resort.[59] Given the timing, this intervention most likely has more to do with allegations about the IMF's waning relevance than anything else.[60] The same might also be said of the Federal Reserve's intervention in late 2007, which uses the South Korean rescue package of 1998 to illustrate the Fund's relative expertise in providing or facilitating such financing.[61] Both statements are in this way part of an attempt to recover and reiterate lessons already learned. By mid-2008, however, the Asian crisis starts to appear within broader discussions about the future of global governance. The organization at the forefront of this process is the ECB, which begins in late 2007 to craft a grand narrative about the evolution of international cooperation. The Asian crisis functions within this in two distinct but complementary ways.

First, it enables a general lesson to be drawn regarding the relation between globalization, crisis, and international reform:

> It is obvious that the systemic changes we are observing in the world's economic and financial system require systematic changes in the policy framework. The rules of the game need to adapt in order to keep pace with developments. This recognition is not new. It was felt already in the 1970s with the breakdown of the Bretton Woods system. And it was felt very strongly in the aftermath of the Asian crisis ten years ago.[62]

In this passage, erstwhile ECB president Jean-Claude Trichet alludes to a sequence of three crises, configuring these into a narrative understanding of the forces that underpin political and economic history. Globalization drives structural change, structural change creates new forms of global crisis, and new forms of global crisis reveal gaps in existing systems of governance. Global stability in turn hinges on the adaptability of international institutions, and crisis prevention—to the extent that such a thing is even possible—becomes "a constant task that requires continuous scrutiny and effort" on the part of the international community.[63] In this schema, the task of crisis prevention is at once both never and always the same—never, because each new solution always has its particulars, and always, because these solutions never actually solve the problem that prompts them (namely, the emergent properties of globalization itself). The result is a very specific vision of history, in which crisis and reform figure as alternating phases in an expansive process of economic globalization.

The second key function performed by the Asian crisis is to retroactively mark a watershed in the globalization of governance. As an intimation of the possibility for crisis, the events of 1997–1998 are far from unique: "It is clear, [the Asian] crisis was not the first one . . . and it certainly was not the last one."[64] But as an expression of the possibility for governance, the Asian crisis is a singular and decisive turning point. "It was the Asian crisis," Trichet reminds us, "that revealed a number of vulnerabilities in national and international financial systems," and it was these vulnerabilities "that led to an enormous reform agenda at the international level."[65] This in itself is not a particularly unusual statement to be hearing from someone like Trichet. If he returns to the scene of the late 1990s, it is most likely because in its own time, the Asian crisis prompted numerous calls for a "new international financial architecture." It is, however, a somewhat stranger thing to say if we consider that back then, these calls were widely deemed to have failed, producing a lot of talk but little in the way of concrete reform.[66] Trichet therefore enacts a kind of rediscovery, wherein the very suggestion or prospect of reform in the wake of the Asian crisis is apperceived as a foretelling of those changes that eventually do emerge through the crisis of 2008. The temporal logic at work here is one of afterwardness or belatedness, whereby the past is returned to in ways that produce fundamentally new understandings of why things happen when they do. This amounts to a form of renarrativization premised on the archetype of revelation, and in the present context, it yields two distinct visions for the future of financial governance.

The first of these concerns the issue of financial sector policy coordination. When looking back on the legacy of the Asian crisis, all four organizations consistently emphasize the creation of the Financial Stability Forum (FSF) in 1999, yet the way in which they do this changes over time. Initially, the ECB focuses on the Forum's promotion of standards and codes.[67] In so doing, it draws an implicit link between the Asian crisis and the idea of voluntary microprudential reform. But in mid-2008, after the FSF presents its report on the ongoing financial turmoil, the ECB instead focuses on the membership and mandate of the Forum, pointing out how it was created in order to enable "a synthetic diagnosis of the state of global finance."[68] This produces a subtle yet important shift in the legacy of the Asian crisis, which is now linked to a new form of coordination under the FSF rather than the substantive content of its early initiatives. At around the same time, the US Treasury makes similar remarks,[69] and by late 2008, the FSF is identified by both organizations as being at the heart of ongoing efforts to understand the multilevel interface between micro- and macroprudential risk.[70] These efforts constitute a clear departure from the approach to financial regulation that the FSF pioneered in the aftermath of the Asian crisis, and yet they are presented here as a continuation of that earlier reform agenda. The Asian crisis is in this way retrofitted with new historical meaning and significance. Its preexisting legacy is not effaced in response to the crisis of 2008, but instead reimagined so as to incorporate subsequent shifts in the international agenda for regulatory reform. Indeed, after the FSF becomes the Financial Stability Board (FSB) and assumes a more central role within the global regulatory system, the Federal Reserve even draws a link between this new body and the Asian crisis, explicitly portraying the latter as a precursor to the former.[71] This is precisely the kind of expansive, backward-looking extrapolation characteristic of revelation in a historical key. Rather than simply marking the emergence of a global agenda for domestic reform, the Asian crisis is now also seen to underpin the creation of an institution capable of one day envisioning a much more extensive kind of international supervisory cooperation.

A similar process can be observed in relation to multilateralism more generally. In late 2007, the ECB begins to portray the Asian crisis as part of a shift toward more inclusive forms of global governance. Initially this involves focusing on the creation of the G20 in 1999, which it suggests was motivated by a post-1997 insight into the importance of emerging markets.[72] But as the G20 becomes a more central forum for discussing crisis response measures in 2009, the ECB makes a second move, reading this new development back into the very inception of the G20:

> While the G7 still have an important role to play, the financial crisis has confirmed the need to reinforce global governance at the level of a more inclusive international informal entity . . . the creation of the G20 after the Asian crisis . . . was an important step to involve the emerging economies more closely in the process of global economic governance. And I am therefore, in the present very demanding circumstances, in full accord with this strengthened role of the G20. The aspect that impresses me most about this emerging global forum is the virtually universal consensus on global economic issues that has been reached.[73]

Once again, this move does not fundamentally alter the overarching structure of the ECB's cooperation narrative. Instead, what we see is the same basic narrative being extended forward in order to encompass the ongoing rise of the G20. But by depicting this development as an outgrowth of the post-1997 reform agenda, the Asian crisis is effectively recast as its harbinger: the unprecedented degree of policy coordination, the sustained dialogue on financial sector reform, even the attempts to address current account imbalances: all are taken to be signs of a new multilateralism, and all are traced back to 1997, for in revealing the scope of global interdependence then, it was the Asian crisis that gave to the world the forum it would need to weather the coming storm.

All this tells us something important not about historical providence, fate, destiny, or progress, but rather the enduring pull these notions continue to exert over the historical imagination and, in particular, the way this plays out through the relation that those responsible for managing the flow of history maintain with the practical and historical past. If the Asian crisis is apperceived by members of the ECB as a key moment in the globalization of governance, it is because they remember the threat it originally seemed to pose, and remain committed to the idea that it must be part of a story in which they emerge as victorious. Similarly, if the staff of the IMF returns to the primal scene of the Great Depression, enshrined in the story of the twentieth century through so many narrative histories, it is because they too want to find signs in the present of a multilateral spirit for which they see themselves as ambassadors. In both instances, the appeal of the past is a promise to reveal—not simply reiterate—the shape of history.

Eternally Returning to Crisis

In the final analysis, Trichet, Strauss-Kahn, and their ilk seem to be gripped by a strange fascination with past crises—but why, exactly? What can be gained by compulsively revisiting prior scenes of crisis? These questions point back not only to the position these individuals occupy within the financial system, but also to the function that historical discourse performs within the world of policymaking elites. Financial economics long ago parted ways with the idea of history, developing instead an increasingly elaborate set of abstract numerical models. Some of these have been a blessing for those attempting to make money in the markets, but they have proved far less useful to those charged with regulating and managing global finance. When it comes to the bigger questions about where we are, how we got here, and what comes next, the age-old arts of rhetoric and narrative remain indispensable. In this sense, global finance continues to depend on historical discourse, and especially when things seem to defy neat forms of explanation. The return to prior episodes of crisis is above all a return to history, and it is repeated most vigorously when history itself seems to be falling apart.

After and with Eliade, this process can be grasped as a form of modern, quasi-historical ritual. In this, it is the discourse of history itself that is called on to help diagnose and treat contemporary events as particular forms of crisis. The appeal of crisis is precisely that it helps reinstitute history as a terrain on which to act. But there are at least two distinct ways in which the past can be called on to deliver the present over to history. The first runs through the archetype of recurrence, yielding narrative projections that announce history as either already or on the cusp of repeating itself. Visions of recurrence carry within them a strong tendency to reproduce existing modes of crisis management. The second, however, runs through the archetype of revelation, yielding narratives that retroactively invest past crises with new meanings. This is a fundamentally creative process. It is not about reasserting existing patterns so much as extrapolating backward on the basis of these. Revelation thus allows the past to transform even the most unforeseen of events into a filling out of some long-latent destiny. When this occurs, the past functions as a means of reinventing rather than reproducing existing modes of crisis management.

Despite these differences, the archetypes of recurrence and revelation are not mutually exclusive; indeed, they are often combined, such as when the prior turning of a cycle is recast as a step toward some grander realignment. Moreover, neither archetype is tied to a particular event by anything other than the prevailing correlates of historical discourse. The one constant is the broader process to which both belong: the ritual return to the past. This ritual transforms the past itself into a means of reconciling the promise of history with the terror it has produced, and it has significant implications for how we engage the contemporary discourse of financial crisis. While the managers of global finance might claim to have the truth of history on their side, there is nothing self-evident about what they do. Both history and crisis acquire their form through a contingent and self-referential conjuring of crisis histories. Without this conjuring, the present itself is unintelligible, and there is no way to devise practical plans about how it may be governed, negotiated, or managed. Crisis management therefore depends on a kind of magic trick. When faced with unprecedented events, the managers of global finance quite simply must stand up and recount to each other the names and dates of history, until the present before them assumes a shape they can understand and respond to using the tools at their disposal.

No one, of course, is supposed to see the trick behind the magic, but once we do, the normative question becomes whether to abandon the discourse of crisis altogether. This would be a grave mistake. The crisis event may well be a "metaphysical fiction," but abandoning the worlds of fiction will do nothing to strip them of their magic.[74] History too has a metaphysics that cannot be divorced from fiction, and crisis remains deeply inscribed within the historical imagination of our times. The task of critique must therefore be to somehow navigate this knotting up of crisis, history, and fiction. The potential pitfalls are clear. As Janet Roitman points out, to talk and think with crisis is to risk reproducing a host of "existing dichotomies and extant hierarchies: public-private, economy-society, morality-politics, material-ideal, and so forth."[75] Yet to do away with crisis is to forgo what is still one of the most powerful ways in which prevailing histories might be contested. And so, I think, we must craft another relationship with the strange power of crisis thinking. Rather than rejecting the magic it entails, the discourse of crisis should be strategically embraced and deployed by anyone who refuses to wish away the terror of financial history, by anyone who resents our self-appointed crisis managers for subsuming it over and again beneath triumphant narratives of multilateral progress. But if the trick that crisis managers employ is to conjure history while appearing to do nothing of the sort, then that of critique must be the opposite: to cultivate an appearance of truth and objectivity, while knowing all the while these are nothing more than the bootstraps on which we choose to tug. This would be a way of working with instead of against the logic of the strange loop—a way of facing up to the repressed origins of history in fiction, rather than clinging to those "benign versions of historical reality constructed as a screen" to protect us from this trauma.[76]

CHAPTER 5

Names of History

History haunts finance in unexpected ways. This chapter moves away from insider discourses on financial crisis, focusing instead on popular culture and contemporary film in particular. Films about finance have always flourished against the backdrop of market turbulence, rising unemployment, and a growing concern regarding the place that financial logics occupy within society. The most recent boom in financial film is no different. In the wake of the subprime crisis, there has been a raft of new titles that take financial turmoil as their theme, ranging from popular dramas and comedies, such as Nicholas Jarecki's *Arbitrage* and Adam McKay's *The Other Guys*, through to critical documentaries and avant-garde interventions, including Charles Ferguson's *Inside Job* and Melanie Gilligan's *Crisis in the Credit System*.[1] According to Jeff Kinkle and Alberto Toscano, these films and the genres in which they work should be appraised on the basis of their ability to represent financial capitalism in its totality—that is, to intimate or reveal the ways in which finance capital organizes social and material life.[2] On such a test, few financial films fare well. Oliver Stone's *Wall Street* franchise, for example, would fail because it opts to "*personify* systemic and impersonal phenomena," rather than showing them for what they are.[3] This may well be the case, but the iconic status of *Wall Street*'s Gordon Gekko hints at another, altogether stranger function for film in relation to financial history.[4]

Two years after Gekko is reprised in *Wall Street: Money Never Sleeps* (2010), the actor Michael Douglas, who plays Gekko in both movies, appears alongside clips from the original film in a FBI public service announcement on insider trading.[5] In the announcement, Douglas reminds us that while "the movie was fiction, the problem is real."[6] He then goes on to direct viewers to a tip line they can use to report suspected instances of financial fraud. Meanwhile, Jordan Belfort—a real-life stockbroker who publicized his crimes in two autobiographies—becomes the namesake for Leonardo DiCaprio's character in Martin Scorsese's Oscar-nominated *The Wolf of Wall Street* (2013).[7] Finally, Eric Packer—a figure already known in the literary world as the protagonist of Don DeLillo's *Cosmopolis*—is played by *Twilight* heartthrob Robert Pattinson in David Cronenberg's 2012 film adaptation, which enjoys unexpected success at the box office in France and Italy.[8] Varied though they are, these vignettes all point to something peculiar about the power of personae in contemporary financial film. Names, much like crises, keeping returning from the past—but why, and to what end?

Writing of Konrad Becker's *Strategic Reality Dictionary*, Brian Holmes notes a fascination with the power of dead mediums—"historical figures from the esoteric annals of cultural intelligence, whom themselves 'channeled' earlier inventors, spies, organizers or psychic wardens."[9] Such figures, Holmes argues, are for Becker not simply a resource for "new agents of deceit and domination," but also for those who might seek to turn the occult arts of oppression into tools of emancipation.[10] In this respect, there is nothing predestined about the influence that figures from the past may exert over the present; the power of dead mediums is a creative power, consisting in a passage back through the historical archive and a reenergizing of the change horizons associated with its various personae. The key to such a process, I argue, is the *proper name*. Proper names appear in historical discourse alongside event names and place names, but the names we use to denote history's great characters—from Joan of Arc all the way back to Genghis Khan or Emperor Nero—are more than a means of signifying influential persons from the past. In the words of Deleuze and Guattari, they are "fields of intensity" with "a magic all their own," peculiar zones through which present-day subjects may pass and emerge from anew.[11] A name of history is thus a *diagram*—"an abstract sequence of possibilities" that may or may not be actualized within the context of a later present—and the circulation of history's names is itself a mode of history production, leveraging temporal distance and established sequences into new trajectories and effects.[12]

Attending to the circulation of proper names puts financial film in a new light. In the contemporary postcrisis landscape, names of finance circulate through works of cinematic fiction. The names themselves, however, whether fictional or fictionalized, partake in the same productive, quasi-historical process with which Deleuze and Guattari were concerned. Just as the name "Joan of Arc" did some centuries ago (and perhaps still does today), the names "Gekko," "Belfort," and "Packer" jump from one present to the next, passing through different media genres along the way, diagramming distinct forms of conduct and mobilizing specific ways of world making. And so the names of financial film reveal another set of history's strange loops, this time premised on the performative power of the proper name and the transmission of names through popular culture.

Capitalist Irrealism

This line of argument entails a departure from fashionable forms of ideology-critique, which would have us interrogate cultural products like film through a concept of the map rather than the diagram. In the present context, the thrust of such approaches can be captured with a simple question: If capital defies representation, then why do we see so many films about money and finance? Monetary and financial operations form one of the most phantom-like dimensions of contemporary capitalism, and yet it is they—rather than more recognizable forms of production, consumption, or exchange—that provide the mise-en-scène for most recent films that deal with questions of economy.[13] What are we to make of this? Are such films, to the extent that they fail to adequately disclose the worlds of money and finance, just so many bricks in the wall of what Mark Fisher has termed "capitalist realism,"[14] that imaginary screen that masks our role in performing capital and blocks out means of producing history otherwise? The history of financial film is ambiguous on this.

For as long as capitalist finance has existed, it has prompted artists, and especially writers, to reconstruct and explore the modalities of money's worlds. In this regard, early forays into financial filmmaking are indebted to works of realist fiction. One of the first known examples of financial film is David Griffith's *A Corner in Wheat*, a silent short produced in 1909 and based on Frank Norris's novel *The Pit*.[15] The film relies heavily on montage, using the technique to tell Norris's story of how a lone speculator on the Chicago wheat exchange brings famine and hardship to farmers and the urban poor.[16] Another realist novel, Émile Zola's *L'Argent*, forms the basis for Marcel L'Herbier's 1928 film of the same name, which again uses montage to link the workings of a stock exchange (this time the Paris Bourse) to activities and outcomes beyond its walls.[17] According to Kinkle and Toscano, works such as these—and especially *L'Argent*—are model examples of what financial film can do, for by splicing between "disparate characters and locations, sudden reversals of fortune, [and] personal fates buffeted by inscrutable structures," they go some way toward staging the totality of capital as a real abstraction.[18] From this perspective, the medium of film can be seen as providing a unique set of tools for challenging contemporary ideologies of obfuscation.

Kinkle and Toscano develop this position further in their book, *Cartographies of the Absolute*.[19] Returning to Fredric Jameson's concept of "cognitive mapping," they argue that different domains of practice provide their own specific techniques for envisaging how capital structures life.[20] The style and composition of *Das Kapital*, for example, can be read as part of Marx's attempt to deliver capital over to representation, and in much the same way, so too can experiments with the television format (as in the HBO series *The Wire*) or the use of visualization technologies to reveal flows of people and containers in cities and across oceans.[21] On this reading, the promise of not only film, but also art and science, resides in their potential to alter and improve how we imagine the "planetary nexus of capitalist power," such that new visions of the globe might be put to work as a force in the world.[22] Emancipatory conduct therefore hinges on creative agents like the filmmaker, for example, first working to create new cartographies of capital and then insisting that any maps they produce be used to radically transform the territories they represent.

Despite the theoretical sophistication of this account, Kinkle and Toscano make the productive function of film contingent on the work of representation, and in so doing obscure other possible relations between film and financial capitalism. This is evident in their critique of later Hollywood films on finance, from those in "the conspiracy genre of the 1970s and early 80s" to the more recent crop of films that emerged after the 2008 crash.[23] Beyond a few exceptions, Kinkle and Toscano sort these films into two basic categories: either they try but ultimately fail to represent finance capital—as is the case with *Wall Street 2*, which "struggles to make finance *visible*" through clichéd montage[24]—or they don't try at all, opting instead for "a simplistic identification of culprits," or otherwise treating finance capital as a mere "backdrop for the trials and tribulations" of individuals and families.[25] The poverty of contemporary financial film therefore indexes both the resistance of finance capital to representation *and* a lack of ambition among those Hollywood filmmakers who choose to take it as their subject. But is it not possible that films about finance, regardless of their realism, do something other than succeed or fail in revealing the complexity of financial capitalism? What if financial films, no matter how bad some of them may be when appraised in terms of their ability to stage capital in its totality, nevertheless perform a productive function within contemporary capitalism? More pointedly, what if the very tendency to "personify systemic and impersonal phenomena" serves as an input into the very processes through which capital structures life? This is a line of thought worth pursuing if one is willing to entertain the notion that capital is less a totality than an evolving set of operations through which worlds are themselves produced.

The capitalist world may appear as a single reality when imagined through the lens of art, science, or some other realm of practice, but the making of worlds through money is nothing less than an emergent property of the world making we engage in through these and other spheres of action. As Nelson Goodman puts it, "The many stuffs—matter, energy, waves, phenomena—that worlds are made of are made along with the worlds," meaning that worlds are made not from nothing, but *"from other worlds."*[26] In this context, the contemporary power of finance capital resides not simply in the way it has transformed virtual worlds into a new source of valorization, but more profoundly in the way it has shaped the production and actualization of these worlds through a host of institutions not typically thought of as belonging to the financial sector (such as those associated with journalism and policymaking, for example, but also popular culture). Finance capital is therefore not so much a phase or stage of history, somehow uniquely resistant to representation, but rather the name we give to a present in which history's abstract and imagined forms have acquired the ability to actualize themselves—less a mode of production than a machinery of history production.[27]

So far I have discussed this dynamic in relation to different genres of historical discourse, but film too can be grasped in these terms. Given their mutual association with literature, both financial film and historical discourse share a number of important formal characteristics (a tendency to rely on narrative, for example, as well as a conventional focus on events and characters). Financial film also frequently draws on patterns cultivated in historical discourse, such as established plot lines and locations or named events and personae. And so in much the same way that narrative histories can reconfigure the present in which they are mobilized, popular films about finance can perform a nonrepresentational function vis-à-vis financial history. There is, however, a crucial difference. As we saw in the discussion of the black mirror, the components of historical discourse produce financial history by purporting to reveal it. In this sense, a certain standard of realism obtains, albeit one that is grounded only in the conventions of historical writing. With film, there is no such constraint. Even a film that makes no attempt at realism furnishes a world, and through its contribution to a broader repertoire of worlds both actual and virtual, such a film participates in the fundamental *irrealism* of capital.

When viewed in this light, Fisher's "capitalist realism" appears as yet another product of capital's irrealism. It may well be "easier to imagine the end of the world than the end of capitalism," as Fisher and others before him have suggested,[28] but there is simply no good reason to suppose that the worlds of film bear a unilinear relation to the way we imagine and produce history. Popular films about finance might deepen the malaise Fisher calls capitalist realism; they also might challenge and reinvent our present attachments to economy in ways we haven't yet imagined. And if this does indeed happen, there is no guarantee we will like the results either. All depends on what sorts of worlds such films furnish, the kinds of patterns these worlds carry within them, and the way these patterns are put to work in actual contexts. Proper names are a vector for this process.

A Theory of Proper Names

In a letter to Jacob Burckhardt, Nietzsche runs through a list of historical personae and arrives at an unusual conclusion: "Every name in history is I."[29] Rather than a sign or product of his madness, Deleuze and Guattari argue that Nietzsche here lays bare the essence of a name by pushing its power to establish connections to an ideal limit. Nietzsche doesn't lose his mind and then start confusing himself with other people; rather, "there is the Nietzschean subject who passes through a series of states, and who identifies these states with the names of history," such that the names themselves take on a constitutive power.[30] Proper names in this way do more than refer to an already existing individual or subject. Nietzsche-the-self, for example, emerges through an attempt to consume or channel all the names of history, and because of this, the name "Nietzsche" carries within it a latent potential to scramble individual and collective histories. But if names such as Nietzsche's might produce history by leading us to reject or take flight from historical discourse, then others might do so by inflecting or reconfiguring the way we engage it. This prospect warrants a return to the theory of proper names developed in *Anti-Oedipus*.

With the "names of history," Deleuze and Guattari mean to create a concept that might free life from a series of shackles imposed on it by capitalist rule. Among these, two are of particular importance. The first is a mode of historical discourse, integral to modern state power, which works to tie processes of development down to coordinates of linear succession. This applies as much to individual bodies as it does to peoples, nations, and their ways of organizing. The second is a regime of money signs that subordinates the self-organizing power of markets to the circulation and accumulation of capital. Deleuze and Guattari typically refer to this as the "capitalist axiomatic" in order to emphasize its basis in number rather than language.[31] The names of history figure within these conditions as a lightning rod for becoming otherwise. Names, they argue, are signs that do more than signify; they are productive in ways that defy linear causality; above all, they are multiple and performative, providing so many means through which bodies might become subjects and subjects might make history. A proper name, then, is more than a reference to a person; it is an abstract machine or virtual pattern that moves between times, producing present-day subjects in a strange loop back through those of the past.[32]

Of course, some named personae did once exist, and sometimes present-day subjects take these as role models. The theory of names, however, concerns an affective process that undergirds conscious thought and transcends the category of the individual subject.[33] Names are the means through which bodies become subjects, and bodies become subjects through names other than their own. Herein lies the peculiar historicity of the proper name. What matters most about history's names are neither the names themselves nor the persons or personae with which they are associated, but rather the possibilities inscribed into them. These are carried in names as histories, and in particular, as the events and chronologies associated with named persons and personae. Joan of Arc, for example, is associated with the Hundred Years' War and being burned at the stake, and as her name circulates beyond her time, that time is brought into the present through the events and chronologies associated with her name. This is precisely where the mechanics of historical discourse enter into the picture. The names of history become associated with particular events and chronologies through the narrative operations that grasp these together, as well as through the circulation of narratives as histories. Here, however, I want to switch the emphasis from such histories themselves to the names they become encoded into.

Following Jay Lampert, events and chronologies can be imagined as the coexisting period- and succession-related elements of a proper name.[34] The period-related elements consist in the context or surroundings with which the named persona is associated (the Hundred Years' War, for example). The succession-related elements are the chains of cause and consequence in which the named persona is enmeshed through narrative (religious visions, relief missions, alleged heresy, execution, martyrdom, sainthood). Finally, each of these elements provides a multiplicity of contexts and trajectories that coexist with one another in the present (there are many Joan of Arcs, and all are with us today). Taken together, these elements transform the name from a merely referential signifier into a kind of latent, retroactive effect that hinges on the operation of sign systems. This effect is activated when one registers the charge of a name from the past and allows it to shape one's present-day emotions, desires, and actions. In such moments "everything commingles," and one brings not the person but the name back to life as a zone of intensity on the body without organs.[35] As Lampert puts it, "Joan of Arc performed some acts, and now those acts can take place on our bodies, following more or less the same kinds of series, offering more or less the same potentials for decisive changes of direction, creating contexts and milieus for new acts of Joan of Arc."[36]

Who, then, beyond Joan of Arc, is or might become a name of history, and what kinds of effects are associated with such names? According to Lampert, "The names of history are always minority figures."[37] This is consistent with the list of names that Deleuze and Guattari provide throughout *Anti-Oedipus*, which they associate with revolutionary charges that threaten to "throw the [capitalist] machine into a panic"—"a Chinese on the horizon, a Cuban missile-launcher, an Arab hijacker, a Black Panther."[38] It also resonates with a more general opposition between history and becoming that Deleuze and Guattari repeat throughout their oeuvre; the minoritarian figure is a schizo who runs the names of history on his or her body and scrambles the overcoded lines of statist history, the majoritarian a paranoid who insists on keeping the past from the present. The names of history are thus commonly associated with a rejection of history as such, both in the names themselves and in those who run them on their bodies. This, I think, is an unduly restrictive perspective on the status of names within history.

First, there is no good reason to suppose that the names of history and their effects need be revolutionary in character. This assessment hinges on a binary between history and becoming that many new Deleuzians are beginning to challenge. Most recently, Craig Lundy has argued that this binary is an artifact of Deleuze's resistance to historicism in particular, and that his work can be read as positing novelty as emerging through an interchange between the poles of historicism and becoming.[39] On this account, history as we know it is produced through interacting basins of historical causality on the one hand and nonlinear becomings on the other. Clearly, where one ends and the other begins is itself in flux. But while the names of history belong to the order of the strange loop, the circulations through which they take effect vary from milieu to milieu, and this brings with it a range of valences for the name vis-à-vis history. Deleuze and Guattari, for example, were French and wrote in the shadow of 1968. It therefore makes sense that they channeled Joan of Arc and the Black Panthers as lightning rods for revolution. It is equally conceivable, however, that in their time, an entirely different set of names might have circulated among capitalist elites and within the upper echelons of the state. It is also conceivable that persons within these milieux might have been influenced by any one of these names. The same goes for financialized populations in a contemporary context.

Another key point is that the names of history need not refer to an actual person, whether living or dead; they can just as well be the names of fictional personae. This is in keeping with how the names of history are grounded in the operation of sign systems. The crucial point, which de Certeau and others have stressed at length, is that historical discourse shares with fiction a dependence on narrative.[40] In both registers, the narrative operation creates meaning where before there was none, configuring events and furnishing worlds with names, dates, and patterns of cause-and-effect (all of which, remember, are the very properties from which names derive their diagrammatic powers). It is thus the institution of writing per se, rather than historical writing in particular, that provides present-day subjects with a repertoire of names to resonate with; as a result, the names of history may circulate in discursive registers beyond those in which they first surfaced. This much is at least implicit in Deleuze and Guattari's idea of the "Joan of Arc effect," for "Joan of Arc" is as much a myth as it is the name of a once-living person.[41] There were, for example, already two French films about her life before they wrote *Anti-Oedipus*, and the earliest of these—Carl Dreyer's *The Passion of Joan of Arc*—comes on the back of a further five hundred years of national mythmaking.[42] And so "by our century," as Lampert notes, "the Joan of Arc effect has already been reshaped by innumerable interpretations of Joan of Arc, which have added to the ways that the events may now resonate in us."[43] The power of the name and the nature of its effects are in this way carried and reconfigured not just through the fictions of history but also through works of historical fiction. We can press this even further, though, for the lines between fiction and history have always been unclear, and over the past century, they have been made muddier still by modes of representation associated first with literary modernism and then later with postmodern historical film.[44] The result is that names for personae that never once existed now travel through and across different media types and genres, taking their place alongside the 'real' names, dates, and events of history. And so the names of history merge with the names of fiction. It makes no difference whether a person actually existed if their name, just like Joan of Arc's, circulates through both fictional and historical orders of discourse, for it is the proper name itself that functions as a performative force within history. It is the proper name that is charged with patterns and possibilities, carrying within these a power to produce new subjectivities, new trajectories, new effects, and it is through the circulation of such names in any one present that we emerge as actors on the world historical stage. Financial film is thus like history: a Gekko effect, a Belfort effect, a Packer effect—all the names of finance, and not just the names in history books.

The Gekko Effect

In the early morning hours of Thursday, August 15, 2013, 21-year-old Moritz Erhardt collapsed in the shower of his student accommodation, suffering a fatal seizure after working without sleep for 72 hours straight.[45] He was nearing the end of a summer internship with the investment division at Bank of America Merrill Lynch in London. Soon after being discovered dead by his colleagues, images began to circulate in the international press of Erhardt wearing a pinstriped shirt, red suspenders, and his hair slicked back with gel. The intern, or so the story went, had modeled himself on Michael Douglas's character in *Wall Street*.[46] It later came to light that the photo was taken at a costume party, to which Erhardt went dressed as Gordon Gekko.[47] The story, however, hints at the enduring reach and power of Gekko's name.

Since *Wall Street* was released in 1987, the name "Gekko" has become synonymous with ambition and avarice in a financial industry setting. Erhardt's death registers the first of these drives, taking one of Gekko's many memorable lines—"Lunch is for wimps"—to its lethal conclusion. It is the second drive, however, that propels Gekko into the popular imagination as a kind of financial demiurge. "Greed, for lack of a better word, is good," declares Gekko in the first film. "Greed clarifies, cuts through, and captures the essence of the evolutionary spirit." These lines have been replayed and reprinted ever since, weaving the name "Gekko" into the fictive fabric of financial history. In 2010, for example, Douglas's Gekko appears on the cover of *Forbes Magazine India* with the title "Greed Is Back." The tagline below reads like gothic horror: "The spirit of Gordon Gekko refuses to be exorcized from Wall Street or Hollywood."[48] "Gekko" the name marks this spirit, which haunts the collective financial psyche as a dark creative force. "Greed works," it tells us. But how exactly does one work with greed like Gekko? What kind of instructions does the name "Gekko" carry? These emerge through the linked plot worlds of each film, along with the historical markers that frame both *Wall Street* tales.

The original film is set during the height of a hostile takeover boom in the United States. Gekko is a ruthless corporate raider who lures an ambitious young stockbroker, Bud Fox, into helping him manipulate the stock price of a small airline company using inside information. After a falling out, Fox decides to sabotage Gekko but later changes his mind and agrees to turn state's evidence. The film ends with Fox about to provide the authorities with the information they need to convict Gekko. The sequel is set some years later, during the onset and immediate wake of a global financial crash. Gekko emerges from jail as a reformed Cassandra-like figure, whose critique of financial derivatives attracts the attention of Jake Moore, an idealistic investment banker trading for a top firm. Gekko tricks Moore into helping him regain entry into the markets. He also uses Moore to exact revenge on an old rival, Bretton James, who we learn was involved in putting Gekko behind bars.

As these brief synopses show, Gekko inhabits a world punctuated by bouts of financial expansion and contraction. The first film establishes this using a series of generic period markers: power suits, telephone trades, mergers and acquisitions—all of these situate Gekko in a bullish equity market sometime in the mid-1980s. In the sequel, though, Gekko appears alongside more specific markers that place him at the tail end of a later boom in structured finance. In a talk to promote his new book, for example, Gekko describes derivatives as "weapons of mass destruction," and in various other scenes, US Treasury and Federal Reserve officials discuss toxic assets, credit default swaps, and the need to bail out financial institutions hit by nonperforming subprime mortgages. These period-related elements place Gekko's return within the subprime-cum-global crisis of 2008. They also situate his broader career trajectory within a particular patterning of financial history.[49]

After decades of Keynesian controls on banking, Gekko's corporate raids in the first film figure as the driving force behind an ongoing subordination of industry to finance. Gekko is in this way not so much a reflection of financial capitalism as its bearer or personification. This is precisely what he says when he attributes evolutionary properties to greed—the desire for money engenders a financial logic that cuts through and replaces archaic modes of accumulation, lifting the money economy itself onto a new and higher plane. Gekko enacts this transition by treating financial gain as above all a "game between people." In such a game, industry is nothing more than a machine to be stripped for scrap. The business of finance, on the other hand, knows no natural limits; it is a machine that trades in whispers. Gekko's rumor spreading is thus a kind of weightless business model premised on the deep psychological traits of those around him: credulity, avarice, myopia. His eventual incarceration marks the intervention of the law as an artificial limit on his powers, as well as those of the financial sector more broadly.

Fast-forward twenty or so years and Gekko emerges from prison to find a world transformed by further rounds of deregulation and financial innovation. "I once said greed is good," he reflects, "[but] now it seems it's legal." Gekko, however, always says only half of what he means, and as the sequel progresses, it reveals his critique of "steroid banking" to be little more than a means of engineering his financial comeback. In fact, Gekko's reprisal is all about comebacks, returns, and cycles. Gekko appears in the original film as the consummation of a historical period unique for its financial excesses, but in the sequel, that period is folded into a longer cycle of boom and bust. Crucially, this pattern of recurrent bubbles is rendered as a kind of cosmic order that feeds on and regulates human psychology. The sequel opens and closes, for example, with Moore describing the Cambrian explosion—an unexpected wave of radiation that gave birth to life on earth—as "the mother of all bubbles." The rest of the film is littered with references to financial bubbles that eventually burst, ranging from the dot-com frenzy and the Roaring Twenties all the way back to the Dutch tulip mania of the 1630s. Gekko's advice for the young Moore is to embrace such cycles and ride their natural rhythms.

Moore is a green energy enthusiast who hopes to fund cold fusion, and so for him, finance is a means of enabling further leaps in planetary evolution.

But in a pivotal scene, Gekko ridicules Moore's idealism by pointing him to a framed illustration of tulip price data. "No one knows what to do except repeat the insanity until the next bubble," he tells Moore, and "that will be the big one, the turning point, *tulip mania*." There is no point trying to escape this fate, he explains; the important thing is to somehow gain from it. He later drives this point home by leaving the painting behind for Moore, as a kind of cruel lesson, after emptying a Swiss bank account of the inheritance he promised to Moore's cause. Finally, the film ends with a resurgent Gekko—who has just had his nemesis Bretton James arrested—telling Moore that "green is the new bubble," and Moore admitting, somewhat despairingly, that "bubbles . . . never die."

Across both films, then, the history of finance appears as a story of recurrent bubbles marked by greed, fraud, and incarceration. Within this pattern, Gekko is interchangeable with James and, by extension, all other market participants throughout history, for every boom and bust provides someone with an opportunity to mount their comeback. Gekko, however, negotiates this pattern in a particular way. His method is that of spreading rumors rather than peddling stock or analyzing data. His goal, too, is unconventional: not money itself or the things it can buy but money as an index of power—"It's all about the game between people." And when the law eventually does intervene, it marks only an arbitrary limit on his method. The name "Gekko" thus diagrams a manipulative drive to differential acquisition, premised on the treatment of psychology as natural, finance as magical, and the law as artificial. To run the Gekko effect is to channel and enact these dispositions in one's own time.

The Belfort Effect

Five months after the Erhardt-as-Gekko story goes viral, reports begin to surface of a rush on London movie theaters.[50] Financial and service sector firms across the city are booking private screenings for their staff of Scorsese's new film, *The Wolf of Wall Street*, and before long, the tabloids are publishing photographs of office workers in costume as retro-traders, wearing "colourful braces, silk patterned ties, bright socks, expensive loafers, and gelled-back hair."[51] In New York, there are reports of Wall Street traders

howling and cheering during an advance screening of the film.[52] The name
behind the buzz is one Jordan Belfort, a young stockbroker convicted for
multiple counts of securities fraud during the early and mid-1990s.

Unlike Gekko, Belfort is an actual person who can and does speak for
himself. Since his release from prison in 2006, he has published two autobiographies and is currently on tour as a motivational speaker.[53] The fact
that Belfort's road to rehabilitation resembles the one taken by Gekko in
the *Wall Street* sequel—where he too is on the public speaker circuit—is
one of many strange loops that connect the names "Gekko" and "Belfort,"
which circulate through space and time in similar ways. Both, for example,
enter financial history through the portal of the trade press (Gekko graces
the cover of *Fortune Magazine* during the opening scenes of *Wall Street*,
while Belfort comes to public attention through a short profile published
in a 1991 issue of *Forbes Magazine*).[54] Belfort's name also travels between
different presents, from the recovery years of the original *Forbes* article to
the mid- and postcrisis years of his books and Scorsese's film, echoing how
Gekko's name resurfaces at various points after it first appears in 1987. To
a certain extent, "Belfort" is the new "Gekko." In its propagation through
film, though, the name "Belfort" acquires a charge distinct from the one
carried in "Gekko."

The Wolf of Wall Street is set during the aftermath of a stock market
crash. Belfort is an ambitious trainee at a Wall Street firm that goes under
just one month into his career as a licensed broker, leaving him out of work
in a bear market. Belfort reluctantly takes up a sales position at a suburban
penny-stock brokerage, but soon realizes his commission rate is 50 percent.
He seizes on this by assembling a crack sales team and setting up his own
"pump-and-dump" operation in Long Island, New Jersey, buying stocks
cheap, talking these up to petty investors, then selling them off once a
price differential has been created. Through various stages, the firm grows
into a big Wall Street player, and with the money coming in, Belfort builds
himself a life of unparalleled excess. With the FBI on his tail, he descends
into recklessness and drug-fueled frenzy. After being arrested and indicted,
he agrees to cooperate with the authorities in return for a reduced sentence.

The fictionalized Belfort operates alongside the same period markers as
the real one. Both begin their careers as brokers on October 19, 1987, the

day of a stock market dive known to financial historians as Black Monday. The film is also littered with recognizable names from the corporate world: Belfort starts out at L. F. Rothschild, a merchant and investment bank that led the boom in high-tech initial public offerings (IPOs) during the mid-1980s. He also alludes to the activities of Goldman Sachs, Lehman Brothers, and Merrill Lynch while justifying the dealings of his firm, Stratton Oakmont. Other period-related elements include Stratton's heavy reliance on telephone trading, and the name of its first IPO, Steven Madden Ltd., a New York fashion company specializing in shoes. All of these markers situate Belfort's deeds within the context of a bull market sometime in the 1990s. In the film, though, it is not so much the cycles of finance as the psychology of the upswing that Belfort embodies and exploits. He begins as a nearly-ran—someone who just missed out on a bonanza and is determined to make up for it, no matter where this takes him or whom he has to trample over. As it happens, this takes him *off* Wall Street, where he learns how to piggyback on the aspirations and ambitions of others like himself. "Every person you're on the phone with," he tells us, "they want to get rich, and they want to get rich quickly. Everybody wants something for nothing." Belfort's signature move is to turn other people's interest in money into a means of financing his own desire. How so?

Belfort builds his fortune by using "rat holes," or dummy investor accounts, to hide and maintain a stake in the companies whose stock he is pushing. This kind of securities fraud can take a variety of forms and does so as the size of Belfort's operation grows, but in every instance, Belfort's schemes hinge on the art of rhetoric and narrative. He begins, for example, by selling stock to clients through off-the-cuff stories about the future of the companies whose stock he's pushing, about his client's future riches if they are smart enough to invest, and so on. When he starts his own operation, he develops these tropes into a standardized script for his employees to use. And when he renames the firm "Stratton Oakmont," he turns the firm name itself into a story element—not just any company but "a company that our clients can believe in." This is his business model in a nutshell: to talk people into a fantasy future he has projected for them and then pocket their willingness to pay for it. Why he wants this money is an altogether different question.

According to Noam Yuran, money carries "an empty negative desire"—it wants and makes subjects that help it multiply.[55] If that is the case, then Belfort wants more than what money wants; he wants and makes money not out of a love for money but in connection with a desire to live out the fullest possible range of earthly pleasures. This is straightforwardly so in the sense that Belfort sees money as a way of buying "better food, better cars, better pussy," not to mention better drugs. But he doesn't just use money to pay for "blue chip" hookers and stockpiles of Quaaludes. Belfort sees money itself as a drug (his favorite "of all the drugs under God's blue heaven"), and when he listens to it what he hears sounds a lot like sex ("You want to know what money sounds like?" he asks at one point: "Fuck this, shit that, cunt, cock, asshole."). This is what Belfort really means when he says money "makes you a better person." Money works neither as a simple means nor an end in itself, but as a way beyond fantasy through to actual investments of energy in body parts, substances, and their seemingly endless permutations. We see this too in his response to the law; even as it approaches and threatens his freedom, Belfort refuses to give up on his desire: "The show goes on!" he cries.

In this respect, Belfort could not appear any more different from Gekko. The closest we get to seeing Gekko in a sensuous key is when he sucks on his cigars, and even here he is calm and collected, strategic and calculating. The same could be said of Gekko's interest in modern art, which for him is, above all, a means of intimidating rivals. But any comparison between Gekko and Belfort is complicated by two facts. The first is that "Belfort" is both a proper name and a named person. This means that Belfort-the-subject comes into being through a world already populated with names. The second is that when Belfort begins his career as a broker, he does so while the first *Wall Street* film is playing in movie theaters. And so Belfort-the-subject emerges through a milieu in which the name of Gekko looms large.

For this reason, a comparison is not the best way of thinking the relation between the names "Belfort" and "Gekko." The latter can cleanly diagram a wily trader precisely because it indexes a fictional person. "Belfort," on the other hand, is a messier affair because Belfort-the-subject channels the names of finance. We hear as much from Belfort himself, who tells us in his memoirs that one of his many nicknames was "Gordon Gekko."[56] But when a kid from the Bronx runs the Gekko effect, he becomes something different entirely—at once more base, unhinged, and self-destructive. "Belfort" is not the new "Gekko," then. Belfort-the-subject emerges through Gekko-the-name, and his fictionalization gives birth to Belfort-the-name as a name of finance. It is telling that in the film, Belfort's operation moves to Wall Street, when in actuality it remained at the periphery in Long Island. With this shift of location, the name "Belfort" comes to diagram a way of working on Wall Street that differs markedly from the one associated with "Gekko." The name "Belfort" diagrams a drive not to differential acquisition but to absolute expenditure—a drive to talk wealth out of its purely financial circulations and sink it instead into physical ones with the fury of pure abandon. This, at least for now, is the shape of the Belfort effect.

The Packer Effect

Somewhere between "Belfort" and "Gekko" is another zone, marked out by the name Eric Packer. "Packer" is a relatively new addition to the names of finance. It first appeared in Don DeLillo's novel *Cosmopolis*, which was published in 2003 as the United States recovered from the dot-com crash and the terrorist attacks of 9/11.[57] Much has since been written about *Cosmopolis*, but in the aftermath of the subprime episode, it was widely celebrated for the critical perspective on finance it develops and enables.[58] Joseph Vogl, for example, describes the novel as "an allegory of modern financial capitalism," arguing that the figure of Packer can be interpreted as "the fallen angel of an illusion" (namely, the illusion that financial markets efficiently allocate resources and smoothly regulate the reproduction of the social body).[59] It is in this context that Canadian film director David Cronenberg decided to develop a film adaption of *Cosmopolis*. "The world seems to have caught up with that book," he explains in an interview with the *New York Times*.[60] But what kind of world does the name "Packer" carry into the present, and what becomes of that present when "Packer" catches up with it?

Cronenberg's adaptation is largely faithful to its source material; he claims to have started work on the screenplay by extracting all spoken dialogue from the novel. And so the novel and the film share the same setting and basic structure, taking place in New York and following Packer's journey across the city one day in a limousine. Packer is a young and gifted fund manager on his way to a run-down barbershop on the West Side. He is losing large amounts of money on an aggressive carry-trade position, which he refuses to wind back despite pleas from his wife and a string of employees. As his journey progresses, everything descends into chaos; protesters attack the financial district, the managing director of the International Monetary Fund is assassinated, the holdings of Packer Capital are decimated, and the global economy is engulfed in turmoil. The story cuts off with Packer's death, which he seeks out by shedding his security entourage and confronting a disgruntled ex-employee who has been making threats on his life.

Cosmopolis revels in irrealism; it unfolds less through dramatic action than the concatenation of numerical and dream logics, which eventually tip over into an amorphous death spiral. We don't know what dies or who does the killing, only that everything ends in ruin. None of this, however, would be possible were it not for the unique qualities of Packer's present, which is marked by a number of ongoing developments in the social field. These include escalating technological change, unprecedented optimism in financial markets, and a mounting backlash against the depredations of neoliberal economy. DeLillo establishes this by dating his novel; the events transpire "In the Year 2000" on "A Day in April" (which was in fact when the dot-com bubble began to burst, as well as the high-water mark for the alter-globalization movements of the 1990s). The film, however, provides no dates, and almost all other historical markers are stripped out of Packer's world. Only the primacy of the yuan in FOREX markets—which Cronenberg substitutes for the Japanese yen—hints at an altered geoeconomic landscape. It is a time, in other words, in which virtual money and computerized trading have seemingly vanquished history, leaving only the self-referential temporality of financial markets themselves. The problem, as Packer's art dealer puts it, is that the present is "too contemporary" (27).

Packer navigates this present through a host of visual interfaces and charting techniques. His success is based on a talent for recognizing patterns in information, and throughout the film, Packer encounters present and former employees who are learning or have failed to grasp his "infinitesimal" (191) data analytics. But what exactly does he want? What drives Packer to ruin as he is driven across town? It isn't acquisition or expenditure, but the lure of money's very movement—its swirling currents and waves of expansion. Packer repeatedly stops to eat or have sex, but never with overt enjoyment. These pleasures pale in comparison with those afforded by his gleaming screens and the price changes they register. Everything else is either a relic or an obstacle: the individuated object is a relic ("even the word computer" [104] feels out of date), while the body in particular is an obstacle. In the novel we learn this through the narrator's voice, which repeatedly dwells on Packer's disappointment with his body.[61] In the film, however, it is Packer's chief of theory that puts this idea in words: "People will not die. Isn't this the creed of the new culture? People will be absorbed in streams of information" (104). Packer is the vanguard of this new culture, yet he struggles to keep up with his own aspirations. It is this tension that constitutes the sequence-related elements of his name. "Money is talking to itself" (77) and Packer wants in on the conversation; "the [yen/yuan] is making a statement" (21), and all he and his team need to do is "read it. ... Then leap" (21). But no matter how hard he tries and no matter which models he uses, Packer can't hear the statement the yuan is making. This is precisely because the dynamics of the financial world are inhuman. The financial world is a numerical world, and the numbers refuse to conform to his visions of order and balance. As this becomes clearer, Packer refuses to acknowledge it, insisting on the existence of a deeper order, hidden somewhere beneath the stream of numbers at his fingertips, but every new attempt at divination only derails and imperils him further. Like Icarus, he aims too high and ends up melting down. The crucial difference is that when Packer falls, he brings the cosmos with him.

If one asks what this tale means, the answer would seem clear: it is a cautionary tale, maybe a parody too.[62] But if one asks instead what the name "Packer" does, the answer is the inverse: "Packer" diagrams a drive to go further, to stop at nothing, to extend and ultimately become one with the deterritorializing logics of money itself. In this respect, the name carries the psychic correlate of money's own desire—if money could have its way, as Deleuze and Guattari say, it would "dispatch itself straight to the moon."[63] Packer lives to push money to this limit even if it kills him, to say nothing of the world around him. He lives, in other words, as a striving force to free both financial circulation and human life from their earthly drags. The

Packer effect is thus a kind of exit velocity, a perilous drive toward the next and highest stage of virtual money: the capitalist singularity. Think Elon Musk.

Desiring-Finance Otherwise

These readings of Gekko, Belfort, and Packer provide more than a new vantage point on the genre of financial film; they also tell us something about the dynamics of financial markets themselves. In particular, they highlight the destabilizing power of what Deleuze and Guattari call "desiring-production" in relation to the logics of capitalist finance. Orthodox economic thinking disavows this power by reducing desire to interest and consigning any surplus to the domain of irrationality. In the neoclassical tradition, for example, the subject is rendered a subject of interest through representative agent modeling, which ascribes to all agents a fixed set of behavioral axioms.[64] The subject, on this view, is little more than a hedonic calculator. To the extent that mainstream financial economics has a microfoundation, it is this; asset prices move as market participants receive and react to relevant information. But as Adam Smith and his contemporaries were well aware, the subject of interest (or *homo economicus*) is everywhere haunted by unreason, exhibiting tendencies that do not properly belong to either cognition or ratiocination.[65] Put simply, people are moved by more than interest.

The names of history are a way of thinking finance not through interest but the passions. *Homo historia* engages economy through names from the past. Some of these are names for well-known events like the Great Depression, which are repeatedly returned to as a means of putting the present into some kind of historical perspective. This process proceeds through the narrative operation and a host of patterns associated with historical discourse, ranging from specific figurations of crisis to the broader archetypes of recurrence and revelation. As we have seen, this is a process undergirded by uncertainty, fear, and a desire to counteract such emotions with the consolations of historical thought. Other names, though, are names for persons or personae, and while these proper names do populate conventional forms of historical discourse, they also emerge and circulate through other media types and genres. The name "Gordon Gekko," for example, is propagated through film but spills over into the trade press and popular culture at large, assuming a place alongside the 'real' names, dates, and events of history. These names are the basis for a different mode of history production, premised less on narrative reasoning than the conductive power of event sequences themselves. Proper names share with event names a dependence on historical discourse, but unlike event names, they carry within them the deeds and fates of named personae, which circulate as ways of *becoming* and *being* rather than merely understanding. Proper names directly engage the passions as effects, registering in subjects as fields of intensity; they therefore function not as models but as diagrams; semiotic platforms that format passions and produce subjects with distinct methods, stratagems, and goals. They are desiring-machines that plug into and reconfigure the horizons of the economic machine. It is this hooking up to and reformatting of desire's coordinates that the term *desiring-production* is meant to capture.

In Deleuze and Guattari's estimation, the circulation of history's names will unleash desiring-production from the shackles of capital. Yet in the contemporary context, the names that circulate through financial film carry with them what can only be described as dubious trajectories. Gekko, Belfort, and Packer are all highly masculinized personae, and though each of their names diagrams the production of a specific form of financial subjectivity, none of these seem too far removed from the kind of bloody-mindedness produced through the figure of homo economicus. "Gekko" is the most straightforward in this regard. The Gekko effect turns finance into an invidious social game that plays out within and for the money economy; it diagrams a mode of conduct that consists in putting rumors to work so as to conjure wealth as a means to power. This is a variant on the subject of interest: rational economic man retooled and rewired for purely relative gains.

The effects of "Belfort" and "Packer" are somewhat more complicated. The Belfort effect makes finance antisocial, setting up a game of tearing down taboos and breaking through onto the body without organs. This game plays out within and against the money economy, turning the power of stories into a siphon running from the numerical world down into the physical. The subject who plays this game is as much a subject of desire as a subject of interest, reproducing capitalist finance at the same time as they plunder the profits it creates. The Packer effect, however, initiates a game that can only be described as asocial—a kind of autistic accelerationism that plays out within but ultimately aims beyond the frontiers of extant money economies. The subject who plays this game serves neither themselves nor capital. They threaten the survival of capital by striving to unleash the purely numerical logics of money, but by the very same token, they threaten to turn economy itself against the human. In this respect, the name "Packer" diagrams an aggressive and ambiguous revolution; it configures desire as a leap through technology into an unknown and unknowable future. This future could be postcapitalist; it could be posthuman; it could be a new and hitherto unimaginable form of posthuman capitalism. There is simply no way to tell; we are in truly speculative territory here.

At any rate, these are three names that circulate on the social body on capital today. There are others of course; historical discourse provides a pool of names that grows, shrinks, and mutates with the loops through which names themselves circulate. But if these particular names work as cogs in the desiring-machines that produce contemporary finance, then where are the names that might provide diagrams for desiring-finance otherwise? Where are the names that might take us beyond the worlds enacted through "Gekko," "Belfort," and "Packer"?

Exits to the Future

History has always looked to the past, but modern historical thinking made the future its ultimate horizon. The concept of crisis was pivotal in this regard, providing a means of imagining the present as part of a developmental process into which humanity itself might intervene. More than a history of crisis thinking alone, this gave rise to an ever-expanding array of crisis narratives in which world history was formatted as a series of cycles and epochs, turning points and thresholds. In this respect, the age of financial capitalism is less unique than commonly thought. Despite various transformations in the money form and the myriad instruments now traded on financial markets, historical change is still imagined and produced through narratives of crisis and the futures onto which these open out. This is one way of understanding the sense of fear and opportunity that emerged in late 2008—as a reminder of just how central the concept of crisis is to the imaginary institution of history, financial or otherwise. "Crisis marks history and crisis generates history," no matter the sign under which these concepts are mobilized.[1]

But all is not continuity. If we live in financial times, then these take shape through novel modes of history production that rest as much on recollected histories of finance as they do the registers of historical theory or philosophy. Beyond the mobilization of concepts like history and crisis is a whole set of strange feedback loops between the discourse of financial history on the one hand and processes of historical change or development on the other. These loops were readily apparent in the wake of 2008, when financial journalists and regulators returned not only to the concept of crisis, but also to familiar figurations of crisis, to signal crisis events, and to established narrative accounts of those prior episodes, turning all of these abstract historical patterns to the task of apprehending and negotiating a world in apparent free fall. In popular culture too, coordinates of financial history were dug up and remixed in the medium of film, where iconic names served as yet another vector for the recursive action of the past on the present. This analysis suggests two further lines of thought, which by way of conclusion I briefly take up here. The first relates to a new series of loops at work in the contemporary, postcrisis moment, the second to a related question of futurity.

Already a decade has passed since 2008, and in that time, it has become harder than ever before to get a handle on the character of the present, which feels like uncharted territory one moment and business as usual the next. The future of the capitalist state, for example, is even more uncertain than it was during the subprime years, the multilateral project is coming apart at the seams, no longer in step with the spirit of the times, and a new populism is sweeping the Western world, giving rise to a range of unfamiliar political and economic imaginaries. And yet markets are once again in the throes of a new-era technology boom, the revolving door between Wall Street and the White House continues to turn, and the myth of a golden age still captures minds as ever before. From a metahistorical perspective, what must be acknowledged is how the crisis of 2008 has been transformed into a name and a date, receding from the present and entering into the virtual storehouse of history, where it lurks, ready to return in any number of later presents. And when it does, there is no telling what it will bring with it. New crises will be conjured into being, and in this process, old meanings will be reborn, transfigured, and put to work in ways we cannot foresee. There will be no final word on the place of the subprime crisis within history. But already, in the present marked out by its separation from this past, we can begin to glimpse some of the strange ways that history continues to feed on itself.

The figure of the cycle, for example, is once again doing the rounds, remaking the anxieties of millennials in the image of an ecstatic fury first announced by millenarian Christians. For all its technological savvy, the alt-right movement is mobilizing an age-old faith in renewal through destruction. The first half of this equation is clear enough, most notably in Donald Trump's 2016 campaign slogan, "Make America Great Again" (which is itself a recycled version of Ronald Reagan's in 1980). The second, destructive element is perhaps a little more controversial, although no less apparent to many. It is also a cornerstone of the philosophy of history to which Trump's election time chief strategist Steve Bannon publicly subscribed on more than one occasion. I am referring here to the Strauss-Howe generational theory, which featured prominently in Bannon's 2010 film about the financial crisis, *Generation Zero*, and can be seen at work in his subsequent statements on US politics both during and after his time with Trump.[2] America, or so the story goes, has entered into the final and most violent phase of an eighty-year cycle that will end in the regeneration of economic, political, and civil life. In this vision, past eras are recruited as so many signs of a coming renewal: the "high" of postwar prosperity, the "awakening" of the 1960s, the "unraveling" of the 1990s, and finally the "crisis" of the new millennium—all are cast as steps toward a grander realignment that will reset the clock on American history. That year zero turns out to be 1930 will surprise some, but the popularity of this vision is a testimony to the enduring appeal and productive power of cyclical thought, which has long been an effective way of reinstituting familiar realities. In this case, the cycle promises a return to American hegemony.

There is, of course, something revelatory about this vision, which turns each of the aforementioned eras into episodes whose true meaning has until now lain latent. A similar logic can be found at work elsewhere too, most notably in the narratives surrounding new labor-saving technologies, which bear all the marks of a traumatic figure fulfillment. Here the signal decade is not the 1930s but the 1970s. In its own time, the crisis of the 1970s was narrated as a failure of the Keynesian state and its efforts to moderate wage demands, sending a message to workers and governments alike that their interests were aligned with those of business. As the 1980s unfolded, these became the interests of banking and finance, with workers seeking wealth not only in personal debt, but also in financial assets and homeownership. But in the wake of the subprime episode, the 1970s are reemerging as a harbinger for the sense of complete and utter redundancy that haunts the figure of the worker. To a certain extent, Marxist commentators have always understood the crisis of the 1970s as brought on by the mechanization of industry, which could no longer afford to employ workers instead of machines. Today, however, this narrative has spread across the political divide, with Silicon Valley visionaries taking their place alongside those on the avant-garde Left to announce the coming end of wage labor; an inexorable consequence, we are told, of the new smart machine revolution.[3] They disagree of course on what should take its place, but to posit this as a moment of decision is already to practice the premise of crisis, and to diagnose the contemporary in these terms is precisely a return to the past through the archetype of revelation. The revelatory mode thus continues to offer consolation, not so much through the trappings of familiarity but in the prospect that every new challenge and setback will one day be redeemed. Whether they will remains to be seen, and always so, for any promise of redemption is a promise redeemed in a time to come.

Finally there are the names of finance, which continue to circulate in ways that defy not only the simple division between past and present but also between the categories of the historical and the fictional, producing unconscious intensities in the strangest of places. Here I will give just the one example, of a deleted scene from the *Wall Street* sequel, which surfaced on YouTube in late 2016.[4] In the clip, Donald Trump walks into a barbershop somewhere in London, only to find Gordon Gekko in the chair beside him talking about scooping up distressed securities.[5] An awkward conversation ensues in which Trump, apparently old friends with Gekko, repeatedly calls him "Gordo," and Gekko sells Trump on investing with his new hedge fund. The scene was most likely intended to bolster the realism of Gekko, but one side effect is to unmask the irrealism of Trump, whose name has long been associated in New York and beyond with the demiurgic powers of Gekko, conveying a drive to make larger-than-life deals and fortunes no matter what the fallout. Today, the name "Trump" circulates in precisely the same ways that "Gekko" does, shifting between the genres of fact and fiction with impunity, having been emblazoned across everything from books and buildings to billboards, university logos, and packets of steak, not to mention magazine covers, newspapers and websites, and now countless items of

White House memorabilia. The two names also share an affinity through the context in which they first emerged, whose potential they put into circulation wherever they appear. "The '80s are no longer, Gordo," says Trump, but in this we should take no solace; their names are precisely a means by which to bring that era back to life, a loop through which to reanimate the spirit of the 1980s, diagramming a method and destination that encapsulates all the worst extremes of financial masculinity at the time. We are still only beginning to see what kinds of worlds the Trump effect might bring into being, but one thing is for sure: whatever they are, they won't be pretty.

And so we arrive again at the question of the future. In a time when the historical process feeds so thoroughly on historical discourse, what has or will become of the future? One answer is that the future hangs in the balance, waiting to be won or lost. The late Susan Strange was very much of this mind, seeing the recurrent fear of crisis as exerting a constraining influence over progressive politics. According to this view, the presence of the past not only leads us to approach the new through the lens of the old; it also threatens to limit present actions to those once pursued in the past. This brings with it the possibility that the future might offer little more than an endless replay of those patterns already identified with capitalist history. Strange rejected this scenario as an abrogation of possibility itself. Rather than "hoping for the best but expecting and preparing for the worst," those who have the time to spare should spend it attempting to break through the resignation that historical discourse cultivates in us. "We have to invent a new kind of polity," she argued, "but we cannot yet imagine how it might work."[6] Strange's assessment is in keeping with a broader sentiment on the philosophical Left, which sees the status of the future as the defining battleground of contemporary politics. The story goes like this. As the cultural scene descends into parody and pastiche, so too does the historical imagination, leaving it beached on the shores of an island from which there is no escape. Some call it "postmodernity," others "capitalist realism," but the upshot is the same: it is easier to imagine the end of the world than the end of capitalism.[7] The precise origins of this phrase remain uncertain, but over the past ten or so years, it has become lodged in the space between critical theory and popular culture, where it now serves as shorthand for all the ways in which neoliberal ideology works to narrow down or close up the horizons of history.[8] Beyond a diagnosis of the times, though, the phrase also carries within it a very specific injunction: to somehow jump-start the will to history and once again deliver the future over to utopian dreaming and design. "The problem to be solved," as Fredric Jameson once put it, "is that of breaking out of the windless present of the postmodern back into real historical time, and a history made by human beings."[9]

But what if there is no real history to break back into? What becomes of the future then? This, I suppose, is the main provocation of this book. If critical thinkers are reluctant or unable to relinquish the will to history, it is because so much rests on it. As Hayden White explains, "With the discovery that the time of history was different from the time of nature, man also came to believe that historical time could be affected by human action and purposiveness in ways that natural time could not, that history could be 'made' as well as 'suffered,' and that a historical knowledge true to its 'concept' provided the prospects for a science of society that balanced the claims of experience with the insistencies of expectation, hope, and faith in the future."[10] In other words, not only modern knowledge but associated notions of freedom too became woven into the discourse of history, turning its pronouncements on the nature of time into promises of secular salvation. The problem, however, is that historicism never managed to provide an experience true to this ambition. If the historical future is held up as a horizon of possibility, subject to the will of humanity, then it comes home to roost as something else—a mounting senselessness—to which our routine response is yet another return to the promise of historical discourse. We go on thinking and acting historically, no matter how inhuman and anhistorical the world becomes.

In many ways this is the ultimate paradox of our times: that the historical imagination lags behind the developments it helps produce. This is certainly so in the financial context, as I have endeavored to show throughout this book, but there is a broader issue here too concerning the interface between historical imagination on the one hand and a society's technical structures of communication on the other. In technical terms, historical knowledge emerged through writing, narrative discourse, and a scriptural economy of texts first written and later printed. The postwar critique of historiography was articulated in response to this apparatus, with particular emphasis being placed on the way authoritative myths worked to shore up the belief that social reality could be "both lived and realistically comprehended as a story."[11] But a lot has changed since the 1960s. After decades of deregulation and further rounds of technological change, new forms of communication have fundamentally reconfigured not just the financial industry, but also our very means of rendering its logics intelligible. On one side are the pricing formulas, trading algorithms, and other more mundane media technologies that structure contemporary financial activity. These open financial markets up to an endless array of statistically projected futures, which haunt the narrative operation as so many reminders of the unknown interactions that produce new events. On the other side are the social media platforms, smartphone screens, and digital archives that pervade the texture of everyday life, all of which both multiply the presence of the past and accelerate the speed at which it circulates through the present, enabling events to partake in an even greater number of replays, short circuits, and transmutations than was possible in the age of regular mass media. "Reality, it seems, has been deregulated, and nothing is business as usual anymore," least of all history.[12]

But if the question of history now seems to hinge on that of technology, then to a certain extent it always has. As Erik Davis reminds us, "New technologies of perception and communication open up new spaces, and these spaces are always mapped, on one level or another, through the imagination."[13] The historical imagination emerged as a means of navigating the space opened up by writing, later evolving into a system for governing the politics and economics of the modern nation. The problem is that this system, which instituted notions of linear time and secular progress at the heart of the industrial and technological enterprise, has produced a social machine that no longer corresponds to these coordinates. The historical imagination is out of sync with the world it has produced, continuing to arrange the flow of social time into a sequence of stages when everywhere past and future suffuse the present, and yet it remains hooked up to that world too, feeding so many imagined histories back-into the strange loops of our time.

All of this means we cannot afford to think of history as a trajectory that simply yields to our attempts to direct, shape, or deflect it, much less one that will reveal an inner essence to us providing we spend enough time sifting through the traces it leaves behind. When we think and speak historically, we do not get closer to revealing some process called "history"; we wrap ourselves in the garb of a concept, living through it as we give life to it as a force in the world. Even when we are not aware, we channel the patterns of the past—by reaching for an anchor, by using a concept, by repeating a cliché about history repeating itself (or us not forgetting it), by setting out to pass some threshold on the horizon, when tomorrow will finally be incommensurable with today, when we will finally bend the world to our purposes. But there is no authentic or primordial plane of historical time to which we can return, only rabbit hole after rabbit hole of a history produced through strange loops. History, for want of a better word, escapes our imagination not simply because it exceeds our image of it, but because it feeds on that image, over and again, confronting us with an ever-evolving set of fantasies about our power to master and remake the systems in which we find ourselves enmeshed.

With regard to the question of the future, the challenge is to somehow cultivate a distance from these fantasies, to engage the historical imagination without taking it at face value, to put its repertoire of forms to work without mistaking the maps for the territory—in other words, to develop a posthistorical imagination better fit for contemporary times. "Everywhere," writes Arthur Kroker, "the structural logic of the will to history comes into contact with its historical antimatter—the eclipse of historical narratives— and the result is a future of annihilation. Not annihilation in the form of the disappearance of things or the definite end of historical events, but annihilation as an eclectic, unpredictable but no less spectacular, series of openings."[14] Navigating these will depend on our ability to think beyond the historical—not an end to history, but an exit from belief in the cultural edifice of historical society.

Notes

Preface

1. Douglas Hofstadter, *I Am a Strange Loop* (New York: Basic Books, 2007).

Introduction

1. Secret Agent, "We Lived in Financial Times," *Financial Times*, February 10, 2012, https://www.ft.com/content/b879c584-517c-11e1-a99d-00144feabdc0.

2. See, for example, Andrew Leyshon and Nigel Thrift, "The Capitalization of Almost Everything: The Future of Finance and Capitalism," *Theory, Culture and Society* 24, no. 7–8 (2007): 97–115; and Koray Çalışkan and Michel Callon, "Economization, Part 1: Shifting Attention from the Economy towards Processes of Economization," *Economy and Society* 38, no. 3 (2009): 369–98, each of which provides a different take on this theme.

3. Kerwin Lee Klein, *From History to Theory* (Berkeley: University of California Press, 2011), 86.

4. Gillian Tett, "Wall Street's Crash Course," *Financial Times*, August 26, 2007.

5. There are different versions of this narrative associated with social theory and political economy, respectively. For those on the postmodern Left, emphasis is usually placed on what becomes of culture once money is detached from the circuit of production and enters into a purely symbolic "space of flows" (Manuel Castells, *The Rise of the Network Society* [Oxford: Blackwell, 1996], 472). For example, see Jean Baudrillard, "Transeconomics," in *The Transparency of Evil: Essays on Extreme Phenomena*, trans. James Benedict (London: Verso, 1993), 26–35; Fredric Jameson, "Culture and Finance Capital," in *The Cultural Turn: Selected Writings on the Postmodern, 1983–1998* (London: Verso, 1998), 136–61; Karin Knorr Cetina and Urs Bruegger, "Global Microstructures: The Virtual Societies of Financial Markets," *American Journal of Sociology* 107, no. 4 (2002): 905–50; Benjamin Lee and Edward LiPuma, *Financial Derivatives and the Globalization of Risks* (Durham, NC: Duke University Press, 2004); and the discussion of these and other texts in Andreas Langenohl, "'In the Long Run We Are All Dead': Imaginary Time in Financial Market Narratives," *Cultural Critique* 70 (Fall 2008): 5–13. Langenohl usefully terms this the "detachment thesis," which he summarizes as follows: "In informational capitalism, trade

is primarily trade with symbols, [which] escapes the limitations of space, creates or destroys capital in real time, and functions independently of the somewhat retarded accumulation logic of industrial capitalism." Ibid., 8.

More traditional political economists also stress the idea of "a prolonged split between the divergent real and financial economies" (Giovanni Arrighi, *The Long Twentieth Century: Money, Power, and the Origins of Our Times* [London: Verso, 1994], 82]), but typically go on to identify a distorting impact of the latter on the former and an eventual reversion from finance-led back to production-based accumulation. For example, see Robert Boyer, "Is the Finance-Led Growth Regime a Viable Alternative to Fordism?" *Economy and Society* 29, no. 1 (2000): 111–45; Engelbert Stockhammer, "Financialisation and the Slowdown of Accumulation," *Cambridge Journal of Economics* 28, no. 5 (2004): 719–41; Greta Krippner, "The Financialization of the American Economy," *Socio-Economic Review* 3, no. 2 (2005): 173–208; and to a certain extent, Richard Posner, *A Failure of Capitalism: The Crisis of '08 and the Descent into Depression* (Cambridge, MA: Harvard University Press, 2009). These kinds of arguments bear a close relation to a broader set of narratives about the socially corrosive power of markets and money in modern life, which are rooted in the Polanyian tradition. For a discussion of the "disembedding narrative" in contemporary social sciences, see Martijn Konings, *The Emotional Logic of Capitalism: What Progressives Have Missed* (Stanford, CA: Stanford University Press, 2015), especially chaps. 1 and 2.

6. Pioneering works in this tradition include Georges Bataille's *The Accursed Share: An Essay on General Economy*, vol. 1, trans. Robert Hurley (Brooklyn: Zone Books, 1991); Claude Lévi-Strauss's *The Savage Mind* (Chicago: University of Chicago Press, 1966); Lewis Mumford's *The Myth of the Machine*, vol. 2: *The Pentagon of Power* (New York: Harcourt Brace Jovanovich, 1970); Clifford Geertz's *The Interpretation of Cultures* (New York: Basic Books, 1973); and Jean-Joseph Goux's *Symbolic Economies: After Marx and Freud*, trans. Jennifer Curtiss Gage (Ithaca, NY: Cornell University Press, 1990).

Contemporary applications of this argumentation to finance in particular can be found in Jonathan Nitzan and Shimshon Bichler, *Capital as Power: A Study of Order and Creorder* (London: Routledge, 2009); Arjun Appadurai, "The Ghost in the Financial Machine," *Public Culture* 23, no. 3 (2011): 517–39; Mark Jacobs, "Financial Crises as Symbols and Rituals," in *The Oxford Handbook of the Sociology of Finance*, ed. Karin Knorr Cetina and Alex Preda (Oxford: Oxford University Press, 2012), 376–92; Joseph Vogl, *The Specter of Capital*, trans. Joachim Redner and Robert Savage (Stanford, CA: Stanford University Press, 2015); and Ivan Ascher, *Portfolio Society: On the Capitalist Mode of Prediction* (Brooklyn: Zone Books, 2016).

7. For a fuller appreciation of this trajectory, compare Mike Hill and Warren Montag's *The Other Adam Smith* (Stanford, CA: Stanford University Press, 2015) with Philip Mirowski's *More Heat Than Light: Economics as Social Physics, Physics as Nature's Economics* (Cambridge: Cambridge University Press, 1992).

8. Keynes, for example, criticized equilibrium theory for wishing away the

sequential character of time, describing it as a "pretty, polite technique" for managing our fundamental ignorance of the future. See John Maynard Keynes, "The General Theory of Employment," *Quarterly Journal of Economics* 51, no. 2 (1937): 215. Other key interventions in this vein include Gregory Shackle, *Time in Economics* (Amsterdam: North-Holland, 1958), and John Hicks, "Some Questions of Time in Economics," in *Evolution, Welfare, and Time in Economics: Essays in Honor of Nicholas Georgescu-Roegen*, ed. Andrew Tang, Fred Westfield, and James Worley (Lexington, MA: Lexington Books, 1976), 135–51. Robinson's key contribution was to shift the discussion of time in economics from the level of subjective experience to that of events and their place within a broader process of development. "It is only by interpreting history," she argued, "including the present in history, that economics can aspire to be a serious subject" (in Joan Robinson, "Time in Economic Theory," *Kyklos* 33, no. 2 [1980]: 224). See also her essay "History Versus Equilibrium" in Joan Robinson, *Collected Economic Papers*, vol. 2 (Oxford: Basil Blackwell, 1979), 48–58.

For a more detailed discussion of Robinson's ideas about historical time and their place in the modern canon, see George Feiwel's "Joan Robinson Inside and Outside of the Stream" and Harvey Gram's "Ideology and Time: Criticisms of General Equilibrium," both in *Joan Robinson and Modern Economic Theory*, ed. George Feiwel (Basingstoke: Macmillan, 1989), chaps. 1 and 8, respectively. Robinson's subsequent influence on historical methodology is discussed in Michael Turk, "The Arrow of Time in Economics: From Robinson's Critique to the New Historical Economics," *European Journal of the History of Economic Thought* 17, no. 3 (2010): 471–92.

9. Joan Robinson, "What Are the Questions?" *Journal of Economic Literature* 15, no. 4 (1977): 1322.

10. Robinson, "Time in Economic Theory," 219.

11. Hyman Minsky, "Secrets of the Temple: How the Federal Reserve Runs the Country," *Challenge* 31, no. 3 (1988): 62.

12. This of course is a rather broad claim. In "The Arrow of Time," Turk provides a detailed illustration of the way Robinson's conception of time carries through into the "new historical economics," by which he means to designate a set of literatures in economics dealing with spatial agglomeration, scale effects, and path dependency. The shared ground between Robinson's vision and Marx's method in volume 1 of *Capital* is discussed in Feiwel's "Joan Robinson Inside and Outside of the Stream." I am suggesting here that the net can be widened to include New Institutional Economics (NIE), as well as the so-called Old Institutional Economics (OIE) associated with evolutionary thought. These traditions either focus on the literal bequest of the past to the present (as in the case of NIE) or combine this with a concern for the forward-moving evolution of institutions, legal structures, and organizational forms (as in OIE). In either instance, the sequential character of chronological time functions as a limit to historical thought. I develop this argument further in Chapter 1, where I take up the Marxist, Keynesian, and evolutionary approaches to crisis thinking in some detail.

13. Prominent examples of recent work in this vein include Vogl's *Specter of*

Capital and Ascher's *Portfolio Society*, as well as Arjun Appadurai, *The Future as Cultural Fact: Essays on the Global Condition* (London: Verso, 2013); Douglas Holmes, *Economy of Words: Communicative Imperatives in Central Banks* (Chicago: University of Chicago Press, 2013); Jens Beckert, *Imagined Futures: Fictional Expectations and Capitalist Dynamics* (Cambridge, MA: Harvard University Press, 2016); Jens Beckert and Richard Bronk, eds., *Uncertain Futures: Imaginaries, Narratives, and Calculation in the Economy* (Cambridge: Cambridge University Press, 2018); and Martijn Konings, *Capital and Time: For a New Critique of Neoliberal Reason* (Stanford, CA: Stanford University Press, 2018). On the emerging field of finance and society studies, see Dick Forslund and Thomas Bay, "The Eve of Critical Finance Studies," *Ephemera: Theory and Politics in Organization* 9, no. 4 (2009): 285–99; Thomas Bay and Christophe Schinkus, "Critical Finance Studies: An Interdisciplinary Manifesto," *Journal of Interdisciplinary Economics* 24, no. 1 (2012): 1–6; and Amin Samman, Nathan Coombs, and Angus Cameron, "For a Post-Disciplinary Study of Finance and Society," *Finance and Society* 1, no. 1 (2015): 1–5.

14. Thorstein Veblen, "Why Is Economics Not an Evolutionary Science?" *Quarterly Journal of Economics* 12, no. 4 (1898): 389.

15. Michel Foucault, *The Birth of Biopolitics: Lectures at the Collège de France, 1978–79*, trans. Graham Burchell (Basingstoke: Palgrave Macmillan, 2008). In the following discussion, quotations are acknowledged by page numbers in parentheses in the body of text.

16. I am thinking here of international organizations like the World Bank and the International Monetary Fund, as well as central banks across the Western world, including the Bank of England, the European Central Bank, and the US Federal Reserve, all of which have moved well beyond a stance of laissez-faire when it comes to supporting the market. The change at the international level became a heated topic of discussion in development studies after the Asian crisis of the late 1990s and was diagnosed with acuity by Charles Gore in "The Rise and the Fall of the Washington Consensus as a Paradigm for Developing Countries," *World Development* 28, no. 5 (2000): 789–804. The shift in central banking practice was noticed somewhat later, after the extraordinary measures introduced to contain the subprime crisis. For a discussion of contemporary central banking as a form of activist neoliberal governance, see Konings, *Capital and Time*, especially chaps. 9–11.

17. He dwells, for example, on the way child rearing, education, health care, and migration are all refigured as "elements which may or may not improve human capital." Foucault, *The Birth of Biopolitics*, 230.

18. Wendy Brown, *Undoing the Demos: Neoliberalism's Stealth Revolution* (Brooklyn: Zone Books, 2015). In the following discussion, quotations are acknowledged by page numbers in parentheses in the body of text.

19. As Brown sees it, "The neoliberal triumph of *homo oeconomicus* . . . is undermining democratic practices and a democratic imaginary by vanquishing the subject that governs itself through moral autonomy and governs with others through popular sovereignty." She continues: "The argument is that economic values have not simply

supersaturated the political or become predominant over the political. Rather, a neoliberal iteration of *homo oeconomicus* is extinguishing the agent, the idiom, and the domains through which democracy . . . materializes." Ibid., 79.

20. The clue is in the taxonomic lexicon, which connects Aristotle's thoughts on the spheres of economy and polis, through Latin translation in the West, to the burgeoning knowledge practices associated with the Enlightenment. *Homo economicus* is materialized through the modern project of political economy; *homo legalis* through jurisprudence; *homo politicus* through the idea and practice of popular sovereignty, and so on. See Brown, *Undoing the Demos*, chap. 3.

21. Michel de Certeau, *The Writing of History*, trans. Tom Conley (New York: Columbia University Press, 1988), 6.

22. See Gilles Deleuze and Félix Guattari, *Anti-Oedipus: Capitalism and Schizophrenia*, trans. Robert Hurley, Mark Seem, and Helen Lane (London: Continuum, 2007), 21–23, 92–95.

23. Paul Valéry, *Reflections on the World Today*, trans. Francis Scarfe (London: Thames and Hudson, 1951), 13, emphasis in original.

24. "Historicality," as Heidegger puts it, "is prior to what is called 'history.' . . . [It] stands for the state of Being that is constitutive for Dasein's 'historizing' as such; [and] only on the basis of such 'historicizing' is anything like 'world-history' possible or can anything belong historically to world-history" (in Martin Heidegger, *Being and Time*, trans. John Macquarrie and Edward Robinson [Oxford: Basil Blackwell, 1987], 41).

25. Joseph Vogl, *The Ascendancy of Finance*, trans. Simon Garnett (Cambridge: Polity Press, 2017).

26. The history of financialization is very much still being written, but key texts include Arrighi's *The Long Twentieth Century*; Barry Eichengreen's *Globalizing Capital: A History of the International Monetary System* (Princeton, NJ: Princeton University Press, 1996); Jan Toporowski's *The End of Finance: Capital Market Inflation, Financial Derivatives and Pension Fund Capitalism* (London: Routledge, 2000); Ronen Palan's *The Offshore World: Sovereign Markets, Virtual Places and Nomad Millionaires* (Ithaca, NY: Cornell University Press, 2003); Dick Bryan and Mike Rafferty's *Capitalism with Derivatives: A Political Economy of Financial Derivatives, Capital and Class* (Basingstoke: Palgrave Macmillan, 2005); Donald MacKenzie's *An Engine, Not a Camera: How Financial Models Shape Markets* (Cambridge, MA: MIT Press, 2006); Martijn Konings's *The Development of American Finance* (Cambridge: Cambridge University Press, 2011); and Greta Krippner's *Capitalizing on Crisis: The Political Origins of the Rise of Finance* (Cambridge, MA: Harvard University Press, 2012).

In recent years, attention has turned not only to the future and newly emergent financial technologies, such as high-frequency trading and block-chain payment systems, but also to the past and, in particular, to a set of foundational innovations in state financing and banking operations associated with the early modern period. On the former, see Donald MacKenzie, "Mechanizing the Merc: The Chicago Mercantile Exchange and the Rise of High-Frequency Trading," *Technology and*

Culture 56, no. 3 (2015): 646–75; Adam Hayes and Paolo Tasca, "Blockchain and Crypto Currencies," in *The FinTech Book: The Financial Technology Handbook for Investors, Entrepreneurs and Visionaries*, ed. Susanne Chishti and Janos Barberis (Chichester: Wiley, 2016), 217–20; and Mark Buitenhek, "Understanding and Applying Blockchain Technology in Banking: Evolution or Revolution?" *Journal of Digital Banking* 1, no. 2 (2016): 111–19. On the latter, see Samuel Knafo, "The State and the Rise of Speculative Finance in England," *Economy and Society* 37, no. 2 (2008): 172–92; Nina Boy, "Sovereign Safety," *Security Dialogue* 46, no. 6 (2015): 530–47; and Stefano Sgambati, "Rethinking Banking: Debt Discounting and the Making of Modern Money as Liquidity," *New Political Economy* 21, no. 3 (2016): 274–90.

27. Peter Osborne, *The Politics of Time: Modernity and Avant-Garde* (London: Verso, 1995), ix.

28. Reinhart Koselleck, *Critique and Crisis: Enlightenment and the Pathogenesis of Modern Society* (Oxford: Berg, 1988).

29. Arrighi, *The Long Twentieth Century*.

30. The phrase originates in Fernand Braudel's *Civilization and Capitalism: 15th–18th Century*, vol. 3: *The Perspective of the World*, trans. Siân Reynolds (Berkeley: University of California Press, 1992), 246, but was popularized by Arrighi's use of it in *The Long Twentieth Century*, 6. Joshua Clover provides an interesting take on its significance in his essay, "Autumn of the System: Poetry and Financial Capital," *Journal of Narrative Theory* 41, no. 1 (2011): 34–52. Clover also provides references to a range of Marxist thinkers in whose work the cyclical figure of financial expansion can be found, including David Harvey and Robert Brenner. To this list I would add William Sewell, who positions speculative bubbles within the broader "cyclical quality of capitalist temporality" (in "The Temporalities of Capitalism," *Socio-Economic Review* 6, no. 3 [2008]: 519–20). For a critique of the tendency to view financial speculation as a natural outgrowth of capitalist expansion, see Samuel Knafo, "Liberalisation and Political Economy of Financial Bubbles," *Competition and Change* 13, no. 2 (2009): 128–44.

31. Harold James, *The Creation and Destruction of Value: The Globalization Cycle* (Cambridge, MA: Harvard University Press, 2009).

32. In theoretical terms, the argument put forward in such accounts is that periods of openness or integration are underpinned by the stabilizing function of a hegemonic state or regime. See, for instance, Charles Kindleberger, *The World in Depression, 1929–1939* (London: Allen Lane, 1973); Stephen Krasner, "State Power and the Structure of International Trade," *World Politics* 28, no. 3 (1976): 317–47; Robert Keohane, *After Hegemony: Cooperation and Discord in the World Political Economy* (Princeton, NJ: Princeton University Press, 1984); and Stephen Gill, *American Hegemony and the Trilateral Commission* (Cambridge: Cambridge University Press, 1990). Despite decades of sustained criticism, stories of a twinned American and global decline continue to capture the world historical imagination. Isabelle Grunberg has explained this as an attachment to the mythological content of such narratives, which provide a means through which to express deeper fears relating to the prospect of

decline and fall. For the relevant textual evidence, see Isabelle Grunberg, "Exploring the 'Myth' of Hegemonic Stability," *International Organization* 44, no. 4 (1990): 431–77.

33. In particular, see Mircea Eliade, *The Myth of the Eternal Return: Or, Cosmos and History*, trans. Willard Trask (Princeton, NJ: Princeton University Press, 1991).

34. For instance, see Joseph Schumpeter, *Business Cycles: A Theoretical, Historical, and Statistical Analysis of the Capitalist Process* (London: McGraw-Hill, 1939); Charles Kindleberger, *Manias, Panics and Crashes* (London: Macmillan, 1978); Hyman Minsky, *Stabilizing an Unstable Economy* (New York: McGraw-Hill, 1986); and Carmen Reinhart and Kenneth Rogoff, *This Time Is Different: Eight Centuries of Financial Folly* (Princeton, NJ: Princeton University Press, 2009).

35. The definitive account of globalization through a narrative lens remains Angus Cameron and Ronen Palan's *The Imagined Economies of Globalization* (London: Sage, 2004).

36. I borrow these terms from Martijn Konings and Andreas Langenohl, respectively. See note 5.

37. Jameson, "Culture and Finance Capital," 136–61.

38. Jean-François Lyotard, quoted in Klein, *From History to Theory*, 92.

39. Jameson, *The Cultural Turn*, 160.

40. Jean Baudrillard, *Simulations*, trans. Paul Foss, Paul Patton, and Philip Beitchman (New York: Semiotext(e), 1983), 71.

41. Fredric Jameson, "Future City," *New Left Review* 21 (May–June 2003): 76.

42. Jameson, *The Cultural Turn*, 154.

43. Ibid.

44. Hayden White, "The Historical Event," *Differences* 19, no. 2 (2008): 9–34, 31 (fn. 4), emphasis in original.

45. This argument comes in many flavors, from the epistemological narrativism of analytic philosophers like Louis Mink to the ontological narrativism of continentals like Paul Ricoeur. I provide more detail on these and other versions of the claim that "historians cannot do without narrative" in Chapter 2.

46. Douglas Hofstadter, *I Am a Strange Loop* (New York: Basic Books, 2007), xii, emphases in original.

47. Dilthey, for example, saw historical works not simply as the product of the historian's own imaginative encounter with the past, but also as the spur to a similar process within the reader, for whom a work's narrative would offer itself as a means of reexperiencing the past through a later present. See Wilhelm Dilthey, *The Formation of the Historical World in the Human Sciences: Selected Works*, vol. 3. trans. Rudolf Makkreel and Frithjof Rodi (Princeton, NJ: Princeton University Press, 2002), 235. Along with thinkers like Droysen, Dilthey forms part of a broader German tradition that runs from the mid-nineteenth century, via twentieth-century hermeneutics, to the kind of approach to historical concepts developed by Koselleck from the 1950s onward. On Dilthey in particular, see Rudolf Makreel, *Dilthey: Philosopher of the Human Studies* (Princeton, NJ: Princeton University Press, 1992). For the broader

intellectual context, see Frederick Beiser, *The German Historicist Tradition* (Oxford: Oxford University Press, 2011).

48. See Hayden White, *The Practical Past* (Evanston, IL: Northwestern University Press, 2014).

49. The key texts in this tradition are John Dunn's *The Political Thought of John Locke: An Historical Account of the Argument of the "Two Treatises of Government"* (Cambridge: Cambridge University Press, 1969); J. G. A. Pocock's *The Machiavellian Moment: Florentine Political Thought and the Atlantic Republican Tradition* (Princeton, NJ: Princeton University Press, 1975); and Quentin Skinner's *The Foundations of Modern Political Thought*, vols. 1 and 2 (Cambridge: Cambridge University Press, 1978). For early statements of the theoretical and methodological underpinnings of these works, see J. G. A. Pocock, "The History of Political Thought: A Methodological Enquiry," in *Philosophy, Politics and Society*, ed. Peter Laslett and W. G. Runciman (Oxford: Blackwell, 1962), 183–202; John Dunn, "The Identity of the History of Ideas," *Philosophy* 43, no. 164 (1968): 85–104; and Quentin Skinner, "Meaning and Understanding in the History of Ideas," *History and Theory* 8, no. 1 (1969): 3–53.

50. For his own reflections on what it means to think history through genealogy, see Michel Foucault, "Nietzsche, Genealogy, History," in *Language, Counter-Memory, and Practice: Selected Essays and Interviews*, ed. Donald Bouchard (Ithaca, NY: Cornell University Press, 1977), 139–64.

Chapter 1

1. Koselleck's key works in this regard include *Critique and Crisis: Enlightenment and the Pathogenesis of Modern Society* (Oxford: Berg, 1988); "Some Questions Regarding the Conceptual History of Crisis," in *The Practice of Conceptual History: Timing History, Spacing Concepts*, trans. Todd Presner (Stanford, CA: Stanford University Press, 2002), 236–47; and "Crisis," *Journal of the History of Ideas* 67, no. 2 (2006): 357–400.

2. Koselleck, *The Practice of Conceptual History*, 237. As he points out, this apparent two-sidedness is in fact a foundational unity, reflecting how modern ideas of subjective critique and objective crisis were still "conceptually fused" under the Greek notion of *krisis*. Koselleck, "Crisis," 359.

3. Janet Roitman, *Anti-Crisis* (Durham, NC: Duke University Press, 2014); in the following discussion, quotations are acknowledged by page numbers in parentheses in the body of text.

4. Koselleck, "Crisis," 370, quoted in Roitman, *Anti-Crisis*, 18.

5. With Aristotle, for example, decisions in the courts are the means through which individuals become citizens and the political order becomes just. See Aristotle, *Politics*, trans. Ernest Barker (Oxford: Oxford University Press, 1998), 84–97.

6. Koselleck, "Crisis," 359.

7. Ibid., 359–60.

8. Koselleck, *The Practice of Conceptual History*, 245.

9. Randolph Starn, "Historians and Crisis," *Past and Present* 52, no. 1 (1971): 4.

10. Koselleck, *The Practice of Conceptual History*, 237.

11. Quoted in Starn, "Historians and Crisis," 4.

12. Koselleck, "Crisis," 361–67.

13. Ibid., 362–63, 368–70.

14. Ibid., 368–81.

15. Ibid., 389.

16. Roitman, *Anti-Crisis*, 18.

17. In Jacob Burckhardt, *Reflections on History*, trans. M. D. Hottinger (Indianapolis, IN: Liberty Fund, 1979), 213–68. In the following discussion, quotations are taken from this edition and are acknowledged by page numbers in parentheses in the body of text.

18. Quoted in James Martin, "The Theory of Storms: Jacob Burckhardt and the Concept of Historical Crisis," *Journal of European Studies* 40, no. 4 (2010): 323. Martin also provides an extended discussion of Burckhardt's political leanings, developing a rare counterbalance to conventional accounts that portray him as either a liberal humanist on the one hand or a proto-fascist on the other. In truth, his worldview is not so easy to pin down.

19. Burckhardt, *Reflections on History*, 216, 248–29. See also Jacob Burckhardt, *Judgments on History and Historians*, trans. Harry Zohn (Indianapolis, IN: Liberty Fund, 1999), 68, 164–65.

20. Starn, "Historians and Crisis," 9.

21. Koselleck, "Crisis," 374.

22. Ibid., 374.

23. Joseph Vogl, *The Specter of Capital*, trans. Joachim Redner and Robert Savage (Stanford, CA: Stanford University Press, 2015), 25.

24. For a broader discussion, see Liana Vardi, *The Physiocrats and the World of the Enlightenment* (Cambridge: Cambridge University Press, 2012).

25. For a discussion of scarcity and the physiocrats, see Michel Foucault's *Security, Territory, Population: Lectures at the Collège de France, 1977–1978*, trans. Graham Burchell (Basingstoke: Palgrave Macmillan, 2007), 29–49. Foucault is expressly interested in developing a genealogy of government rather than a history of concepts, but he too notes how "the event" of scarcity seems to disappear within the theoretical and practical universe of the physiocrats, its very suggestion being "gradually corrected, compensated for, checked, and finally nullified" (40) through a series of individual and collective mechanisms characteristic of untrammeled market society.

26. Paul Mattick, *Economic Crisis and Crisis Theory* (London: Merlin Press, 1981), 23, emphasis added.

27. William Stanley Jevons, "Commercial Crises and Sun-Spots," *Nature* 19, no. 472 (1878): 33–37.

28. This terminology was first used by Léon Walras, who founded the general equilibrium framework with his *Elements of Pure Economics*, trans. William Jaffé (London: Routledge, 2003).

29. Mattick, *Economic Crisis and Crisis Theory*, 30–31.

30. For example, see Robert Lucas, "An Equilibrium Model of the Business Cycle," *Journal of Political Economy* 83, no. 6 (1975): 1113–44; Robert Lucas, *Studies in Business-Cycle Theory* (Cambridge, MA: MIT Press, 1983); and James Hartley, Kevin Hoover, and Kevin Salyer, eds., *Real Business Cycles: A Reader* (London: Routledge, 1998).

31. Fredric Jameson, *The Political Unconscious: Narrative as a Socially Symbolic Act* (London: Routledge, 2002), 13.

32. See Adam Smith's *The Wealth of Nations* (Chicago: University of Chicago Press, 1976), 302–4, and *The Theory of Moral Sentiments* (Indianapolis, IN: Liberty Fund, 1979), 182–84. For a complementary discussion, see David Blaney and Naeem Inayatullah, "Undressing the Wound of Wealth: Political Economy as a Cultural Project," in *Cultural Political Economy*, ed. Jacqueline Best and Matthew Paterson (London: Routledge, 2010), 29–47.

33. See Joseph Schumpeter, *Theory of Economic Development* (Brunswick, NJ: Transaction Publishers, 1980).

34. Joseph Schumpeter and Richard Clemence, *Essays on Entrepreneurs, Innovations, Business Cycles, and the Evolution of Capitalism* (Brunswick, NJ: Transaction Publishers, 1989), 112–17.

35. According to Hayek, every market agent must be involved in the process of economic discovery, because without competition for customers, producers would be unable to identify and meet the diverse demands of individuals. See Friedrich von Hayek, *Law, Legislation and Liberty*, vol. 3: *Political Order of a Free People* (Chicago: University of Chicago Press, 1979), 67–68. On reward and punishment, see *The Constitution of Liberty* (Chicago: University of Chicago Press, 1960), 71–84, and *Law, Legislation and Liberty*, vol. 2: *The Mirage of Social Justice* (Chicago: University of Chicago Press, 1976), 107–32.

36. Friedrich von Hayek, *Prices and Production* (London: Routledge and Kegan Paul, 1931), 98ff.

37. Marx's writings on crisis are notoriously fragmented, and this has spawned an entire cottage industry in critical exegesis. I focus here on the comments in volume 3 of *Capital*, as it is these that have come to underpin the orthodox branch of Marxist crisis theory. See Karl Marx, *Capital: A Critique of Political Economy*, vol. 3 (Moscow: Progress Publishers, 1977), esp. 247–59.

38. David Ricardo, *On the Principles of Political Economy and Taxation* (London: J. M. Dent, 1969), 64–76.

39. Karl Marx, *Grundrisse: Foundations of the Critique of Political Economy*, trans. Martin Nicolaus (Harmondsworth: Penguin Pelican, 1973), 754.

40. Koselleck, "Crisis," 395.

41. Marx, *Capital*, 3: 251–55.

42. Ibid., 257–59. See also Karl Marx and Friedrich Engels, *The Communist Manifesto: A Modern Edition*, trans. Samuel Moore (London: Verso, 1998), 41–42.

43. During the twentieth century, there were countless reformulations of Marx's theory. Useful overviews are provided in Michael Bleaney, *Underconsumption Theories:*

A History and Critical Analysis (New York: International Publishers, 1976); Anwar Shaikh, "An Introduction to the History of Crisis Theories," in *U.S. Capitalism in Crisis*, ed. Anwar Shaikh (New York: URPE, 1978), 219–41; James O'Connor, *The Meaning of Crisis: A Theoretical Introduction* (Oxford: Basil Blackwell, 1987); and Simon Clarke, *Marx's Theory of Crisis* (Basingstoke: Macmillan Press, 1994).

44. For example, see Ernest Mandel, *Late Capitalism*, trans. Joris De Bres (London: Verso, 1998); Anwar Shaikh, "Political Economy and Capitalism: Notes on Dobb's Theory of Crisis," *Cambridge Journal of Economics* 2, no. 2 (1978): 233–51; and Paul Mattick, *Economics, Politics, and the Age of Inflation* (London: Merlin Press, 1980).

45. More precisely, Luxemburg argues that a structurally induced underconsumption renders capitalist societies dependent on external sources of demand, which are secured by states through an imperial conquest of the noncapitalist world. See Rosa Luxemburg, *The Accumulation of Capital*, trans. Agnes Schwarzschild (London: Routledge, 2003), 247–306.

46. See Paul Baran and Paul Sweezy, *Monopoly Capital: An Essay on the American Economic and Social Order* (New York: Monthly Review Press, 1968), 117–214.

47. David Harvey, *The Limits to Capital* (London: Verso, 1982).

48. John Maynard Keynes, *The General Theory of Employment, Interest and Money* (London: Macmillan, 1936).

49. In fact, once divorced from their claims about the structural basis of underconsumption, Baran and Sweezy's account of crisis management ends up looking remarkably similar to Alvin Hansen's vision of the "smoothed" or "managed" business cycle. See Hansen's *Fiscal Policy and Business Cycles* (New York: Norton, 1941). Paul Samuelson coined the term *neoclassical synthesis* in the third edition of his textbook, *Economics* (New York: McGraw-Hill, 1955), 212. The idea of a synthesis between Keynesian and neoclassical ideas was first suggested shortly after the publication of *The General Theory*, by John Hicks in "Mr. Keynes and the 'Classics': A Suggested Interpretation," *Econometrica* 5, no. 2 (1937): 147–59.

50. Jan Toporowski, *Theories of Financial Disturbance: An Examination of Critical Theories of Finance from Adam Smith to the Present Day* (Cheltenham: Edward Elgar, 2005), 88, 94–95, 134. As Keynes himself put it in *The General Theory* (320), it is only "with markets organized and influenced as they are at present" that uncertainty can breed permanent under-investment—meaning that epochal crisis hinges on a coupling of industry to the cycles of finance.

51. See Hyman Minsky, *Stabilizing an Unstable Economy* (New York: McGraw-Hill, 1986).

52. Thorstein Veblen, *The Place of Science in Modern Civilization and Other Essays* (New York: Huebsch, 1919), 436.

53. We know from one of his reading lists that Keynes used Veblen's *Theory of Business Enterprise* (New Brunswick, NJ: Transaction Publishers, 1978) while lecturing at Cambridge before World War I. See Toporowski, *Theories of Financial Disturbance*, 80.

54. "Accumulation regime" refers to a sustainable pattern of investment and

consumption within a capitalist social formation; "mode of regulation" refers to the ensemble of norms and institutions that stabilize this pattern and enable its reproduction.

55. At one point, he describes them as "chance discoveries made in the course of human struggles." Alain Lipietz, *Mirages and Miracles: The Crisis in Global Fordism*, trans. David Macey (London: Verso, 1987), 15.

56. Michel Aglietta, *A Theory of Capitalist Regulation: The U.S. Experience*, trans. David Fernbach (London: New Left Books, 1979), 383.

57. Ronen Palan, "Transnational Theories of Order and Change: Heterodoxy in International Relations Scholarship," *Review of International Studies* 33, no. 1 (2007): 47–69.

58. See Alain Lipietz, "From Althusserianism to Regulation Theory," in *The Althusserian Legacy*, ed. E. Ann Kaplan and Michael Sprinker (London: Verso, 1993), 99–138. See also Robert Boyer, "Is a Finance-Led Growth Regime a Viable Alternative to Fordism?" *Economy and Society* 29, no. 1 (2000): 111–45.

59. Louis Althusser, *For Marx*, trans. Ben Brewster (Harmondsworth: Penguin, 1969), 100. Compare with Lipietz, "From Althusserianism to Regulation Theory," 127.

60. Lipietz, "From Althusserianism to Regulation Theory," 120–38.

61. Régis Debray, *Prison Writings*, trans. Rosemary Sheed (London: Penguin, 1975), 87–160. In the following discussion, quotations are taken from this edition and are acknowledged by page numbers in parentheses in the body of text.

62. For example, see George Cooper, *The Origin of Financial Crises: Central Banks, Credit Bubbles and the Efficient Market Fallacy* (New York: Vintage Books, 2008); Costas Lapavitsas, *Profiting without Producing: How Finance Exploits Us All* (London: Verso, 2014); Anastasia Nesvetailova, *Financial Alchemy in Crisis: The Great Liquidity Illusion* (London: Pluto Press, 2010); and Bill Lucarelli, *The Economics of Financial Turbulence: Alternative Theories of Money and Finance* (Cheltenham: Edward Elgar, 2011). On the Regulation approach in particular, see Henk Overbeek, "Transnational Class Formation and Concepts of Control: Towards a Genealogy of the Amsterdam Project in International Political Economy," *Journal of International Relations and Development* 7, no. 2 (2004): 113–41; Ronen Palan, "Is the Competition State the New, Post-Fordist, Mode of Regulation? Regulation Theory from an International Political Economic Perspective," *Competition and Change* 10, no. 2 (2006): 246–62; and Robert Boyer, "The Global Financial Crisis in Historical Perspective: An Economic Analysis Combining Minsky, Hayek, Fisher, Keynes and the Regulation Approach," *Accounting, Economics and Law* 3, no. 3 (2013): 93–139.

63. Roitman, *Anti-Crisis*, 11.

64. Colin Hay, "Crisis and the Structural Transformation of the State: Interrogating the Process of Change," *British Journal of Politics and International Relations* 1, no. 3 (1999): 317–44.

65. Ibid., 333, 335.

66. Colin Hay, "Narrating Crisis: The Discursive Construction of the Winter of Discontent," *Sociology* 30, no. 2 (1996): 253–77, at 261.

67. For the paradigmatic expression of this view, see Wesley Widmaier, Mark Blyth, and Leonard Seabrooke, "Exogenous Shocks or Endogenous Constructions? The Meanings of Wars and Crises," *International Studies Quarterly* 51, no. 4 (2007): 747–59, esp. 752–53. The broader disciplinary context for this intervention is laid out in the introductory chapter of Rawi Abdelal, Mark Blyth, and Craig Parsons, eds., *Constructing the International Economy* (Ithaca, NY: Cornell University Press, 2010), 1–19.

68. Blyth invokes the American economist Frank Knight in order to emphasize what he sees as the epistemological character of uncertainty. See Frank Knight, *Risk, Uncertainty, and Profit* (Chicago: University of Chicago Press, 1921). Keynes offered a more extreme, ontological account of uncertainty in his *Treatise on Probability*, which was originally published in the same year as Knight's book. Keynes's treatise can be found in his *Collected Writings*, vol. 3 (New York: St. Martin's Press, 1973).

69. Mark Blyth, *Great Transformations: Economic Ideas and Institutional Change in the Twentieth Century* (Cambridge: Cambridge University Press, 2002), 8.

70. Ibid., 32.

71. Mark Blyth, "Powering, Puzzling, or Persuading? The Mechanisms of Building Institutional Orders," *International Studies Quarterly* 51, no. 4 (2007): 761; and Leonard Seabrooke, "The Everyday Social Sources of Economic Crises: From 'Great Frustrations' to 'Great Revelations' in Interwar Britain," *International Studies Quarterly* 51, no. 4 (2007): 795.

72. Widmaier, Blyth, and Seabrooke, "Exogenous Shocks or Endogenous Constructions?" 748, 749.

73. Over the last decade or so, Jessop has published extensively on what he calls the cultural political economy of crisis construal and construction. Key texts include Bob Jessop, "Critical Semiotic Analysis and Cultural Political Economy," *Critical Discourse Studies* 1, no. 2 (2004): 159–74; Bob Jessop and Ngai-Ling Sum, "Towards a Cultural International Political Economy: Poststructuralism and the Italian School," in *International Political Economy and Poststructural Politics*, ed. Marieke de Goede (Basingstoke: Palgrave, 2006), 157–76; Bob Jessop, "Crisis Construal in the North Atlantic Financial Crisis and the Eurozone Crisis," *Competition and Change* 19, no. 2 (2015): 95–112; and Bob Jessop, "The Symptomatology of Crises, Reading Crises and Learning from Them: Some Critical Realist Reflections," *Journal of Critical Realism* 14, no. 3 (2015): 238–71. On the broader framework that underpins this analysis of crisis, see Ngai-Ling Sum and Bob Jessop, *Towards a Cultural Political Economy: Putting Culture in its Place in Political Economy* (Cheltenham: Edward Elgar, 2013), especially parts 1 and 2.

74. Jessop, "Critical Semiotic Analysis," 166–70; Sum and Jessop, *Towards a Cultural Political Economy*, 72–90.

75. Jessop, "Critical Semiotic Analysis," 162–63.

76. Bob Jessop, "The Knowledge-Based Economy," *Naked Punch Review* 10 (2008): 83–44.

77. Hay, "Narrating Crisis," 253.

78. For example, see John Bellamy Foster and Fred Magdoff, *The Great Financial Crisis: Causes and Consequences* (New York: Monthly Review Press, 2009), and Andrew Kliman, *The Failure of Capitalist Production: Underlying Causes of the Great Recession* (London: Pluto, 2012).

79. Paul Mason, *Postcapitalism: A Guide to Our Future* (London: Allen Lane, 2015).

80. Michael Bordo and Harold James, "The Great Depression Analogy," *Financial History Review* 17, no. 2 (2010): 127.

Chapter 2

1. Johan Huizinga, "A Definition of the Concept of History," in *Philosophy and History: Essays Presented to Ernst Cassirer*, ed. Ernst Cassirer, Raymond Klibansky, and H. J. Paton (New York: Harper and Row, 1963), 3.

2. Michel de Certeau, *The Writing of History*, trans. Tom Conley (New York: Columbia University Press, 1988), 3.

3. Ibid., 4.

4. Rainer Maria Rilke, *The Notebooks of Malte Laurids Brigge*, trans. Burton Pike (London: Dalkey Archive Press, 2008), 11.

5. de Certeau, *The Writing of History*, 2–5. In the following discussion, quotations are acknowledged by page numbers in parentheses in the body of text.

6. Ian Buchanan, *Michel de Certeau: Cultural Theorist* (London: Sage, 2000), 81–82.

7. Michel de Certeau, *The Practice of Everyday Life*, trans. Steven Rendall (Berkeley: University of California Press, 1984), 131–53.

8. Michel de Certeau, *Heterologies: Discourse on the Other*, trans. Brian Massumi (Minneapolis: University of Minnesota Press, 1986), 219.

9. See Peter Novick, *That Noble Dream: The "Objectivity Question" and the American Historical Profession* (Cambridge: Cambridge University Press, 1988), especially chap. 4, and Joan Wallach Scott, "History in Crisis: The Others' Side of the Story," *American Historical Review* 94, no. 3 (1989): 680–92.

10. de Certeau, *Heterologies*, 219.

11. Ibid.

12. Hayden White, "The Practical Past," *Historein*, 10 (2010): 10–19.

13. Michael Oakeshott, *On History and Other Essays* (Indianapolis, IN: Liberty Fund, 1999), 1–48.

14. Of course, for de Certeau, this very idea of a purely deontological relation to the past is part of the operation that guarantees the functionality of historical discourse.

15. White, "The Practical Past," 11, emphasis in original.

16. This is why White speaks of an "exclusion of rhetoric from historiology." Ibid., 9. For more on this, see "The Politics of Historical Interpretation: Discipline and De-Sublimation," in Hayden White, *The Content of the Form: Narrative*

Discourse and Historical Representation (Baltimore, MD: Johns Hopkins University Press, 1987), 58–82.

17. White, "The Practical Past," 7. He briefly discusses each of these three forms, but for a deeper analysis of postmodern fiction and its reinvention of the historical novel, see Linda Hutcheon, *A Poetics of Postmodernism: History, Theory, Fiction* (London: Routledge, 1988), and Amy Elias, *Sublime Desire: History and Post-1960 Fiction* (Baltimore, MD: Johns Hopkins University Press, 2001).

18. White, "The Practical Past," 13.

19. Wilhelm Dilthey, *The Formation of the Historical World in the Human Sciences: Selected Works*, vol. 3, trans. Rudolf Makkreel and Frithjof Rodi (Princeton, NJ: Princeton University Press, 2002), 235.

20. Georg Wilhelm Friedrich Hegel, *The Philosophy of History*, trans. John Sibree (New York: Dover, 1956), 60.

21. For example, see Harry Barnes, *A History of Historical Writing* (New York: Dover, 1963); John Burrow, *A History of Histories: Epics, Chronicles, Romances and Inquiries from Herodotus and Thucydides to the Twentieth Century* (London: Allen Lane, 2007); and George Iggers, Q. Edward Wang, and Supriya Mukherjee, *A Global History of Historiography* (Harlow: Pearson Longman, 2008). All three of these histories focus on historical writing in general, but the question of narrative figures prominently throughout each. For shorter discussions that deal specifically with the place of narrative within historiography, see the various contributions in Robert Canary and Henry Kozicki, eds., *The Writing of History: Literary Form and Historical Understanding* (Madison: University of Wisconsin Press, 1978) and Geoffrey Roberts, ed., *The History and Narrative Reader* (London: Routledge, 2001).

22. Burrow, *A History of Histories*.

23. At this point, history was not yet an established university subject, and Ranke's appointment in Berlin reflected a national agenda for educational reform led by Prussian education minister Wilhelm von Humboldt. See Donald Kelley, "History and the Life Sciences in the Early Nineteenth Century: Wilhelm von Humboldt and Leopold von Ranke," in *Leopold von Ranke and the Shaping of the Historical Discipline*, ed. George Iggers and James Powell (Syracuse, NY: Syracuse University Press, 1990), 21–35.

24. Leopold von Ranke, "Preface to the First Edition of *Histories of the Latin and German Nations* (1824)," in *The Modern Historiography Reader: Western Sources*, ed. Adam Budd (London: Routledge, 2009), 172.

25. Quoted in Marnie Hughes-Warrington, *Fifty Key Thinkers on History*, 2nd ed. (London: Routledge, 2008), 294.

26. On this issue, see the various contributions in Iggers and Powell, *Ranke and the Shaping of the Historical Discipline*.

27. For example, see Edward Hallett Carr, *What Is History?* 2nd ed. (Harmondsworth: Penguin, 1987), 8; and Stephen Bann, *The Clothing of Clio: A Study of the Representation of History in Nineteenth-Century Britain and France* (Cambridge: Cambridge University Press, 1984), 30.

28. Fernand Braudel, "The Situation of History in 1950," in *On History*, trans. Sarah Matthews (Chicago: University of Chicago Press, 1980), 11.

29. For similar critiques of narrative history from later Annales school historians, see the contributions of François Furet and Jacques Le Goff in *Historical Studies Today*, ed. Felix Gilbert and Stephen Graubard (New York: Norton, 1972).

30. The phrase *total history* first appears in the writing of Lucien Febvre, who, along with Marc Bloch, was a key figure in the first generation of *Annalistes* and a major influence on Braudel. See André Burguière, *The Annales School: An Intellectual History*, trans. Jane Marie Todd (Ithaca, NY: Cornell University Press, 2009), 133ff. Burguière himself was part of a fourth generation of *Annalistes*, and his insider account provides the most comprehensive portrait to date of the school's founding and development.

31. According to Geoffrey Roberts, the apparent eclipse of narrative was "an illusory effect," reflecting "the transitory prominence of certain schools and fashions within history (the French Annales school, various types of Marxism, quantitative history, the new social history in Britain, the United States, Germany and elsewhere)." From his "Introduction: The History and Narrative Debate, 1960–2000," in *The History and Narrative Reader*, 3.

32. W. B. Gallie, *Philosophy and the Historical Understanding* (London: Chatto and Windus, 1964); Arthur Danto, *Analytical Philosophy of History* (Cambridge: Cambridge University Press, 1965); and Louis Mink, "Philosophical Analysis and Historical Understanding," *Review of Metaphysics* 21, no. 4 (1968): 667–98.

33. William Dray, *Philosophy of History* (Englewood Cliffs, NJ: Prentice Hall, 1964), 1.

34. Louis Mink, "Narrative Form as Cognitive Instrument," in *The Writing of History: Literary Form and Historical Understanding*, ed. Robert Canary and Henry Kozicki (Madison: University of Wisconsin Press, 1978), 143f.

35. White, *The Content of the Form*, 31. See also 220, fn. 10.

36. For an indication of the subsequent debates, see Hans Kellner, "Narrativity in History: Post-Structuralism and Since," *History and Theory* 26, no. 4 (1987): 1–29; Frank Ankersmit, "Historiography and Postmodernism," *History and Theory* 28, no. 2 (1989): 137–53; and Keith Jenkins, ed., *The Postmodern History Reader* (London: Routledge, 1997). Jenkins's anthology also reprints short key texts on history from Foucault (36–38), Barthes (120–23), and Lyotard (124–26).

To this list of names, one should really add Louis Althusser. Although Althusser was less explicit in his discussion of narrativity than, say, Barthes or Lyotard, his concept of ideology combined insights from Lacanian psychoanalysis and structural linguistics in ways that bear a significant resemblance to what White calls the "semiologically oriented approach" to narrative. Indeed, Althusser was one of White's primary touchstones in this regard, encapsulating for him a much broader tendency at the time to distinguish between the "imaginary" elaborations of narrative discourse and the order of the "real" these worked to cover over. "Behind this formulation," White observed, "lay a vast mass of highly problematical theories of language, discourse, consciousness, and ideology, with which the names of both Lacan and Althusser especially were associated." In White, *The Content of the Form*, 36.

37. Ibid., 31.

38. For useful introductory texts, see Martin Heidegger, *The Concept of Time: The First Draft of Being and Time*, trans. Ingo Farin (London: Continuum, 2011); Hans-Georg Gadamer, "The Historicity of Understanding," in *Critical Sociology*, ed. Paul Connerton (Harmondsworth: Penguin, 1965), 117–33; and Paul Ricoeur, "History and Hermeneutics," *Journal of Philosophy* 73, no. 19 (1976): 683–95.

39. This shift is clearly registered in the kinds of themes that animate anthologies on the philosophy of history. Compare, for example, William Dray, ed., *Philosophical Analysis and History* (Westport, CT: Greenwood Press, 1966), with Frank Ankersmit and Hans Kellner, eds., *A New Philosophy of History* (Chicago: University of Chicago Press, 1995).

40. Hayden White, *Metahistory: The Historical Imagination in Nineteenth-Century Europe* (Baltimore, MD: John Hopkins University Press, 1973).

41. In order to make this argument, White develops a formal typology that emphasizes the reliance of narrative histories on interdependent "modes of emplotment, argument, and ideological implication." Ibid., 29. He then posits that these three aspects of a work are grasped together through one of four modal tropes (metaphor, metonymy, synecdoche, and irony).

42. Hayden White, *Tropics of Discourse: Essays in Cultural Criticism* (Baltimore, MD: John Hopkins University Press, 1978), 88, emphasis in original.

43. See Hayden White, "The Burden of History," *History and Theory* 5, no. 2 (1966): 111–34.

44. White, *The Content of the Form*, 66–68 passim. This is why some have described White's brand of narrativism as "impositionalist." For example, see Andrew Norman, "Telling It Like It Was: Historical Narratives on Their Own Terms," *History and Theory* 30, no. 2 (1991): 120–22.

45. White quotes Schiller in order to develop this notion of the historical sublime, but he immediately observes that the same words "could have been written by Nietzsche" (in *The Content of the Form*, 69). The relevant passages in Nietzsche can be found in his essay "On the Uses and Disadvantages of History for Life," in *Friedrich Nietzsche: Untimely Meditations*, ed. Daniel Breazeale (Cambridge: Cambridge University Press, 1997), 57–124.

46. Here White reveals another debt, this time to the category of *inventio* in classical rhetoric and its recovery in the writings of late Renaissance thinkers like Giambattista Vico.

47. Paul Ricoeur, *Time and Narrative*, vol. 1, trans. Kathleen McLaughlin and David Pellauer (Chicago: University of Chicago Press, 1984), 52–87. Ricoeur also deals with the relation of narrative to time and history in two early essays: "Narrative Time," *Critical Inquiry* 7, no. 1 (1980): 169–90; and "The Narrative Function," in *Hermeneutics and the Human Sciences: Essays on Language, Action and Interpretation*, ed. John Thompson (Cambridge: Cambridge University Press, 1981), 274–96.

48. Ricoeur, *Time and Narrative*, 3. Other prominent advocates of an ontological rather than impositional narrativism include David Carr and Jerome Bruner. See Carr's "Narrative and the Real World: An Argument for Continuity," *History and Theory* 25, no. 2 (1986): 117–31, and Bruner's "The Narrative Construction of Reality," *Critical Inquiry* 18, no. 1 (1991): 1–21.

49. Ricoeur, "Narrative Time," 178.

50. Ricoeur, "The Narrative Function," 294.

51. Ricoeur follows Aristotle in using *emplotment* to designate the general means by which narrative understanding is created. White also employs the term, but for him, it refers more specifically to the kinds of meaning that a sequence of events can be given through narrativization, such as those typified by the modes of romance, comedy, tragedy, and satire. For the relevant definitions, see Ricoeur, *Time and Narrative*, 31–51, and White, *Metahistory*, 7–11.

52. In *Time and Narrative* (206–25), Ricoeur demonstrates this point through an analysis of Fernand Braudel's most famous book, *The Mediterranean and the Mediterranean World in the Age of Phillip II*, vols. 1 and 2, trans. Siân Reynolds (New York: Harper and Row, 1972–1974).

53. Danto, *Analytical Philosophy of History*, 168.

54. See Ricoeur, *Time and Narrative*, 52–87.

55. Alain Badiou, *Being and Event*, trans. Oliver Feltham (London: Continuum, 2005). For an indication of this work's reception on translation into English, see Adrian Johnston's *Badiou, Žižek, and Political Transformations: The Cadence of Change* (Evanston, IL: Northwestern University Press, 2009), as well as the discussion in Slavoj Žižek and Costas Douzinas, eds., *The Idea of Communism* (London: Verso, 2010), which collects the proceedings from a conference called in response to the publication of Badiou's "The Communist Hypothesis" in the *New Left Review* 49 (January–February 2008): 29–42. See also Alain Badiou, *The Communist Hypothesis*, trans. David Macey and Steve Corcoran (London: Verso, 2010).

56. In actual fact, the concept of the event occupies a more nuanced position in the history of Marxist philosophy. As Nathan Coombs has shown, a concept of the novelty-bearing event has been tacitly included in this tradition from its very inception, connecting the lineage of Hegel, Marx, and Lenin to that of Althusser, Badiou, and Meillassoux. See Coombs's *History and Event: From Marxism to Contemporary French Theory* (Edinburgh: Edinburgh University Press, 2015).

57. Paul Ricoeur, *Memory, History, Forgetting*, trans. Kathleen Blamey and David Pellauer (Chicago: University of Chicago Press, 2004). I provide an overview of the broader turn to memory in historical studies in chapter 4 of this book.

58. Ricoeur, *Time and Narrative*, 208.

59. Ricoeur, *Memory, History, Forgetting*, 56–92, 234–92.

60. Ibid., 412–56.

61. Ibid., 506.

62. See Saul Friedlander, ed., *Probing the Limits of Representation: Nazism and the "Final Solution"* (Cambridge, MA: Harvard University Press, 1992).

63. Hayden White, *Figural Realism: Studies in the Mimesis Effect* (Baltimore, MD: Johns Hopkins University Press, 1999), 27–42.

64. Ibid., 39. See also White's essay, "The Modernist Event," reprinted in *Figural Realism*, 66–86.

65. Ibid., 69.

66. The classic text in this regard remains Baudrillard's *The Gulf War Did Not Take Place*, trans. Chris Turner (Bloomington: Indiana University Press, 1995). More detail on the underlying argumentation can be found elsewhere, though, such as in *Simulations*, trans. Paul Foss, Paul Patton, and Philip Beitchman (New York: Semiotext(e), 1983), esp. 61–75; "Superconductive Events," in *The Transparency of Evil: Essays on Extreme Phenomena*, trans. James Benedict (London: Verso, 1993), 36–43; and "Real Event, Fated Event: Singularity of the Event," in *Impossible Exchange*, trans. Chris Turner (London: Verso, 2001), 132–38.

67. White, *Figural Realism*, 72–74.

68. Hayden White, "The Historical Event," *Differences* 19, no. 2 (2008): 26. In the following discussion, quotations are acknowledged by page numbers in parentheses in the body of text.

69. de Certeau, *Heterologies*, 200.

70. Douglas Hofstadter, *I Am a Strange Loop* (New York: Basic Books, 2007), 102.

Chapter 3

1. Paul Valéry, *Reflections on the World Today*, trans. Francis Scarfe (London: Thames and Hudson, 1951), 13.

2. The International Monetary Fund, for example, made numerous and explicit comparisons to the 1930s in its *World Economic Outlook, April 2009: Crisis and Recovery* (Washington, DC: IMF, 2009). I analyze such policy discourses at length in Chapter 4.

3. Asset-backed securities (ABSs), mortgage-backed securities (MBSs), and credit default obligations (CDOs) are just some of the structured products implicated in the subprime crisis.

4. Research in this vein has focused on issues such as the relation between monetary policy and asset-price bubbles, the effectiveness of monetary and fiscal stimulus, and possible exit strategies from crisis response measures. For example, see Steven Gjerstad and Vernon Smith, "Monetary Policy, Credit Extension, and Housing Bubbles: 2008 and 1929," *Critical Review* 21, no. 2–3 (2009): 269–300; Miguel Almunia, Agustín Bénétrix, Barry Eichengreen, Kevin O'Rourke, and Gisela Rua, "From Great Depression to Great Credit Crisis: Similarities, Differences and Lessons," *Economic Policy* 25, no. 62 (2010): 219–65; and Kris James Mitchener and Joseph Mason, "Blood and Treasure: Exiting the Great Depression and Lessons for Today," *Oxford Review of Economic Policy* 26, no. 3 (2010): 510–39.

5. See Liaquat Ahamed, *Lords of Finance: The Bankers Who Broke the World* (London: William Heinemann, 2009); Paul Krugman, *The Return of Depression Economics*

and the Crisis of 2008 (New York: Norton, 2009); and Robert Skidelsky, *Keynes: The Return of the Master* (London: Allen Lane, 2009).

6. Lionel Barber, "How Gamblers Broke the Banks," *Financial Times,* December 15, 2009.

7. Valéry, *Reflections on the World Today,* 13.

8. Ibid.

9. See Arnaud Maillet, *The Claude Glass: Use and Meaning of the Black Mirror in Western Art* (New York: Zone Books, 2004), esp. 85–101. Maillet has many interesting things to say about the object's relation to religious superstitions, but it is the mirror's role in landscape painting that I am alluding to here.

10. See the Preface in Karl Marx, *A Contribution to the Critique of Political Economy* (New York: International Publishers, 1970).

11. On the market-making power of the printing press and the novel, see Jürgen Habermas, *The Structural Transformation of the Public Sphere: An Inquiry into a Category of Bourgeois Society,* trans. Thomas Burger (Cambridge, MA: MIT Press, 1989). In relation to finance in particular, see Joyce Goggin, "Learning Finance through Fiction: *Cecilia* and the Perils of Credit," *Finance and Society* 1, no. 1 (2015): 61–74. Goggin argues that both the form and content of early realist novels were integral to the creation of a culture at ease with financial market speculation. For a broader and more detailed version of this argument, see Mary Poovey's *Genres of the Credit Economy: Mediating Value in Eighteenth- and Nineteenth-Century Britain* (Chicago: University of Chicago Press, 2008).

12. Philip Cerny, "The Dynamics of Financial Globalization: Technology, Market Structure and Policy Response," *Policy Sciences* 27, no. 4 (1994): 319–42; Manuel Castells, *The Rise of the Network Society* (Oxford: Blackwell, 1996).

13. Key political economy texts on these practices include Thorstein Veblen, *The Theory of Business Enterprise* (New Brunswick, NJ: Transaction, 1978); John Kenneth Galbraith, *The New Industrial State* (London: Pelican, 1968); and Edward Herman and Noam Chomsky, *Manufacturing Consent: The Political Economy of the Mass Media* (New York: Pantheon Books, 1988).

14. "Model T Advertising," Henry Ford Organization, accessed November 24, 2015, https://www.thehenryford.org/exhibits/showroom/1908/ads.html; Lucy Hughes-Hallett, *The Pike: Gabriele D'Annunzio—Poet, Seducer and Preacher of War* (London: Fourth Estate, 2013), 71–8.

15. Raymond Williams, *Marxism and Literature* (Oxford: Oxford University Press, 1977), 97–99.

16. See György Lukács, *History and Class Consciousness: Studies in Marxist Dialectics,* trans. Rodney Livingstone (London: Merlin Press, 1971).

17. John Guillory, "Genesis of the Media Concept," *Critical Inquiry* 36, no. 2 (2010): 353–62.

18. This particular use of the mediation concept can be traced back to Hegel via Lukács. See Andrew Arato, "Esthetic Theory and Cultural Criticism," in *The Essential Frankfurt School Reader,* ed. Andrew Arato and Eike Gebhardt (London: Continuum, 1982), 199–219.

19. Guy Debord, *The Society of the Spectacle*, trans. Donald Nicholson-Smith (New York: Zone Books, 1994), 24; Jean Baudrillard, *Simulations*, trans. Paul Foss, Paul Patton, and Philip Beitchman (New York: Semiotext(e), 1983), 99.

20. Debord, *Society of the Spectacle*, 114; Guy Debord, *Comments on the Society of the Spectacle*, trans. Malcolm Imrie (London: Verso, 1998), 12.

21. According to Baudrillard, capitalism moves through three distinct orders of appearance (or simulacra) associated with the logics of counterfeit, production, and simulation. For more detail on these and their intersection with reigning laws of value, see Baudrillard, *Simulations*, 81–152. In relation to the third simulacrum, he declares: "We come out of history in order to enter into simulation." In "L'an 2000 ne passera pas," *Traverses* 33, no. 4 (1985): 8–16, quoted in Kuan-Hsing Chen, "The Masses and the Media: Baudrillard's Implosive Postmodernism," *Theory, Culture and Society* 4, no. 1 (1987): 72.

22. Gordon Clark, Nigel Thrift, and Adam Tickell, "Performing Finance: The Industry, the Media and Its Image," *Review of International Political Economy* 11, no. 2 (2004): 289.

23. On mimetic rationality and reflexivity in networked financial markets, see Mark Taylor, *Confidence Games: Money and Markets in a World without Redemption* (Chicago: University of Chicago Press, 2008), 285–87; Shaun French, Andrew Leyshon, and Nigel Thrift, "A Very Geographical Crisis: The Making and Breaking of the 2007–2008 Financial Crisis," *Cambridge Journal of Regions, Economy and Society* 2, no. 2 (2009): 287–302; and Jodi Dean, *Blog Theory: Feedback and Capture in the Circuits of Desire* (Cambridge: Polity Press, 2010), 4–14.

24. Duncan Wigan, "Financialisation and Derivatives: Constructing an Artifice of Indifference," *Competition and Change* 13, no. 2 (2009): 158. Since at least the 1960s, this market-completion fantasy has been the animating force behind orthodox finance theory.

25. On this, see Donald MacKenzie, *An Engine, Not a Camera: How Financial Models Shape Markets* (Cambridge, MA: MIT Press, 2006); and Joseph Vogl, *The Specter of Capital*, trans. Joachim Redner and Robert Savage (Stanford, CA: Stanford University Press, 2015), 58–82.

26. Gillian Tett, "Wall Street's Crash Course," *Financial Times*, August 26, 2007.

27. This is not to say that television coverage was an inconsequential form of mediation during the subprime crisis. The point is rather that the rolling news format—with its ceaseless announcements of an event's arrival—is part and parcel of spectacular or simulated time. For an analysis of how television coverage, alongside online and print journalism, helped produce a sense of world historical crisis in 2008, see James Brassett and Chris Clarke, "Performing the Sub-Prime Crisis: Trauma and the Financial Event," *International Political Sociology* 6, no. 1 (2012): 4–20.

28. Although different from one another in many ways, each of these publications is based in a major international financial center and has syndication networks that target other hubs of high finance. The *Economist* and the *Financial Times* are based in London, publishing additional print editions for North America, Europe, and the

Asia Pacific; *Forbes* and the *Wall Street Journal* are based in New York, publishing additional print editions for Europe and Asia.

In a corpus of 1,085 texts drawn from these four titles, the events of the 1930s are referred to in 235 separate articles. This corpus was constructed out of comment or opinion pieces that met three criteria: (1) they addressed ongoing financial turmoil, (2) they appeared in the native print edition of each publication, and (3) they were published between January 2007 and December 2009. Key search phrases used were "credit squeeze," "credit crunch," "financial crisis," and "global financial crisis"—a series intended to capture relevant articles at various different stages of the subprime episode. WSJ articles were retrieved from the Proquest database. For each of the other publications, articles were retrieved through the archive and search services on their respective websites.

The aggregate count and list of relevant article subcategories for each publication are as follows: *Economist* (273)—"Leaders," "Special Reports," and "Briefings,"; *Financial Times* (385)—"Editorial Comment" and "Columns"; *Forbes* (194)—"Fact and Comment," "Current Events," and "Columns"; and *Wall Street Journal* (234)—"Editorial" and "Commentary." References to the Great Depression are more numerous and frequent following the collapse of Lehman Brothers in September 2008, reaching their peak in the fourth quarter of that year. This obtains across each of the four publications. The *Economist* invokes it on a total of eighty separate occasions, the *Financial Times* on forty-seven, *Forbes* on sixty-two, and the *Wall Street Journal* on forty-six.

29. *Economist*, "The Alchemists of Finance," May 17, 2007.

30. Tett, "Wall Street's Crash Course."

31. The *Economist* pursues this line further in early 2009. By comparing the statements of Depression-era economist and failed investor Irving Fisher to those of former Citigroup head Chuck Prince, it suggests that each gave voice to a procyclical bias inherent to the psychology of financial markets. "How to Play Chicken and Lose," January 22, 2009.

32. See *Economist*, "The Great American Slowdown," April 10, 2008; "Paradise Lost," May 15, 2008; "Britain's Sinking Economy," July 3, 2008.

33. *Economist*, "Unhappy America," July 24, 2008.

34. Cited in Martin Wolf, "A Turning Point in Managing the World's Economy," *Financial Times*, April 22, 2008.

35. Ken Fisher, "Dear Abby," *Forbes Magazine*, April 21, 2008.

36. David Roche, "Recession Is Inevitable," *Wall Street Journal*, March 14, 2008.

37. David Malpass, "Credit Crisis Hits Home," *Forbes Magazine*, April 21, 2008.

38. John Berlau, "Maybe the Banks Are Just Counting Wrong," *Wall Street Journal*, September 20, 2008.

39. Gary Becker, "We're Not Headed for a Depression," *Wall Street Journal*, October 7, 2008.

40. A. Gary Shilling, "Worse Is Yet to Come," *Forbes Magazine*, September

29, 2008; "Heard on the Street: Financial Analysis and Commentary," *Wall Street Journal*, October 9, 2008.

41. Martin Wolf, "It's Time for Comprehensive Rescues of Financial Systems," *Financial Times*, October 7, 2008; *Economist*, "Into the Storm," October 23, 2008.

42. Ian Bremmer and Nouriel Roubini, "Expect the World Economy to Suffer through 2009," *Wall Street Journal*, January 23, 2009.

43. See David Malpass, "Recession, Taxes and Moral Hazard," *Forbes Magazine*, April 16, 2007, and Steven Forbes, "Do Bad Economic Ideas Ever Die?" *Forbes Magazine*, July 2, 2007.

44. Steven Forbes, "How Capitalism Will Save Us," *Forbes Magazine*, November 10, 2008; George Bush, "The Surest Path Back to Prosperity," *Wall Street Journal*, November 15, 2008.

45. *Economist*, "Capitalism at Bay," October 16, 2008.

46. Martin Wolf, "Global Imbalances Threaten the Survival of Liberal Trade," *Financial Times*, December 2, 2008.

47. *Economist*, "Farewell, Free Trade," December 18, 2008. See also "Government and Business in America: Piling On," May 28, 2009.

48. *Economist*, "The Nuts and Bolts Come Apart," March 26, 2009; Steven Forbes, "Uh-oh," *Forbes Magazine*, March 2, 2009.

49. Steven Forbes, "The World Bank Should Resign," *Forbes Magazine*, June 18, 2007.

50. Forbes, "How Capitalism Will Save Us"; Martin Wolf, "Congress Decides It's Worth Risking Depression," *Financial Times*, September 30, 2008.

51. Aaron Friedberg and Gabriel Schoenfeld, "The Dangers of a Diminished America," *Wall Street Journal*, October 21, 2008.

52. *Financial Times*, "Editorial: A Survival Plan for Global Capitalism," March 8, 2009.

53. Amity Shlaes, "Ugly View from Below," *Forbes Magazine*, March 30, 2009.

54. *Economist*, "World Trade: Unpredictable Tides," July 23, 2009; Martin Wolf, "How the Noughties Were a Hinge of History," *Financial Times*, December 23, 2009.

55. *Economist*, "The Great Stabilisation," December 17, 2009.

56. *Economist*, "World Trade."

57. Steven Forbes, "The Real Peace Prize Winner," *Forbes Magazine*, November 16, 2009.

58. Steven Forbes, "True Catastrophes," *Forbes Magazine*, August 24, 2009.

59. Wolf, "How the Noughties Were a Hinge of History."

60. The *Financial Times* and the *Wall Street Journal*, for example, ask whether markets might have reached a trough as they did in 1932. See Martin Wolf, "Why Fairly Valued Stock Markets Are an Opportunity," *Financial Times*, November 25, 2008; and James Stewart, "Retiree Hell Isn't as Bad as You Might Think It Is," *Wall Street Journal*, January 28, 2009. Meanwhile, both the *Economist* and *Forbes* recommend buying stocks even with default rates at Depression-era levels. See *Economist*, "When the Golden Eggs Run Out,"

December 4, 2008, and David Dreman, "It's Time to Buy," *Forbes Magazine*, December 8, 2008).

61. Ken Fisher, "The Bear Market Is Over," *Forbes Magazine*, August 24, 2009.

62. James Stewart, "The Year of Investing Cautiously," *Wall Street Journal*, September 9, 2009.

63. Steven Forbes, "Hank, Meet Herb," *Forbes Magazine*, January 7, 2008.

64. Steven Forbes, "Herbert Hoover Obama," *Forbes Magazine*, June 30, 2008.

65. Paul Johnson, "Let Economies Cure Themselves," *Forbes Magazine*, September 1, 2008.

66. James Grant, "The Confidence Game," *Wall Street Journal*, October 18, 2008.

67. *Economist*, "America's Bail-Out Plan: The Doctor's Bill," September 25, 2008.

68. *Financial Times*, "Editorial: The Bail-Out Failure and Blame Game," September 30, 2008.

69. *Economist*, "When Fortune Frowned," October 9, 2008. See also *Financial Times*, "Editorial: Nationalise to Save the Free Market," October 13, 2008.

70. *Financial Times*, "Nationalise to Save the Free Market."

71. David Malpass, "Curbing Washington's Growing Power," *Forbes Magazine*, November 10, 2008.

72. Robert Barro, "What Are the Odds of a Depression?" *Wall Street Journal*, March 4, 2009.

73. Daniel Henninger, "Is This the End of Capitalism?" *Wall Street Journal*, April 2, 2009.

74. Amity Shlaes, "The New PC," *Forbes Magazine*, September 3, 2009.

75. Compare *Economist*, "Government and Business in America" with Wolf, "How the Noughties Were a Hinge of History."

76. *Economist*, "Capitalism at Bay."

77. For example see Harold James, *The Creation and Destruction of Value: The Globalization Cycle* (Cambridge, MA: Harvard University Press, 2009); Michael Bordo and Harold James, "The Great Depression Analogy," *Financial History Review* 17, no. 2 (2010): 127–40; James Livingston, "Their Great Depression and Ours," in *The Great Credit Crash*, ed. Martijn Konings (London: Verso, 2010), 31–46; and Peter Temin, "The Great Recession and the Great Depression," *Daedalus* 139, no. 4 (2010): 115–24.

78. Barry Eichengreen, *Hall of Mirrors: The Great Depression, the Great Recession, and the Uses—and Misuses—of History* (Oxford: Oxford University Press, 2015).

79. Maillet, *The Claude Glass*, 85–101.

80. Ibid., 142.

81. Debord, *Society of the Spectacle*, 114.

Chapter 4

1. Quoted in Quentin Peel, "Europe Writes a History of Crisis Management," *Financial Times*, October 9, 2008.

2. Thomas Oatley, *A Political Economy of American Hegemony: Buildups, Booms, and Busts* (Cambridge: Cambridge University Press, 2015).

3. Daniel Drezner, *The System Worked: How the World Stopped Another Great Depression* (Oxford: Oxford University Press, 2014).

4. For example, see Hyman Minsky, *Can "It" Happen Again? Essays on Instability and Finance* (New York: M. E. Sharpe, 1982); J. Bradford Delong, "Financial Crises in the 1890s and the 1990s: Must History Repeat?" *Brookings Papers on Economic Activity* 1999, no. 2 (1999): 253–94; and Carmen Reinhart and Kenneth Rogoff, *This Time Is Different: Eight Centuries of Financial Folly* (Princeton, NJ: Princeton University Press, 2009).

5. Mircea Eliade, *The Myth of the Eternal Return: Or, Cosmos and History*, trans. Willard Trask (Princeton, NJ: Princeton University Press, 1991), 149.

6. Kerwin Lee Klein, "On the Emergence of Memory in Historical Discourse," *Representations* 69 (Winter 2000): 128. The boom in memory studies gathered pace in the 1990s, prompting Klein and others to voice concerns about its sustainability and impact on the broader field of historical studies. For example, see Wolf Kansteiner, "Finding Meaning In Memory: A Methodological Critique of Collective Memory Studies," *History and Theory* 41, no. 2 (2002): 179–97, and Gavriel Rosenfeld, "A Looming Crash or a Soft Landing? Forecasting the Future of the Memory Industry," *Journal of Modern History* 81, no. 1 (2009): 122–58. Looking back, it would seem these bearish warnings went unheeded: the market for memory research remains robust, albeit below the historic high of the early-to-mid-2000s.

7. The literature on social, cultural, or collective memory is now vast, and numerous attempts have been made over the years to develop a programmatic research agenda around these concepts. For useful overviews, see Jeffrey Olick and Joyce Robbins, "Social Memory Studies: From 'Collective Memory' to the Historical Sociology of Mnemonic Practices," *Annual Review of Sociology* 24, no.1 (1998): 105–40; and Jeffrey Olick, "Collective Memory: A Memoir and Prospect," *Memory Studies* 1, no. 1 (2008): 23–29. More recently, the intersection between digital media and mnemonic practice emerged as a key focal point for thinking the relation between memory and history. For a critical discussion of this issue, see Jeffrey Andrew Barash, *Collective Memory and the Historical Past* (Chicago: University of Chicago Press, 2016)

8. Barash, *Collective Memory and the Historical Past*.

9. Paul Ricoeur, *Memory, History, Forgetting*, trans. Kathleen Blamey and David Pellauer (Chicago: University of Chicago Press, 2004), 5–55.

10. Ibid., 56–92, 234–92.

11. Michel de Certeau, *The Writing of History*, trans. Tom Conley (New York: Columbia University Press, 1988), 94.

12. James Brassett and Chris Clarke, "Performing the Sub-Prime Crisis: Trauma and the Financial Event," *International Political Sociology* 6, no. 1 (2012): 4–20.

13. Ibid., 14. See also James Brassett, Lena Rethel, and Matthew Watson, "The Political Economy of the Subprime Crisis: The Economics, Politics and Ethics of Response," *New Political Economy* 15, no. 1 (2010): 1–7.

14. James Brassett and Nick Vaughan-Williams, "Crisis *Is* Governance: Sub-Prime, the Traumatic Event, and Bare Life," *Global Society* 26, no. 1 (2012): 19–42.

15. Ibid., 28.

16. For his full thoughts on the matter, see James Brassett, *Affective Politics of the Global Event: Trauma and the Resilient Market Subject* (London: Routledge, 2018).

17. For an important exception to this rule, see Paul Crosthwaite, "Is a Financial Crisis a Trauma?" *Cultural Critique* 82 (Fall 2012): 34–67.

18. Foundational texts on trauma in the humanities include Shoshana Felman and Dori Laub's *Testimony: Crises of Witnessing in Literature, Psychoanalysis and History* (London: Routledge, 1992); Cathy Caruth's *Unclaimed Experience: Trauma, Narrative and History* (Baltimore, MD: Johns Hopkins University Press, 1996); and Dominick LaCapra's *Writing History, Writing Trauma* (Baltimore, MD: Johns Hopkins University Press, 2001). For an indication of the broader literature connecting to questions of international politics, see Jenny Edkins, *Trauma and the Memory of Politics* (Cambridge: Cambridge University Press, 2003); Maja Zehfuss, *Wounds of Memory: The Politics of War in Germany* (Cambridge: Cambridge University Press, 2007); and especially Duncan Bell, ed., *Memory, Trauma and World Politics: Reflections on the Relationship between Past and Present* (Basingstoke: Palgrave Macmillan, 2006).

19. Saul Friedlander, ed., *Probing the Limits of Representation: Nazism and the "Final Solution"* (Cambridge, MA: Harvard University Press, 1992). See also Michael Rothberg, *Traumatic Realism: The Demands of Holocaust Representation* (Minneapolis: University of Minnesota Press, 2000). The idea of trauma as a "limit event" is developed in LaCapra's *Writing History, Writing Trauma*.

20. Kate Lawless, "Unrecyclable Times: The Traumatic Topographies of Global Capitalism in W. G. Sebald's *Austerlitz*," *Word Hoard* 1, no. 2 (2013): 94.

21. Hayden White, "The Historical Event," *Differences* 19, no. 2 (2008): 29, emphasis in original.

22. Ibid., 30, emphasis added.

23. Eliade, *Eternal Return*, 153.

24. Constantin Fasolt, *The Limits of History* (Chicago: University of Chicago Press, 2004).

25. Eliade, *Eternal Return*, 73–92, 112–30.

26. Ibid., 102–12.

27. White, "The Historical Event," 28.

28. "Historiophany" is a neologism intended to specify an epiphany brought on through an apparent manifestation of History in the world. It is a play on "theophany," where of course it is God that appears.

29. The corpus consists of 537 texts and is made up of public statements delivered by representatives of these organizations that meet two further criteria: that they address ongoing financial or economic turmoil and that they were issued between January 2007 and December 2009. To analyze this material, I employed NVivo software as a coding and sorting device. It was used differently at each stage in a three-step procedure. First, a preliminary reading of all texts was undertaken,

enabling past crises to be manually coded no matter how those episodes appear in a text. The economic instability of the interwar years, for example, can appear as the "Great Crash," "1929," the "Great Depression," the "1930s," and so on. These codes then formed the basis for a second round of reading, which focused on the most frequently invoked past crises. Through this reading, the first set of codes was supplemented with a second, which were used to sort references into emergent thematic categories. A reference to the "Great Depression," for example, can concern monetary policy, financial regulation, international trade, and so on. Finally, a third round of chronological reading organized through these code sets was used to explore the ways in which different past crises featured within narratives concerning specific aspects of the then ongoing crisis.

30. Hanjo Berressem, "Crystal History: You Pick Up the Pieces. You Connect the Dots," in *Time and History in Deleuze and Serres*, ed. Bernd Herzogenrath (London: Continuum, 2012), 215.

31. For example, compare Charles Kindleberger, *The World in Depression, 1929–1939* (London: Allen Lane, 1973); Karl Polanyi, *The Great Transformation: The Political and Economic Origins of Our Time* (Boston: Beacon Press, 2001); Marc Trachtenberg, "Keynes Triumphant: A Study in the Social History of Economic Ideas," *Knowledge and Society* 4 (1983): 17–86; and John Gerard Ruggie, "International Regimes, Transactions, and Change: Embedded Liberalism in the Postwar Economic Order," *International Organization* 36, no. 2 (1982): 379–415.

32. Between 2007 and 2009, the Great Depression appears in eighty speeches or statements. Of these, the European Central Bank (ECB) accounts for twenty-six, the International Monetary Fund (IMF) for twenty-five, the US Federal Reserve Bank (Federal Reserve) for sixteen, and the US Treasury for thirteen. At first, references to the 1930s are only intermittent, but in late 2008, they become more frequent, reaching a peak in mid-2009. The IMF and the ECB account for just over half of these, while the remainder is spread more or less evenly between the Federal Reserve and the US Treasury. The return of or to the Great Depression is therefore again a widespread phenomenon, and especially so after the collapse of Lehman Brothers in September 2008. The methodological parameters for these observations are outlined in note 29.

33. Saleh Nsouli, "Lessons from the Recent Financial Crisis and the Role of the Fund," Paris, June 26, 2008, section 1, accessed June 22, 2009, http://www.imf.org/external/np/speeches/2008/062608.htm.

34. Frederic Mishkin, "Global Financial Turmoil and the World Economy," Eliat, July 2, 2008, section 1, accessed July 29, 2009, http://www.federalreserve.gov/newsevents/speech/mishkin20080702a.htm.

35. Jürgen Stark, "EMU: Weathering the Perfect Storm," London, June 25, 2009, section 1, accessed July 15, 2009, http://www.ecb.int/press/key/date/2009/html/sp090625.en.html. See also Michael Barr, "Remarks on Regulatory Reform," Washington, DC, July 15, 2009, section 1, accessed September 18, 2013, http://www.treasury.gov/press-center/press-releases/Pages/tg213.aspx.

36. Rodrigo de Rato, "Confronting the Future with Wisdom and Courage," Washington, DC, July 19, 2007, point 7, accessed May 28, 2009, http://www.imf.org/external/np/speeches/2007/071907.htm.

37. David McCormick, "Remarks at the Peter G. Peterson Institute for International Economics Conference on IMF Reform," Washington, DC, February 25, 2008, section 2, accessed September 18, 2013, http://www.treasury.gov/press-center/press-releases/Pages/hp838.aspx.

38. Lorenzo Smaghi, "From Tuscany's 19th Century Currency, the Fiorino, to the Euro," Florence, May 15, 2008, paragraphs 28–29, accessed October 27, 2009, http://www.ecb.int/press/key/date/2008/html/sp080515_2.en.html.

39. Dominique Strauss-Kahn, "Remarks to the Board of Governors of the IMF," Washington, DC, October 13, 2008, paragraph 12, accessed June 22, 2009, http://www.imf.org/external/np/speeches/2008/101308.htm.

40. Mark Sobel, "Remarks on the Global Financial Crisis and the IMF's Response,'" US Treasury press release, December 2, 2008, section 1, accessed September 18, 2013, http://www.treasury.gov/press-center/press-releases/Pages/hp1307.aspx. Lorenzo Smaghi, "The Financial Crisis and Global Imbalances," Beijing, December 9, 2008, section 2, accessed October 5, 2009, http://www.ecb.int/press/key/date/2008/html/sp081209.en.html.

41. See Kindleberger's *The World in Depression*, for example. Kindleberger's narrative of the Great Depression was carried through into subsequent theories of hegemonic stability within international studies. References to this literature are provided in the Introduction, note 32.

42. I discuss these and other narrated threats of recurrence at length in Chapter 3. For a similar analysis that focuses specifically on trade discourse and policy, see Gabriel Siles-Brügge, "Explaining the Resilience of Free Trade: The 'Smoot-Hawley' Myth and the Crisis," *Review of International Political Economy* 21, no. 3 (2014): 535–74.

43. Lorenzo Smaghi, "The Euro Area's Exchange Rate Policy and the Experience with International Monetary Coordination during the Crisis," Brussels, April 6, 2009, section 1, accessed October 19, 2009, http://www.ecb.int/press/key/date/2009/html/sp090406.en.html. Timothy Geithner, "The United States and China: Cooperating for Recovery and Growth," Beijing, June 1, 2009, section 2, accessed September 18, 2013, http://www.treasury.gov/press-center/press-releases/Pages/tg152.aspx.

44. John Lipsky, "Crisis Lessons for the IMF," New York, December 17, 2008, section 4, accessed May 28, 2009, http://www.imf.org/external/np/speeches/2008/121708.htm.

45. Smaghi, "Financial Crisis and Global Imbalances," section 2.

46. Strauss-Kahn, "Remarks to the Board of Governors," paragraphs 3, 7, and 10.

47. Ibid., paragraph 19.

48. Lipsky, "Crisis Lessons for the IMF," section 4. See also Dominique Strauss-Kahn, "Speech delivered at the 44th SEACEN Governors' Conference," Kuala

Lumpur, February 7, 2009, section 1, accessed June 22, 2009, http://www.imf.org/external/np/speeches/2009/020709.htm.

49. See McCormick, "Remarks on IMF Reform," section 2; and Sobel, "Global Financial Crisis and the IMF," section 1.

50. Dominique Strauss-Kahn, "Multilateralism and the Role of the International Monetary Fund in the Global Financial Crisis," Washington, DC, April 23, 2009, section 1, accessed May 28, 2009, http://www.imf.org/external/np/speeches/2009/042309.htm.

51. Dominique Strauss-Kahn, "Economic Stability, Economic Cooperation, and Peace," Oslo, October 23, 2009, section 2, accessed October 23, 2009, http://www.imf.org/external/np/speeches/2009/102309.htm.

52. An early and influential version of this critical response is outlined in Robert Wade and Frank Veneroso, "The Asian Crisis: The High-Debt Model vs. the Wall Street-Treasury-IMF Complex," *New Left Review* (March–April 1998): 3–23.

53. For example, see Stephan Haggard and Andrew MacIntyre, "The Political Economy of the Asian Economic Crisis," *Review of International Political Economy* 5, no. 3 (1998): 381–92.

54. On this, compare Charles Gore, "The Rise and the Fall of the Washington Consensus as a Paradigm for Developing Countries," *World Development* 28, no. 5 (2000): 789–804; Yujiro Hayami, "From the Washington Consensus to the Post-Washington Consensus: Retrospect and Prospect," *Asian Development Review* 20, no. 2 (2003): 47–54; and Eric Sheppard and Helga Leitner, "*Quo Vadis* Neoliberalism? The Remaking of Global Capitalist Governance After the Washington Consensus," *Geoforum* 41, no. 2 (2010): 185–94.

55. Between 2007 and 2009, the Asian crisis appears in sixty-seven speeches or statements. Of these, the ECB accounts for twenty-nine, the IMF for twenty, the Federal Reserve for eleven, and the US Treasury for seven. The methodological parameters for these observations are outlined in note 29.

56. See Kevin Warsh, "Market Liquidity: Definitions and Implications," Washington, DC, March 5, 2007, section 2, accessed October 6, 2009, http://www.federalreserve.gov/newsevents/speech/warsh20070305a.htm; and David Burton, "Asia: Ten Years On," Singapore, June 5, 2007, section 1, accessed May 28, 2009, http://www.imf.org/external/np/speeches/2007/060507.htm. The Federal Reserve soon joins the IMF in presenting the Asian crisis as a typical banking crisis. See Randall Kroszner, "Analyzing and Assessing Banking Crises," San Francisco, September 6, 2007, section 2, accessed October 6, 2009, http://www.federalreserve.gov/newsevents/speech/kroszner20070906a.htm.

57. Ben Bernanke, then chairman of the Federal Reserve, first articulates this crisis history in a speech entitled "Global Imbalances: Recent Developments and Prospects," Berlin, September 11, 2007, accessed October 6, 2009, http://www.federalreserve.gov/newsevents/speech/bernanke20070911a.htm.

58. On the global narration of state failure in South Korea, see Rodney Bruce Hall, "The Discursive Demolition of the Asian Development Model," *International*

Studies Quarterly 47, no. 1 (2003): 71–99. Jakob Vestergaard has developed a broader but related argument about economic normalization in the wake of the Asian crisis. See his *Discipline in the Global Economy? International Finance and the End of Liberalism* (London: Routledge, 2009).

59. Rodrigo de Rato, "Ten Years after the Asian Currency Crisis," Tokyo, January 22, 2007, point 1, accessed May 28, 2009, http://www.imf.org/external/np/speeches/2007/012207.htm.

60. In late 2007 the IMF faced considerable budgetary pressures, prompting it to lay off fifteen percent of its staff in order to reduce operating expenses. See André Broome, "The International Monetary Fund, Crisis Management and the Credit Crunch," *Australian Journal of International Affairs* 64, no. 1 (2010): 45–46.

61. Frederic Mishkin, "Systemic Risk and the International Lender of Last Resort," Chicago, September 28, 2007, section 3, accessed October 12, 2009, http://www.federalreserve.gov/newsevents/speech/mishkin20070928a.htm.

62. Jean-Claude Trichet, "Reflections on the International Financial Architecture," Salzburg, September 29, 2007, section 3, accessed June 23, 2009, http://www.ecb.int/press/key/date/2007/html/sp070929.en.html.

63. Ibid., section 1.

64. Ibid.

65. Ibid.

66. For an indication of this shift from optimism to disappointment, compare Gregory Noble and John Ravenhill, eds., *The Asian Financial Crisis and the Architecture of Global Finance* (Cambridge: Cambridge University Press, 2000), and Jacqueline Best, "The Limits of Financial Risk Management: Or What We Didn't Learn from the Asian Crisis," *New Political Economy* 15, no. 1 (2010): 29–49.

67. See Trichet, "International Financial Architecture," section 3; and "Reflections on the Global Financial System," Washington, DC, October 20, 2007, section 2, accessed June 23, 2009, http://www.ecb.int/press/key/date/2007/html/sp071020.en.html.

68. Jean-Claude Trichet, "Remarks on the Recent Turbulences in Global Financial Markets," New York, April 14, 2008, section 3, accessed June 23, 2009, http://www.ecb.int/press/key/date/2008/html/sp080414_1.en.html.

69. Clay Lowery, "Remarks at the Annual Conference of the Institute of International Bankers," New York, March 3, 2008, section 4, accessed September 18, 2013, http://www.treasury.gov/press-center/press-releases/Pages/hp855.aspx. David McCormick, "The International Response to Financial Market Turmoil," Chicago, April 16, 2008, section 3, accessed September 18, 2013, http://www.treasury.gov/press-center/press-releases/Pages/hp931.aspx.

70. Trichet, "Turbulences in Global Financial Markets," section 3. Sobel, "Global Financial Crisis and the IMF," section 3.

71. Daniel Tarullo, "International Cooperation to Modernize Financial Regulation," Washington, DC, September 30, 2009, section 1, accessed October 15, 2009, http://www.federalreserve.gov/newsevents/testimony/tarullo20090930a.

htm. For a discussion of this transformation and its likely significance at the time, see Eric Helleiner, "What Role for the New Financial Stability Board? The Politics of International Standards After the Crisis," *Global Policy* 1, no. 3 (2010): 282–90.

72. Trichet, "International Financial Architecture," section 3.

73. Jean-Claude Trichet, "Lessons from the Financial Crisis," Frankfurt, October 15, 2009, section 3, accessed October 23, 2009, http://www.ecb.int/press/key/date/2009/html/sp091015.en.html.

74. Brassett and Clarke, "Performing Sub-Prime," 18.

75. Janet Roitman, *Anti-Crisis* (Durham, NC: Duke University Press, 2014), 90.

76. White, "The Historical Event," 28.

Chapter 5

1. *Arbitrage*, directed by Nicholas Jarecki (2012); *The Other Guys*, directed by Adam McKay (2010); *Inside Job*, directed by Charles Ferguson (2010); *Crisis in the Credit System*, directed by Melanie Gilligan (2008).

2. Jeff Kinkle and Alberto Toscano, "Filming the Crisis: A Survey," *Film Quarterly* 65, no. 1 (2011): 39–51.

3. Ibid., 39, emphasis in original.

4. *Wall Street*, directed by Oliver Stone (1987).

5. *Wall Street: Money Never Sleeps*, directed by Oliver Stone (2010).

6. US Federal Bureau of Investigation, "Financial Fraud Public Service Announcement," video, originally released on February 27, 2012, accessed July 11, 2018, https://www.fbi.gov/video-repository/newss-financial-fraud-public-service-announcement/view.

7. *The Wolf of Wall Street*, directed by Martin Scorsese (2013).

8. *Cosmopolis*, directed by David Cronenberg (2012). For information on the box office performance of the film, see BoxOfficeMojo, "Cosmopolis," accessed July 28, 2015, http://www.boxofficemojo.com/movies/?page=intl&id=cosmopolis.htm.

9. Brian Holmes, "Phantasmagoric Systems: On Konrad Becker's *Strategic Reality Dictionary*," in *Strategic Reality Dictionary: Deep Infopolitics and Cultural Intelligence*, ed. Konrad Becker (Brooklyn: Autonomedia, 2009), 10.

10. Ibid.

11. Gilles Deleuze and Félix Guattari, *Anti-Oedipus: Capitalism and Schizophrenia*, trans. Robert Hurley, Mark Seem, and Helen Lane (London: Continuum, 2007), 95.

12. Jay Lampert, *Deleuze and Guattari's Philosophy of History* (London: Continuum, 2006), 3.

13. For a filmography compiled by a chartered financial analyst, see Usman Hayat, "Top 20 Films About Finance: From Crisis to Con Men," *CFA Institute Enterprising Investor* (blog), September 20, 2013, http://blogs.cfainstitute.org/investor/2013/09/20/20-finance-films-for-entertainment-and-education/.

14. Mark Fisher, *Capitalist Realism: Is There No Alternative?* (Winchester, UK: Zero Books, 2009).

15. *A Corner in Wheat*, directed by David Griffith (1909). Frank Norris, *The Pit: A Story of Chicago* (London: Penguin, 1994).

16. Interestingly, it was discussions with traders at the Chicago wheat exchange that prompted Bertolt Brecht to make his 1932 film, *Kuhle Wampe*, with Slatan Dudow. See Kinkle and Toscano, "Filming the Crisis," 48.

17. Émile Zola, *Money* (Oxford: Oxford University Press, 2014); *L'Argent*, directed by Marcel L'Herbier (1928).

18. Kinkle and Toscano, "Filming the Crisis," 40. See also Alberto Toscano, "Seeing It Whole: Staging Totality in Social Theory and Art," *Sociological Review* 60, S1 (2012): 64–83.

19. Alberto Toscano and Jeff Kinkle, *Cartographies of the Absolute* (Winchester, UK: Zero Books, 2015).

20. For the original formulation of the concept, see Fredric Jameson, "Cognitive Mapping," in *Marxism and the Interpretation of Culture*, ed. Cary Nelson and Lawrence Grossberg (Champaign: University of Illinois Press, 1988), 347–57. Toscano and Kinkle are not alone in returning to this aspect of Jameson's thought. Recent years have witnessed a revival of interest in cognitive mapping among new theorists on the radical Left. For instance, see David Hodge and Hamed Yousefi, eds., "Forum. Paranoid Subjectivity and the Challenges of Cognitive Mapping—How Is Capitalism to Be Represented?" *e-flux Conversations* (March/April 2015), http://conversations.e-flux.com/t/paranoid-subjectivity-and-the-challenges-of-cognitive-mapping-how-is-capitalism-to-be-represented/1080.

21. For an appraisal of Marx's opus on these terms, see Fredric Jameson, *Representing Capital: A Reading of Volume One* (London: Verso, 2011). Toscano and Kinkle discuss *The Wire* and global shipping logistics in *Cartographies of the Absolute*, chaps. 4 and 6, respectively. For an alternative take on the former, see Leigh Clare La Berge, "Capitalist Realism and Serial Form: The Fifth Season of *The Wire*," *Criticism* 52, no. 3–4 (2010): 547–67.

22. Toscano and Kinkle, *Cartographies of the Absolute*, 10.

23. Kinkle and Toscano, "Filming the Crisis," 42.

24. Ibid., 45, emphasis in original.

25. Ibid., 39.

26. Nelson Goodman, *Ways of Worldmaking* (Indianapolis, IN: Hackett Publishing, 1978), 6, emphasis in original.

27. This, I think, is how to read some of Lyotard's more oracular statements about paganism and capital: "The master of our stories is not a pagan god, it is capital." From *Instructions païennes/Pagan Instructions*, translated and quoted in Kerwin Lee Klein's *From History to Theory* (Berkeley: University of California Press, 2011), 92.

28. The phrase appears in Fisher's *Capitalist Realism* as the opening chapter title. For more detail on its use and provenance, see my discussion in the Afterword, including notes 7 and 8.

29. Friedrich Nietzsche, "Letter to Jakob Burckhardt, January 5, 1889," in *Selected*

Letters of Friedrich Nietzsche, ed. Christopher Middleton (Chicago: University of Chicago Press, 1969), 347.

30. Deleuze and Guattari, *Anti-Oedipus*, 22, emphasis in original.

31. Ibid., 267.

32. The "names of history" bear a close resemblance to concepts developed elsewhere in Deleuze and Guattari's oeuvre, including their discussion of Lenin as an "abstract machine" and the influence of "conceptual personae" on the work of philosophy (such as with Plato's Socrates or Nietzsche's Dionysus). For the relevant passages, see *A Thousand Plateaus: Capitalism and Schizophrenia*, trans. Brian Massumi (London: Athlone, 1988), 83–100; and *What Is Philosophy?* trans. Graham Burchell and Hugh Tomlinson (London: Verso, 1994), 64ff.

33. It is a question, as Deleuze and Guattari put it, of "identifying races, cultures, and gods with fields of intensity on the body without organs, [of] identifying personages with states that fill these fields, and with effects that fulgurate within and traverse these fields." *Anti-Oedipus*, 95.

34. Lampert, *Deleuze and Guattari's Philosophy of History*, 5–6.

35. Deleuze and Guattari, *Anti-Oedipus*, 93.

36. Lampert, *Deleuze and Guattari's Philosophy of History*, 3.

37. Ibid., 4.

38. Deleuze and Guattari, *Anti-Oedipus*, 282.

39. Craig Lundy, *History and Becoming: Deleuze's Philosophy of Creativity* (Edinburgh: Edinburgh University Press, 2012). See also Jeffrey Bell and Claire Colebrook, eds., *Deleuze and History* (Edinburgh: Edinburgh University Press, 2009); and Eugene Holland, "Non-Linear Historical Materialism: Or, What Is Revolutionary in Deleuze and Guattari's Philosophy of History?" in *Time and History in Deleuze and Serres*, ed. Bernd Herzogenrath (London: Continuum, 2012), 17–30.

40. Michel de Certeau, *The Writing of History*, trans. Tom Conley (New York: Columbia University Press, 1988).

41. Deleuze and Guattari, *Anti-Oedipus*, 95.

42. *The Passion of Joan of Arc*, directed by Carl Theodor Dreyer (1928).

43. Lampert, *Deleuze and Guattari's Philosophy of History*, 6.

44. For an account of historiography's relation to film and fiction, respectively, see Hayden White's *Figural Realism: Studies in the Mimesis Effect* (Baltimore, MD: Johns Hopkins University Press, 1999), 66–86, and his essay "The Practical Past," *Historein* 10 (2010): 10–19.

45. Elizabeth Day, "Moritz Erhardt: The Tragic Death of a City Intern," *Guardian*, October 5, 2013, http://www.theguardian.com/business/2013/oct/05/moritz-erhardt-internship-banking.

46. For example, see Christian Gysin, "Bank Intern, 21, Who Died After Working 'Eight All-Nighters in Just Two Weeks' Had Modeled Himself on Ruthless Trader Gordon Gekko in Film Wall Street," *Daily Mail Online*, August 21, 2013, http://www.dailymail.co.uk/news/article-2399336/Moritz-Erhardt-death-bank-intern-modelled-Gordon-Gekko-film-Wall-Street.html.

["<","<",">"]

47. Christoph Scheuermann, "High Stakes: Making Sense of a Banking Intern's Death," *Spiegel Online*, October 11, 2013, http://www.spiegel.de/international/europe/how-moritz-erhardt-worked-himself-to-the-top-a-927174.html.

48. S. Srinivasan, "Greed Is Back on Wall Street," *Forbes Magazine India*, October 4, 2010.

49. This mixing of genres is a trademark of Stone's historical fiction, and his use of this technique has been both criticized and celebrated. For further discussion, see White, *Figural Realism*, 66–86.

50. Joshi Hermann, "The Wolf of Wall Street: Why London's Bankers Love Real-Life Fraudster Jordan Belfort," *Evening Standard*, January 16, 2014, http://www.standard.co.uk/lifestyle/london-life/the-wolf-of-wall-street-why-londons-bankers-love-real-life-fraudster-jordan-belfort-9064038.html/.

51. Guy Adams, "Our Hero, The Wolf of Wall Street! City Traders Dress Up to Go to the Cinema in Honour of the Sleazy 80s Crook Whose Story Is Now a Hit Film (So Does This Mean They Think Greed Is Good Again?)," *Daily Mail Online*, January 21, 2014, http://www.dailymail.co.uk/news/article-2543619/How-Wolf-Wall-Street-folk-hero-Britains-bankers-City-traders-dress-honour-sleazy-crook-story-hit-film.html/.

52. Steven Perlberg, "We Saw 'Wolf of Wall Street' with a Bunch of Wall Street Dudes and It Was Disturbing," *Business Insider*, December 19, 2013, http://www.businessinsider.com/banker-pros-cheer-wolf-of-wall-street-2013-12?IR=T/.

53. See Jordan Belfort, *The Wolf of Wall Street* (New York: Random House, 2007), and *Catching the Wolf of Wall Street* (New York: Random House, 2009).

54. Roula Khalaf, "Steaks, Stocks—What's the Difference?" *Forbes Magazine*, October 14, 1991.

55. Noam Yuran, *What Money Wants: An Economy of Desire* (Stanford, CA: Stanford University Press, 2014), 71.

56. Belfort, *The Wolf of Wall Street*, 21.

57. Don DeLillo, *Cosmopolis* (London: Picador, 2011); in the following discussion, quotations are taken from this edition and are acknowledged by page numbers in parentheses in the body of text. All of these quotations also appear in the film adaptation.

58. Though largely confined to the academic world, the boom in post-2008 literature on *Cosmopolis* shows no sign of slowing. For example, see Paul Crosthwaite, "Blood on the Trading Floor: Waste, Sacrifice, and Death in Financial Crises," *Angelaki* 15, no. 2 (2010): 3–18; Alison Shonkwiler, "Don DeLillo's Financial Sublime," *Contemporary Literature* 51, no. 2 (2010): 246–82; Alessandra De Marco, "Don DeLillo's Fiction of Finance Capital," *Literature Compass* 11, no. 10 (2014): 657–66; and Mark Osteen, "The Currency of DeLillo's *Cosmopolis*," *Critique: Studies in Contemporary Fiction* 55, no. 3 (2014): 291–304.

59. Joseph Vogl, *The Specter of Capital*, trans. Joachim Redner and Robert Savage (Stanford, CA: Stanford University Press, 2015), 2, and Vogl, "The End of an Illusion," *Finance and Society* 1, no. 2 (2015): 38.

60. Dennis Lim, "The World Behind the Tinted Window," *New York Times*, August 3, 2012, http://www.nytimes.com/2012/08/05/movies/cosmopolis-cronenbergs-take-on-don-delillo.html?_r=0/.

61. "He'd always wanted to become quantum dust, transcending his body mass, the soft tissue over bones, the muscle and fat. The idea was to live outside the given limits, on a disk, as data, in whirl, in radiant spin, a consciousness saved from void." DeLillo, *Cosmopolis*, 206.

62. As I have already indicated, DeLillo's novel has proved extremely popular in literary criticism, where it has been taken to either mount or enable a form of critique uniquely suited to our financial times. At this level, the character of Packer can be read as an extreme parody of certain forms of financial subjectivity. What is rarely noted, however, is the striking resemblance between Packer's internal monologues on "cybercapital" and the critical analysis of finance provided by many of those who engage with the novel. There is a way of reading *Cosmopolis* as a parody of such critical discourse, but this possibility seems to have been lost on those who readily redeploy its prose *as* critique. I thank John Macintosh for drawing this irony to my attention.

63. "We really haven't seen anything yet!" they add. Deleuze and Guattari, *Anti-Oedipus*, 36–37.

64. James Hartley provides an overview and critique of this methodology in his book, *The Representative Agent in Macroeconomics* (London: Routledge, 2002).

65. For a detailed exploration of this tension in Smith's writings, see Mike Hill and Warren Montag, *The Other Adam Smith* (Stanford, CA: Stanford University Press, 2014). Brian Massumi also engages with Smith and others on the question of rational self-interest in his book, *The Power at the End of the Economy* (Durham, NC: Duke University Press, 2014). In the following discussion, I join Massumi by setting the rational subject of interest against a backdrop of the broader affective tendencies through which subjects are themselves produced.

Afterword

1. Janet Roitman, *Anti-Crisis* (Durham, NC: Duke University Press, 2014), 20.

2. See William Strauss and Neil Howe's *The Fourth Turning: An American Prophecy—What the Cycles of History Tell Us about America's Next Rendezvous with Destiny* (New York: Broadway Books, 1997). Bannon's interest in the theory was picked up by a number of news outlets in early 2017, including *Business Insider*, the *Huffington Post*, and the *Nation*. For a response from one of the original book's authors, including a concise summary of its key claims, see Neil Howe, "Where Did Steve Bannon Get His Worldview? From My Book," *Washington Post*, February 24, 2017, https://www.washingtonpost.com/entertainment/books/where-did-steve-bannon-get-his-world-view-from-my-book/2017/02/24/16937f38-f84a-11e6-9845-576c69081518_story.html?utm_term=.b60951c8d9b8.

3. For example, see Nick Srnicek and Alex Williams, *Inventing the Future: Postcapitalism and a World without Work* (London: Verso, 2015); Douglas Rushkoff, *Throwing Rocks at the Google Bus: How Growth Became the Enemy of Prosperity* (London: Penguin,

2016); Guy Standing, *Basic Income: And How We Can Make It Happen* (London: Pelican, 2017); and Andrew Yang, *The War on Normal People: The Truth about America's Disappearing Jobs and Why Universal Basic Income Is Our Future* (New York: Hachette, 2018).

4. At the time of writing, the full scene can be viewed at https://www.youtube.com/watch?v=cKZp-V1Uwtk, accessed November 26, 2018.

5. It is hardly a coincidence that the scene takes place in a barbershop; both Trump and Gekko have a unique visual signature centered on their respective hairstyles, and the script makes hay of this. At one point in the scene, Trump tells Gekko he'd "look great—really great—in a comb over," to which Gekko responds that he's more of "a gel-man." The point is certainly not lost on Trump either, whose team was very specific about how to shoot his hair:

> The preferred camera angle is Mr. Trump sitting front face to camera slightly favoring his right side, while avoiding left hair part and back and sides of hair and head. Camera eye level or above. If any angle shots need to be taken, please only use Mr. Trump's 3/4 right side angle shot, while still avoiding the back and sides of hair/head. Lighting, warm golden lighting (no red tones please). Can you please include an eye light (if shooting in high definition, eye light needs to be even more powerful). Also, we had more success with being front lit and avoiding strong lighting behind top of hair/head). The result is golden blond hair, warm golden (even tone) tan skin, and a more defined jaw-line. A great reference for Mr. Trump's look is always the boardroom scenes in *Celebrity Apprentice*. Can you please provide a monitor for Mr. Trump to see the shot before he starts.

Email from a Trump assistant, June 5, 2010, reproduced in Zach Schonfeld, "Here Are the Absurd Instructions for Filming Donald Trump in Your Movie," *Newsweek*, October 14, 2016, http://www.newsweek.com/here-are-absurd-instructions-putting-donald-trump-your-movie-509810. The precision of these instructions raises an interesting question about the relationship between Trump-the-name and Trump-the-subject, but this is for another time.

6. Susan Strange, *Mad Money: When Markets Outgrow Governments* (Ann Arbor: University of Michigan Press, 1998), 188, 190.

7. For example, compare Fredric Jameson's "The Antinomies of Postmodernity," in *The Cultural Turn: Selected Writings on the Postmodern, 1983–1998* (London: Verso, 1998), 50–72, with Mark Fisher's *Capitalist Realism: Is There No Alternative?* (Winchester, UK: Zero Books, 2009). Fisher agrees with Jameson's account of postmodernity, but argues that its cultural logics have become "so aggravated and chronic" (7) as to constitute a new historical phase in which alternatives to capitalism are all but impossible to imagine—hence, "capitalist realism." The disappearance of the future is also a key theme in Srnicek and Williams's *Inventing the Future*.

8. The consensus seems to be that the phrase emerged as a recurring theme in exchanges between Fredric Jameson and Slavoj Žižek during the 1990s. These

exchanges, as well as the broader cultural significance of the phrase, are well captured by Clint Burnham:

> Here a meme in the Jameson-Žižek conversation is worth considering, beginning with Jameson's assertion in *Archaeologies of the Future*: "[i]f it is so, as someone has observed, that it is easier to imagine the end of the world than the end of capitalism, we probably need another term to characterize the increasingly popular visions of total destruction and of the extinction of life on Earth." The story of this meme has been ably documented on the *Qlipoth* blog, but a short version is that the phrase first appears in Jameson's essay "The Antinomies of Postmodernity," when he admits that "[i]t seems easier for us to imagine the thoroughgoing deterioration of the earth and of nature than the breakdown of late capitalism; perhaps that is due to some weakness of our imaginations." Žižek in turn cites Jameson—"it seems easier to imagine the 'end of the world' than a far more modest change in the mode of production" and at a certain point the meme continues in Jameson's other writings (including the "Future City" essay), in the *Žižek!* documentary and his speech at Occupy Wall Street, and no doubt into the future. It may be easier to imagine the destruction of the planet than the end of this particular meme.

In Clint Burnham, *Fredric Jameson and the Wolf of Wall Street* (London: Bloomsbury, 2016), 86–87. The relevant passages can be found in Fredric Jameson, "The Antinomies of Postmodernity," in *The Cultural Turn*, 50–72; Slavoj Žižek, "The Spectre of Ideology," in *Mapping Ideology*, ed. Slavoj Žižek (London: Verso, 1994), 1–33; Fredric Jameson, "Journey into Fear," in *Archaeologies of the Future: The Desire Called Utopia and Other Science Fictions* (London: Verso, 2005), 182–210; and Fredric Jameson, "Future City," *New Left Review* 21 (May–June 2003): 65–79. See also *Žižek!* directed by Astra Taylor (2005). Burnham's account is based on Qlipoth, "Easier to Imagine the End of the World . . . " *Qlipoth* (blog), November 11, 2009, http://qlipoth.blogspot.com/2009/11/easier-to-imagine-end-of-world.html.

9. Jameson, "Future City," 76.

10. Hayden White, in the Foreword to Reinhart Koselleck's *The Practice of Conceptual History: Timing History, Spacing Concepts*, trans. Todd Presner (Stanford, CA: Stanford University Press, 2002), xi.

11. Hayden White, *The Content of the Form: Narrative Discourse and Historical Representation* (Baltimore, MD: Johns Hopkins University Press, 1987), x.

12. Erik Davis, *TechGnosis: Myth, Magic and Mysticism in the Age of Information* (London: Serpents Tail, 2004), 268.

13. Ibid., 90.

14. Arthur Kroker, *Exits to the Posthuman Future* (Cambridge: Polity Press, 2014), 79.

Bibliography

Abdelal, Rawi, Mark Blyth, and Craig Parsons, eds. *Constructing the International Economy*. Ithaca, NY: Cornell University Press, 2010.

Adams, Guy. "Our Hero, the Wolf of Wall Street! City Traders Dress Up to Go to the Cinema in Honour of the Sleazy 80s Crook Whose Story Is Now a Hit Film (So Does This Mean They Think Greed Is Good Again?)." *Daily Mail Online*, January 21, 2014. http://www.dailymail.co.uk/news/article-2543619/How-Wolf-Wall-Street-folk-hero-Britains-bankers-City-traders-dress-honour-sleazy-crook-story-hit-film.html/.

Aglietta, Michel. *A Theory of Capitalist Regulation: The U.S. Experience*. Translated by David Fernbach. London: New Left Books, 1979.

Ahamed, Liaquat. *Lords of Finance: The Bankers Who Broke the World*. London: William Heinemann, 2009.

Almunia, Miguel, Agustín Bénétrix, Barry Eichengreen, Kevin O'Rourke, and Gisela Rua. "From Great Depression to Great Credit Crisis: Similarities, Differences and Lessons." *Economic Policy* 25, no. 62 (2010): 219–65.

Althusser, Louis. *For Marx*. Translated by Ben Brewster. Harmondsworth: Penguin, 1969.

Ankersmit, Frank. "Historiography and Postmodernism." *History and Theory* 28, no. 2 (1989): 137–53.

Ankersmit, Frank, and Hans Kellner, eds. *A New Philosophy of History*. Chicago: University of Chicago Press, 1995.

Arato, Andrew. "Esthetic Theory and Cultural Criticism." In *The Essential Frankfurt School Reader*, edited by Andrew Arato and Eike Gebhardt, 185–224. London: Continuum, 1982.

Aristotle. *Politics*. Translated by Ernest Barker. Oxford: Oxford University Press, 1998.

Ascher, Ivan. *Portfolio Society: On the Capitalist Mode of Prediction*. Brooklyn: Zone Books, 2016.

Appadurai, Arjun. "The Ghost in the Financial Machine." *Public Culture* 23, no. 3 (2011): 517–39.

————. *The Future as Cultural Fact: Essays on the Global Condition*. London: Verso, 2013.

Arrighi, Giovanni. *The Long Twentieth Century: Money, Power, and the Origins of Our Times*. London: Verso, 1994.

Badiou, Alain. *Being and Event*. Translated by Oliver Feltham. London: Continuum, 2005.

————. "The Communist Hypothesis." *New Left Review* 49 (January–February 2008): 29–42.

————. *The Communist Hypothesis*. Translated by David Macey and Steve Corcoran. London: Verso, 2010.

Baran, Paul, and Paul Sweezy. *Monopoly Capital: An Essay on the American Economic and Social Order*. New York: Monthly Review Press, 1968.

Barber, Lionel. "How Gamblers Broke the Banks." *Financial Times*, December 15, 2009.

Barnes, Harry. *A History of Historical Writing*, 2nd ed. New York: Dover, 1963.

Barro, Robert. "What Are the Odds of a Depression?" *Wall Street Journal*, March 4, 2009.

Bataille, Georges. *The Accursed Share: An Essay on General Economy*, vol. 1. Translated by Robert Hurley. Brooklyn: Zone Books, 1991.

Bann, Stephen. *The Clothing of Clio: A Study of the Representation of History in Nine-teenth–Century Britain and France*. Cambridge: Cambridge University Press, 1984.

Barash, Jeffrey Andrew. *Collective Memory and the Historical Past*. Chicago: University of Chicago Press, 2016.

Barr, Michael. "Remarks on Regulatory Reform." Washington, DC, July 15, 2009. http://www.treasury.gov/press-center/press-releases/Pages/tg213.aspx.

Baudrillard, Jean. *Simulations*. Translated by Paul Foss, Paul Patton, and Philip Beitchman. New York: Semiotext(e), 1983.

————. "L'an 2000 ne passera pas," *Traverses* 33, no. 4 (1985): 8–16.

————. *The Transparency of Evil: Essays on Extreme Phenomena*. Translated by James Benedict. London: Verso, 1993.

————. *The Gulf War Did Not Take Place*. Translated by Chris Turner. Bloomington: Indiana University Press, 1995.

————. *Impossible Exchange*. Translated by Chris Turner. London: Verso, 2001.

Bay, Thomas, and Christophe Schinkus. "Critical Finance Studies: An Interdisci-plinary Manifesto." *Journal of Interdisciplinary Economics* 24, no. 1 (2012): 1–6.

Becker, Gary. "We're Not Headed For a Depression." *Wall Street Journal*, October 7, 2008.

Beckert, Jens. *Imagined Futures: Fictional Expectations and Capitalist Dynamics*. Cam-bridge, MA: Harvard University Press, 2016.

Beckert, Jens, and Richard Bronk, eds. *Uncertain Futures: Imaginaries, Narratives, and Calculation in the Economy*. Cambridge: Cambridge University Press, 2018.

Beiser, Frederick. *The German Historicist Tradition*. Oxford: Oxford University Press, 2011.

Belfort, Jordan. *The Wolf of Wall Street*. New York: Random House, 2007.

———. *Catching the Wolf of Wall Street*. New York: Random House, 2009.

Bell, Duncan, ed. *Memory, Trauma and World Politics: Reflections on the Relationship between Past and Present*. Basingstoke: Palgrave Macmillan, 2006.

Bell, Jeffrey, and Claire Colebrook, eds. *Deleuze and History*. Edinburgh: Edinburgh University Press, 2009.

Berlau, John. "Maybe the Banks Are Just Counting Wrong." *Wall Street Journal*, September 20, 2008.

Bernanke, Ben. "Global Imbalances: Recent Developments and Prospects." Berlin, September 11, 2007. http://www.federalreserve.gov/newsevents/speech/bernanke20070911a.htm.

Berressem, Hanjo. "Crystal History: You Pick Up the Pieces. You Connect the Dots." In *Time and History in Deleuze and Serres*, edited by Bernd Herzogenrath, 203–28. London: Continuum, 2012.

Best, Jacqueline. "The Limits of Financial Risk Management: Or What We Didn't Learn from the Asian Crisis." *New Political Economy* 15, no. 1 (2010): 29–49.

Blaney, David, and Naeem Inayatullah, "Undressing the Wound of Wealth: Political Economy as a Cultural Project." In *Cultural Political Economy*, edited by Jacqueline Best and Matthew Paterson, 29–47. London: Routledge, 2010.

Bleaney, Michael. *Underconsumption Theories: A History and Critical Analysis*. New York: International Publishers, 1976.

Blyth, Mark. *Great Transformations: Economic Ideas and Institutional Change in the Twentieth Century*. Cambridge: Cambridge University Press, 2002.

———. "Powering, Puzzling, or Persuading? The Mechanisms of Building Institutional Orders." *International Studies Quarterly* 51, no. 4 (2007): 761–77.

Bordo, Michael, and Harold James. "The Great Depression Analogy." *Financial History Review* 17, no. 2 (2010): 127–40.

BoxOfficeMojo. "Cosmopolis." Accessed July 28, 2015. http://www.boxofficemojo.com/movies/?page=intl&id=cosmopolis.htm.

Boy, Nina. "Sovereign Safety." *Security Dialogue* 46, no. 6 (2015): 530–47.

Boyer, Robert. "Is the Finance-Led Growth Regime a Viable Alternative to Fordism?" *Economy and Society* 29, no. 1 (2000): 111–45.

———. "The Global Financial Crisis in Historical Perspective: An Economic Analysis Combining Minsky, Hayek, Fisher, Keynes and the Regulation Approach." *Accounting, Economics and Law* 3, no. 3 (2013): 93–139.

Brassett, James. *Affective Politics of the Global Event: Trauma and the Resilient Market Subject*. London: Routledge, 2018.

Brassett, James, and Chris Clarke. "Performing the Sub-Prime Crisis: Trauma and the Financial Event." *International Political Sociology* 6, no. 1 (2012): 4–20.

Brassett, James, Lena Rethel, and Matthew Watson. "The Political Economy of the Subprime Crisis: The Economics, Politics and Ethics of Response." *New Political Economy* 15, no. 1 (2010): 1–7.

Brassett, James, and Nick Vaughan-Williams. "Crisis *Is* Governance: Sub-Prime, the Traumatic Event, and Bare Life." *Global Society* 26, no. 1 (2012): 19–42.

Braudel, Fernand. *The Mediterranean and the Mediterranean World in the Age of Philip II*, vols. 1–2. Translated by Siân Reynolds. New York: Harper and Row, 1972–1974.

———. *On History.* Translated by Sarah Matthews. Chicago: University of Chicago Press, 1980.

———. *Civilization and Capitalism: 15th–18th Century.* Vol. 3: *The Perspective of the World.* Translated by Siân Reynolds. Berkeley: University of California Press, 1992.

Bremmer, Ian, and Nouriel Roubini. "Expect the World Economy to Suffer through 2009." *Wall Street Journal*, January 23, 2009.

Broome, André. "The International Monetary Fund, Crisis Management and the Credit Crunch." *Australian Journal of International Affairs* 64, no. 1 (2010): 37–54.

Brown, Wendy. *Undoing the Demos: Neoliberalism's Stealth Revolution.* Brooklyn: Zone Books, 2015.

Bruner, Jerome. "The Narrative Construction of Reality." *Critical Inquiry* 18, no. 1 (1991): 1–21.

Bryan, Dick, and Mike Rafferty. *Capitalism with Derivatives: A Political Economy of Financial Derivatives, Capital and Class.* Basingstoke: Palgrave Macmillan, 2005.

Buchanan, Ian. *Michel de Certeau: Cultural Theorist.* London: Sage, 2000.

Buitenhek, Mark. "Understanding and Applying Blockchain Technology in Banking: Evolution or Revolution?" *Journal of Digital Banking* 1, no. 2 (2016): 111–19.

Burckhardt, Jacob. *Reflections on History.* Translated by M. D. Hottinger. Indianapolis, IN: Liberty Fund, 1979.

———. *Judgments on History and Historians.* Translated by Harry Zohn. Indianapolis, IN: Liberty Fund, 1999.

Burguière, André. *The Annales School: An Intellectual History.* Translated by Jane Marie Todd. Ithaca, NY: Cornell University Press, 2009.

Burnham, Clint. *Fredric Jameson and the Wolf of Wall Street.* London: Bloomsbury, 2016.

Burrow, John. *A History of Histories: Epics, Chronicles, Romances and Inquiries from Herodotus and Thucydides to the Twentieth Century.* London: Allen Lane, 2007.

Burton, David. "Asia: Ten Years On." Singapore, June 5, 2007. http://www.imf.org/external/np/speeches/2007/060507.htm.

Bush, George. "The Surest Path Back to Prosperity." *Wall Street Journal*, November 15, 2008.

Çalışkan, Koray, and Michel Callon. "Economization, Part 1: Shifting Attention from the Economy towards Processes of Economization." *Economy and Society* 38, no. 3 (2009): 369–98.

Cameron, Angus, and Ronen Palan. *The Imagined Economies of Globalization.* London: Sage, 2004.

Canary, Robert, and Henry Kozicki, eds. *The Writing of History: Literary Form and Historical Understanding.* Madison: University of Wisconsin Press, 1978.

Carr, David. "Narrative and the Real World: An Argument for Continuity." *History and Theory* 25, no. 2 (1986): 117–31.

Carr, Edward Hallett. *What Is History?* 2nd ed. Harmondsworth: Penguin, 1987.

Caruth, Cathy. *Unclaimed Experience: Trauma, Narrative and History*. Baltimore, MD: Johns Hopkins University Press, 1996.

Castells, Manuel. *The Rise of the Network Society*. Oxford: Blackwell, 1996.

Cerny, Philip. "The Dynamics of Financial Globalization: Technology, Market Structure and Policy Response." *Policy Sciences* 27, no. 4 (1994): 319–42.

Chen, Kuan-Hsing. "The Masses and the Media: Baudrillard's Implosive Postmodernism." *Theory, Culture and Society* 4, no. 1 (1987): 71–88.

Clark, Gordon, Nigel Thrift, and Adam Tickell. "Performing Finance: The Industry, the Media and Its Image." *Review of International Political Economy* 11, no. 2 (2004): 289–310.

Clarke, Simon. *Marx's Theory of Crisis*. Basingstoke: Macmillan Press, 1994.

Clover, Joshua. "Autumn of the System: Poetry and Financial Capital." *Journal of Narrative Theory* 41, no. 1 (2011): 34–52.

Coombs, Nathan. *History and Event: From Marxism to Contemporary French Theory*. Edinburgh: Edinburgh University Press, 2015.

Cooper, George. *The Origin of Financial Crises: Central Banks, Credit Bubbles and the Efficient Market Fallacy*. New York: Vintage Books, 2008.

Cronenberg, David, dir. *Cosmopolis*. 2012.

Crosthwaite, Paul. "Blood on the Trading Floor: Waste, Sacrifice, and Death in Financial Crises." *Angelaki* 15, no. 2 (2010): 3–18

———. "Is a Financial Crisis a Trauma?" *Cultural Critique* 82 (Fall 2012): 34–67.

Danto, Arthur. *Analytical Philosophy of History*. Cambridge: Cambridge University Press, 1965.

Davis, Erik. *TechGnosis: Myth, Magic and Mysticism in the Age of Information*. London: Serpents Tail, 2004.

Day, Elizabeth. "Moritz Erhardt: The Tragic Death of a City Intern." *Guardian*, October 5, 2013. http://www.theguardian.com/business/2013/oct/05/moritz-erhardt-internship-banking.

Dean, Jodi. *Blog Theory: Feedback and Capture in the Circuits of Desire*. Cambridge: Polity Press, 2010.

Debord, Guy. *The Society of the Spectacle*. Translated by Donald Nicholson-Smith. New York: Zone Books, 1994.

———. *Comments on the Society of the Spectacle*. Translated by Malcolm Imrie. London: Verso, 1998.

Debray, Régis. *Prison Writings*. Translated by Rosemary Sheed. London: Penguin, 1975.

De Certeau, Michel. *The Practice of Everyday Life*. Translated by Steven Rendall. Berkeley: University of California Press, 1984.

———. *Heterologies: Discourse on the Other*. Translated by Brian Massumi. Minneapolis: University of Minnesota Press, 1986.

———. *The Writing of History.* Translated by Tom Conley. New York: Columbia University Press, 1988.

Deleuze, Gilles, and Félix Guattari. *A Thousand Plateaus: Capitalism and Schizophrenia.* Translated by Brian Massumi. London: Athlone, 1988.

———. *What Is Philosophy?* Translated by Graham Burchell and Hugh Tomlinson. London: Verso, 1994.

———. *Anti-Oedipus: Capitalism and Schizophrenia.* Translated by Robert Hurley, Mark Seem, and Helen Lane. London: Continuum, 2007.

DeLillo, Don. *Cosmopolis.* London: Picador, 2011.

Delong, J. Bradford. "Financial Crises in the 1890s and the 1990s: Must History Repeat?" *Brookings Papers on Economic Activity* 1999, no. 2 (1999): 253–94.

De Marco, Alessandra. "Don DeLillo's Fiction of Finance Capital." *Literature Compass* 11, no. 10 (2014): 657–66.

Dilthey, Wilhelm. *The Formation of the Historical World in the Human Sciences: Selected Works,* vol. 3. Translated by Rudolf Makkreel and Frithjof Rodi. Princeton, NJ: Princeton University Press, 2002.

Dray, William. *Philosophy of History.* Englewood Cliffs, NJ: Prentice-Hall, 1964.

———, ed. *Philosophical Analysis and History.* Westport, CT: Greenwood Press, 1966.

Dreman, David. "It's Time to Buy." *Forbes Magazine,* December 8, 2008.

Dreyer, Carl Theodor, dir. *The Passion of Joan of Arc.* 1928.

Drezner, Daniel. *The System Worked: How the World Stopped Another Great Depression.* Oxford: Oxford University Press, 2014.

Dunn, John. "The Identity of the History of Ideas." *Philosophy* 43, no. 164 (1968): 85–104.

———. *The Political Thought of John Locke: An Historical Account of the Argument of the "Two Treatises of Government."* Cambridge: Cambridge University Press, 1969.

Economist. "The Alchemists of Finance." May 17, 2007.

———. "The Great American Slowdown." April 10, 2008.

———. "Paradise Lost." May 15, 2008.

———. "Britain's Sinking Economy." July 3, 2008.

———. "Unhappy America." July 24, 2008.

———. "America's Bail-Out Plan: The Doctor's Bill." September 25, 2008.

———. "When Fortune Frowned." October 9, 2008.

———. "Capitalism at Bay." October 16, 2008.

———. "Into the Storm." October 23, 2008.

———. "When the Golden Eggs Run Out." December 4, 2008.

———. "Farewell, Free Trade." December 18, 2008.

———. "How to Play Chicken and Lose." January 22, 2009.

———. "The Nuts and Bolts Come Apart." March 26, 2009.

———. "Government and Business in America: Piling On." May 28, 2009.

———. "World Trade: Unpredictable Tides." July 23, 2009.

———. "The Great Stabilisation." December 17, 2009.

Edkins, Jenny. *Trauma and the Memory of Politics*. Cambridge: Cambridge University Press, 2003.

Eichengreen, Barry. *Globalizing Capital: A History of the International Monetary System*. Princeton, NJ: Princeton University Press, 1996.

———. *Hall of Mirrors: The Great Depression, The Great Recession, and the Uses—and Misuses—of History*. Oxford: Oxford University Press, 2015.

Eliade, Mircea. *The Myth of the Eternal Return: Or, Cosmos and History*. Translated by Willard Trask. Princeton, NJ: Princeton University Press, 1991.

Elias, Amy. *Sublime Desire: History and Post-1960 Fiction*. Baltimore, MD: Johns Hopkins University Press, 2001.

Fasolt, Constantin. *The Limits of History*. Chicago: University of Chicago Press, 2004.

Feiwel, George. "Joan Robinson Inside and Outside of the Stream." In *Joan Robinson and Modern Economic Theory*, edited by George Feiwel, 1–120. Basingstoke: Macmillan Press, 1989.

Felman, Shoshana, and Dori Laub. *Testimony: Crises of Witnessing in Literature, Psychoanalysis and History*. London: Routledge, 1992.

Ferguson, Charles, dir. *Inside Job*. 2010.

Financial Times. "Editorial: The Bail-Out Failure and Blame Game." September 30, 2008.

———. "Editorial: Nationalise to Save the Free Market." October 13, 2008.

———. "Editorial: A Survival Plan for Global Capitalism." March 8, 2009.

Fisher, Ken. "Dear Abby." *Forbes Magazine*, April 21, 2008.

———. "The Bear Market Is Over." *Forbes Magazine*, August 24, 2009.

Fisher, Mark. *Capitalist Realism: Is There No Alternative?* Winchester, UK: Zero Books, 2009.

Forbes, Steven. "The World Bank Should Resign," *Forbes Magazine*, June 18, 2007.

———. "Do Bad Economic Ideas Ever Die?" *Forbes Magazine*, July 2, 2007.

———. "Hank, Meet Herb." *Forbes Magazine*, January 7, 2008.

———. "Herbert Hoover Obama." *Forbes Magazine*, June 30, 2008.

———. "How Capitalism Will Save Us." *Forbes Magazine*, November 10, 2008.

———. "Uh-oh." *Forbes Magazine*, March 2, 2009.

———. "True Catastrophes." *Forbes Magazine*, August 24, 2009.

———. "The Real Peace Prize Winner." *Forbes Magazine*, November 16, 2009.

Forslund, Dick, and Thomas Bay. "The Eve of Critical Finance Studies." *Ephemera: Theory and Politics in Organization* 9, no. 4 (2009): 285–99.

Foster, John Bellamy, and Fred Magdoff. *The Great Financial Crisis: Causes and Consequences*. New York: Monthly Review Press, 2009.

Foucault, Michel. "Nietzsche, Genealogy, History." In *Language, Counter-Memory, and Practice: Selected Essays and Interviews*, edited by Donald Bouchard, 139–64. Ithaca, NY: Cornell University Press, 1977.

———. *Security, Territory, Population: Lectures at the Collège de France, 1977–1978*. Translated by Graham Burchell. Basingstoke: Palgrave Macmillan, 2007.

————. *The Birth of Biopolitics: Lectures at the Collège de France, 1978–79.* Translated by Graham Burchell. Basingstoke: Palgrave Macmillan, 2008.

French, Shaun, Andrew Leyshon, and Nigel Thrift. "A Very Geographical Crisis: The Making and Breaking of the 2007–2008 Financial Crisis." *Cambridge Journal of Regions, Economy and Society* 2, no. 2 (2009): 287–302.

Friedberg, Aaron, and Gabriel Schoenfeld. "The Dangers of a Diminished America." *Wall Street Journal*, October 21, 2008.

Friedlander, Saul, ed. *Probing the Limits of Representation: Nazism and the "Final Solution."* Cambridge, MA: Harvard University Press, 1992.

Gadamer, Hans-Georg. "The Historicity of Understanding." In *Critical Sociology*, edited by Paul Connerton, 117–33. Harmondsworth: Penguin, 1965.

Galbraith, John Kenneth. *The New Industrial State.* London: Pelican, 1968.

Gallie, W. B. *Philosophy and the Historical Understanding.* London: Chatto and Windus, 1964.

Geertz, Clifford. *The Interpretation of Cultures.* New York: Basic Books, 1973.

Geithner, Timothy. "The United States and China: Cooperating for Recovery and Growth." Beijing, June 1, 2009. http://www.treasury.gov/press-center/press-releases/Pages/tg152.aspx.

Gilbert, Felix, and Stephen Graubard, eds. *Historical Studies Today.* New York: Norton, 1972.

Gill, Stephen. *American Hegemony and the Trilateral Commission.* Cambridge: Cambridge University Press, 1990.

Gilligan, Melanie, dir. *Crisis in the Credit System.* 2008.

Gjerstad, Steven, and Vernon Smith. "Monetary Policy, Credit Extension, and Housing Bubbles: 2008 and 1929." *Critical Review* 21, nos. 2–3 (2009): 269–300.

Goggin, Joyce. "Learning Finance through Fiction: *Cecilia* and the Perils of Credit." *Finance and Society* 1, no. 1 (2015): 61–74.

Goodman, Nelson. *Ways of Worldmaking.* Indianapolis, IN: Hackett Publishing, 1978.

Gore, Charles. "The Rise and the Fall of the Washington Consensus as a Paradigm for Developing Countries." *World Development* 28, no. 5 (2000): 789–804.

Goux, Jean-Joseph. *Symbolic Economies: After Marx and Freud.* Translated by Jennifer Curtiss Gage. Ithaca, NY: Cornell University Press, 1990.

Gram, Harvey. "Ideology and Time: Criticisms of General Equilibrium." In *Joan Robinson and Modern Economic Theory*, edited by George Feiwel, 285–302. Basingstoke: Macmillan Press, 1989.

Grant, James. "The Confidence Game." *Wall Street Journal*, October 18, 2008.

Griffith, David, dir. *A Corner in Wheat.* 1909.

Grunberg, Isabelle. "Exploring the 'Myth' of Hegemonic Stability." *International Organization* 44, no. 4 (1990): 431–77.

Guillory, John. "Genesis of the Media Concept." *Critical Inquiry* 36, no. 2 (2010): 321–62.

Gysin, Christian. "Bank Intern, 21, Who Died after Working 'Eight All-Nighters in Just Two Weeks' Had Modeled Himself on Ruthless Trader Gordon Gekko in Film Wall Street." *Daily Mail Online*, August 21, 2013. http://www.dailymail. co.uk/news/article-2399336/Moritz-Erhardt-death-bank-intern-modelled-Gordon-Gekko-film-Wall-Street.html.

Habermas, Jürgen. *The Structural Transformation of the Public Sphere: An Inquiry into a Category of Bourgeois Society*. Translated by Thomas Burger. Cambridge, MA: MIT Press, 1989.

Haggard, Stephan, and Andrew MacIntyre. "The Political Economy of the Asian Economic Crisis." *Review of International Political Economy* 5, no. 3 (1998): 381–92.

Hall, Rodney Bruce. "The Discursive Demolition of the Asian Development Model." *International Studies Quarterly* 47, no. 1 (2003): 71–99.

Hansen, Alvin. *Fiscal Policy and Business Cycles*. New York: Norton, 1941.

Hartley, James. *The Representative Agent in Macroeconomics*. London: Routledge, 2002.

Hartley, James, Kevin Hoover, and Kevin Salyer, eds. *Real Business Cycles: A Reader*. London: Routledge, 1998.

Harvey, David. *The Limits to Capital*. London: Verso, 1982.

Hay, Colin. "Narrating Crisis: The Discursive Construction of the Winter of Discontent." *Sociology* 30, no. 2 (1996): 253–77.

———. "Crisis and the Structural Transformation of the State: Interrogating the Process of Change." *British Journal of Politics and International Relations* 1, no. 3 (1999): 317–44.

Hayami, Yujiro. "From the Washington Consensus to the Post-Washington Consensus: Retrospect and Prospect." *Asian Development Review* 20, no. 2 (2003): 47–54.

Hayat, Usman. "Top 20 Films about Finance: From Crisis to Con Men." *CFA Institute Enterprising Investor* (blog), September 20, 2013. http://blogs.cfainstitute. org/investor/2013/09/20/20-finance-films-for-entertainment-and-education/.

Hayek, Friedrich von. *Prices and Production*. London: Routledge and Kegan Paul, 1931.

———. *The Constitution of Liberty*. Chicago: University of Chicago Press, 1960.

———. *Law, Legislation and Liberty*, vol. 2: *The Mirage of Social Justice*. Chicago: University of Chicago Press, 1976.

———. *Law, Legislation and Liberty*, vol. 3: *Political Order of a Free People*. Chicago: University of Chicago Press, 1979.

Hayes, Adam, and Paolo Tasca. "Blockchain and Crypto Currencies." In *The FinTech Book: The Financial Technology Handbook for Investors, Entrepreneurs and Visionaries*, edited by Susanne Chishti and Janos Barberis, 217–20. Chichester: Wiley, 2016.

"Heard on the Street: Financial Analysis and Commentary." *Wall Street Journal*, October 9, 2008.

Hegel, Georg Wilhelm Friedrich. *The Philosophy of History*. Translated by John Sibree. New York: Dover, 1956.

Heidegger, Martin. *Being and Time*. Translated by John Macquarrie and Edward Robinson. Oxford: Basil Blackwell, 1987.

———. *The Concept of Time: The First Draft of Being and Time*. Translated by Ingo Farin. London: Continuum, 2011.

Helleiner, Eric. "What Role for the New Financial Stability Board? The Politics of International Standards after the Crisis." *Global Policy* 1, no. 3 (2010): 282–90.

Henninger, Daniel. "Is This the End of Capitalism?" *Wall Street Journal*, April 2, 2009.

Henry Ford Organization. "Model T Advertising." Accessed November 24, 2015. https://www.thehenryford.org/exhibits/showroom/1908/ads.html.

Herman, Edward, and Noam Chomsky. *Manufacturing Consent: The Political Economy of the Mass Media*. New York: Pantheon Books, 1988.

Hermann, Joshi. "The Wolf of Wall Street: Why London's Bankers Love Real-Life Fraudster Jordan Belfort." *Evening Standard*, January 16, 2014. http://www.standard.co.uk/lifestyle/london-life/the-wolf-of-wall-street-why-londons-bankers-love-real-life-fraudster-jordan-belfort-9064038.html/.

Hicks, John. "Mr. Keynes and the 'Classics': A Suggested Interpretation." *Econometrica* 5, no. 2 (1937): 147–59.

———. "Some Questions of Time in Economics." In *Evolution, Welfare, and Time in Economics: Essays in Honor of Nicholas Georgescu-Roegen*, edited by Andrew Tang, Fred Westfield, and James Worley, 135–51. Lexington, MA: Lexington Books, 1976.

Hill, Mike, and Warren Montag. *The Other Adam Smith*. Stanford, CA: Stanford University Press, 2015.

Hodge, David, and Hamed Yousefi. eds. "Forum. Paranoid Subjectivity and the Challenges of Cognitive Mapping—How Is Capitalism to Be Represented?" *e-flux conversations* (March/April 2015). http://conversations.e-flux.com/t/paranoid-subjectivity-and-the-challenges-of-cognitive-mapping-how-is-capitalism-to-be-represented/1080.

Hofstadter, Douglas. *I Am a Strange Loop*. New York: Basic Books, 2007.

Holland, Eugene. "Non-Linear Historical Materialism: Or, What Is Revolutionary in Deleuze and Guattari's Philosophy of History?" In *Time and History in Deleuze and Serres*, edited by Bernd Herzogenrath, 17–30. London: Continuum, 2012.

Holmes, Brian. "Phantasmagoric Systems: On Konrad Becker's *Strategic Reality Dictionary*." In *Strategic Reality Dictionary: Deep Infopolitics and Cultural Intelligence*, edited by Konrad Becker, 9–13. Brooklyn: Autonomedia, 2009.

Holmes, Douglas. *Economy of Words: Communicative Imperatives in Central Banks*. Chicago: University of Chicago Press, 2013.

Howe, Neil. "Where Did Steve Bannon Get His Worldview? From My Book." *Washington Post*, February 24, 2017. https://www.washingtonpost.com/entertainment/books/where-did-steve-bannon-get-his-worldview-from-my-book/2017/02/24/16937f38-f84a-11e6-9845-576c69081518_story.html?utm_term=.b60951c8d9b8.

Hughes-Hallett, Lucy. *The Pike: Gabriele D'Annunzio—Poet, Seducer and Preacher of War*. London: Fourth Estate, 2013.

Hughes-Warrington, Marnie. *Fifty Key Thinkers on History*, 2nd ed. London: Routledge, 2008.

Huizinga, Johan. "A Definition of the Concept of History." In *Philosophy and History: Essays Presented to Ernst Cassirer*, edited by Ernst Cassirer, Raymond Klibansky, and H. J. Paton, 1–10. New York: Harper and Row, 1963.

Hutcheon, Linda. *A Poetics of Postmodernism: History, Theory, Fiction*. London: Routledge, 1988.

Iggers, George, Q. Edward Wang, and Supriya Mukherjee. *A Global History of Historiography*. Harlow: Pearson Longman, 2008.

International Monetary Fund. *World Economic Outlook, April 2009: Crisis and Recovery*. Washington, DC: IMF, 2009.

Jacobs, Mark. "Financial Crises as Symbols and Rituals." In *The Oxford Handbook of the Sociology of Finance*, edited by Karin Knorr Cetina and Alex Preda, 376–92. Oxford: Oxford University Press, 2012.

James, Harold. *The Creation and Destruction of Value: The Globalization Cycle*. Cambridge, MA: Harvard University Press, 2009.

Jameson, Fredric. "Cognitive Mapping." In *Marxism and the Interpretation of Culture*, edited by Cary Nelson and Lawrence Grossberg, 347–57. Chicago: University of Illinois Press, 1988.

———. *The Cultural Turn: Selected Writings on the Postmodern, 1983–1998*. London: Verso, 1998.

———. *The Political Unconscious: Narrative as a Socially Symbolic Act*. London: Routledge, 2002.

———. "Future City." *New Left Review* 21 (May–June 2003): 65–79.

———. *Archaeologies of the Future: The Desire Called Utopia and Other Science Fictions*. London: Verso, 2005.

———. *Representing Capital: A Reading of Volume One*. London: Verso, 2011.

Jarecki, Nicholas, dir. *Arbitrage*. 2012.

Jenkins, Keith, ed. *The Postmodern History Reader*. London: Routledge, 1997.

Jessop, Bob. "Critical Semiotic Analysis and Cultural Political Economy." *Critical Discourse Studies* 1, no. 2 (2004): 159–74.

———. "The Knowledge-Based Economy." *Naked Punch Review* 10 (2008): 82–89.

———. "Crisis Construal in the North Atlantic Financial Crisis and the Eurozone Crisis." *Competition and Change* 19, no. 2 (2015): 95–112.

———. "The Symptomatology of Crises, Reading Crises and Learning from Them: Some Critical Realist Reflections." *Journal of Critical Realism* 14, no. 3 (2015): 238–71.

Jessop, Bob, and Ngai-Ling Sum. "Towards a Cultural International Political Economy: Poststructuralism and the Italian School." In *International Political Economy and Poststructural Politics*, edited by Marieke de Goede, 157–76. Basingstoke: Palgrave, 2006.

Jevons, William Stanley. "Commercial Crises and Sun-Spots." *Nature* 19, no. 472 (1878): 33–37.

Johnson, Paul. "Let Economies Cure Themselves." *Forbes Magazine*, September 1, 2008.

Johnston, Adrian. *Badiou, Žižek, and Political Transformations: The Cadence of Change.* Evanston, IL: Northwestern University Press, 2009.

Kansteiner, Wolf. "Finding Meaning in Memory: A Methodological Critique of Collective Memory Studies." *History and Theory* 41, no. 2 (2002): 179–197.

Kelley, Donald. "History and the Life Sciences in the Early Nineteenth Century: Wilhelm von Humboldt and Leopold von Ranke." In *Leopold von Ranke and the Shaping of the Historical Discipline*, edited by George Iggers and James Powell, 21–35. Syracuse, NY: Syracuse University Press, 1990.

Kellner, Hans. "Narrativity in History: Post-Structuralism and Since." *History and Theory* 26, no. 4 (1987): 1–29.

Keohane, Robert. *After Hegemony: Cooperation and Discord in the World Political Economy.* Princeton, NJ: Princeton University Press, 1984.

Keynes, John Maynard. *The General Theory of Employment, Interest and Money.* London: Macmillan, 1936.

———. "The General Theory of Employment." *Quarterly Journal of Economics* 51, no. 2 (1937): 209–23.

———. *Collected Writings*, vol. 3. New York: St. Martin's Press, 1973.

Khalaf, Roula. "Steaks, Stocks—What's the Difference?" *Forbes Magazine*, October 14, 1991.

Kindleberger, Charles. *The World in Depression, 1929–1939.* London: Allen Lane, 1973.

———. *Manias, Panics and Crashes.* London: Macmillan, 1978.

Kinkle, Jeff, and Alberto Toscano. "Filming the Crisis: A Survey." *Film Quarterly* 65, no. 1 (2011): 39–51.

Klein, Kerwin Lee. "On the Emergence of Memory in Historical Discourse." *Representations* 69 (Winter 2000): 127–50.

———. *From History to Theory.* Berkeley: University of California Press, 2011.

Kliman, Andrew. *The Failure of Capitalist Production: Underlying Causes of the Great Recession.* London: Pluto, 2012.

Knafo, Samuel. "The State and the Rise of Speculative Finance in England." *Economy and Society* 37, no. 2 (2008): 172–92.

———. "Liberalisation and Political Economy of Financial Bubbles." *Competition and Change* 13, no. 2 (2009): 128–44.

Knight, Frank. *Risk, Uncertainty, and Profit.* Chicago: University of Chicago Press, 1921.

Knorr Cetina, Karin, and Urs Bruegger. "Global Microstructures: The Virtual Societies of Financial Markets." *American Journal of Sociology* 107, no. 4 (2002): 905–50.

Konings, Martijn. *The Development of American Finance.* Cambridge: Cambridge University Press, 2011.

———. *The Emotional Logic of Capitalism: What Progressives Have Missed.* Stanford, CA: Stanford University Press, 2015.

———. *Capital and Time: For a New Critique of Neoliberal Reason*. Stanford, CA: Stanford University Press, 2018.

Koselleck, Reinhart. *Critique and Crisis: Enlightenment and the Pathogenesis of Modern Society*. Oxford: Berg, 1988.

———. "Some Questions Regarding the Conceptual History of Crisis." In *The Practice of Conceptual History: Timing History, Spacing Concepts*, translated by Todd Presner, 236–47. Stanford, CA: Stanford University Press, 2002.

———. "Crisis." *Journal of the History of Ideas* 67, no. 2 (2006): 357–400.

Krasner, Stephen. "State Power and the Structure of International Trade." *World Politics* 28, no. 3 (1976): 317–47.

Krippner, Greta. "The Financialization of the American Economy." *Socio-Economic Review* 3, no. 2 (2005): 173–208.

———. *Capitalizing on Crisis: The Political Origins of the Rise of Finance*. Cambridge, MA: Harvard University Press, 2012.

Kroker, Arthur. *Exits to the Posthuman Future*. Cambridge: Polity Press, 2014.

Kroszner, Randall. "Analyzing and Assessing Banking Crises." San Francisco, September 6, 2007. http://www.federalreserve.gov/newsevents/speech/kroszner20070906a.htm.

Krugman, Paul. *The Return of Depression Economics and the Crisis of 2008*. New York: Norton, 2009.

La Berge, Leigh Clare. "Capitalist Realism and Serial Form: The Fifth Season of *The Wire*." *Criticism* 52, nos. 3–4 (2010): 547–67.

LaCapra, Dominick. *Writing History, Writing Trauma*. Baltimore, MD: Johns Hopkins University Press, 2001.

Lampert, Jay. *Deleuze and Guattari's Philosophy of History*. London: Continuum, 2006.

Langenohl, Andreas. "'In the Long Run We Are All Dead': Imaginary Time in Financial Market Narratives." *Cultural Critique* 70 (Fall 2008): 3–31.

Lapavitsas, Costas. *Profiting without Producing: How Finance Exploits Us All*. London: Verso, 2014.

Lawless, Kate. "Unrecyclable Times: The Traumatic Topographies of Global Capitalism in W. G. Sebald's *Austerlitz*." *Word Hoard* 1, no. 2 (2013): 94–108.

Lee, Benjamin, and Edward LiPuma. *Financial Derivatives and the Globalization of Risks*. Durham, NC: Duke University Press, 2004.

Lévi-Strauss, Claude. *The Savage Mind*. Chicago: University of Chicago Press, 1966.

Leyshon, Andrew, and Nigel Thrift. "The Capitalization of Almost Everything: The Future of Finance and Capitalism." *Theory, Culture and Society* 24, nos. 7–8 (2007): 97–115.

L'Herbier, Marcel, dir. *L'Argent*. 1928.

Lim, Dennis. "The World behind the Tinted Window." *New York Times*, August 3, 2012. http://www.nytimes.com/2012/08/05/movies/cosmopolis-cronenbergs-take-on-don-delillo.html?_r=0/.

Lipietz, Alain. *Mirages and Miracles: The Crisis in Global Fordism*. Translated by David Macey. London: Verso, 1987.

————. "From Althusserianism to Regulation Theory." In *The Althusserian Legacy*, edited by E. Ann Kaplan and Michael Sprinker, 99–138. London: Verso, 1993.

Lipsky, John. "Crisis Lessons for the IMF." New York, December 17, 2008. http://www.imf.org/external/np/speeches/2008/121708.htm.

Livingston, James. "Their Great Depression and Ours." In *The Great Credit Crash*, edited by Martijn Konings, 31–46. London: Verso, 2010.

Lowery, Clay. "Remarks at the Annual Conference of the Institute of International Bankers." New York, March 3, 2008. http://www.treasury.gov/press-center/press-releases/Pages/hp855.aspx.

Lucarelli, Bill. *The Economics of Financial Turbulence: Alternative Theories of Money and Finance*. Cheltenham: Edward Elgar, 2011.

Lucas, Robert. "An Equilibrium Model of the Business Cycle." *Journal of Political Economy* 83, no. 6 (1975): 1113–44.

————. *Studies in Business-Cycle Theory*. Cambridge, MA: MIT Press, 1983.

Lukács, György. *History and Class Consciousness: Studies in Marxist Dialectics*. Translated by Rodney Livingston. London: Merlin Press, 1971.

Lundy, Craig. *History and Becoming: Deleuze's Philosophy of Creativity*. Edinburgh: Edinburgh University Press, 2012.

Luxemburg, Rosa. *The Accumulation of Capital*. Translated by Agnes Schwarzschild. London: Routledge, 2003.

MacKenzie, Donald. *An Engine, Not a Camera: How Financial Models Shape Markets*. Cambridge, MA: MIT Press, 2006.

————. "Mechanizing the Merc: The Chicago Mercantile Exchange and the Rise of High-Frequency Trading." *Technology and Culture* 56, no. 3 (2015): 646–75.

Maillet, Arnaud. *The Claude Glass: Use and Meaning of the Black Mirror in Western Art*. New York: Zone Books, 2004.

Makreel, Rudolf. *Dilthey: Philosopher of the Human Studies*. Princeton, NJ: Princeton University Press, 1992.

Malpass, David. "Recession, Taxes and Moral Hazard," *Forbes Magazine*, April 16, 2007.

————. "Credit Crisis Hits Home." *Forbes Magazine*, April 21, 2008.

————. "Curbing Washington's Growing Power." *Forbes Magazine*, November 10, 2008.

Mandel, Ernest. *Late Capitalism*. Translated by Joris De Bres. London: Verso, 1998.

Martin, James. "The Theory of Storms: Jacob Burckhardt and the Concept of Historical Crisis." *Journal of European Studies* 40, no. 4 (2010): 307–27.

Marx, Karl. *A Contribution to the Critique of Political Economy*. New York: International Publishers, 1970.

————. *Grundrisse: Foundations of the Critique of Political Economy*. Translated by Martin Nicolaus. Harmondsworth: Penguin Pelican, 1973.

————. *Capital: A Critique of Political Economy*, vol. 3. Moscow: Progress Publishers, 1977.

Marx, Karl, and Friedrich Engels. *The Communist Manifesto: A Modern Edition*. Translated by Samuel Moore. London: Verso, 1998.

Mason, Paul. *Postcapitalism: A Guide to Our Future*. London: Allen Lane, 2015.

Massumi, Brian. *The Power at the End of the Economy*. Durham, NC: Duke University Press, 2014.

Mattick, Paul. *Economics, Politics, and the Age of Inflation*. London: Merlin Press, 1980.

———. *Economic Crisis and Crisis Theory*. London: Merlin Press, 1981.

McCormick, David. "Remarks at the Peter G. Peterson Institute for International Economics Conference on IMF Reform." Washington, DC, February 25, 2008. http://www.treasury.gov/press-center/press-releases/Pages/hp838.aspx.

———. "The International Response to Financial Market Turmoil." Chicago, April 16, 2008. http://www.treasury.gov/press-center/press-releases/Pages/hp931.aspx.

McKay, Adam, dir. *The Other Guys*. 2010.

Mink, Louis. "Philosophical Analysis and Historical Understanding." *Review of Metaphysics* 21, no. 4 (1968): 667–98.

———. "Narrative Form as Cognitive Instrument." In *The Writing of History: Literary Form and Historical Understanding*, edited by Robert Canary and Henry Kozicki, 129–49. Madison: University of Wisconsin Press, 1978.

Minsky, Hyman. *Can "It" Happen Again? Essays on Instability and Finance*. New York: M. E. Sharpe, 1982.

———. *Stabilizing an Unstable Economy*. New York: McGraw-Hill, 1986.

———. "Secrets of the Temple: How the Federal Reserve Runs the Country." *Challenge* 31, no. 3 (1988): 58–62.

Mirowski, Philip. *More Heat Than Light: Economics as Social Physics, Physics as Nature's Economics*. Cambridge: Cambridge University Press, 1992.

Mishkin, Frederic. "Systemic Risk and the International Lender of Last Resort." Speech at the Tenth Annual International Banking Conference, Federal Reserve Bank of Chicago, Chicago, September 28, 2007. http://www.federalreserve.gov/newsevents/speech/mishkin20070928a.htm.

———. "Global Financial Turmoil and the World Economy." Speech at the Caesarea Forum of the Israel Democracy Institute, Eliat, July 2, 2008. http://www.federalreserve.gov/newsevents/speech/mishkin20080702a.htm.

Mitchener, Kris James, and Joseph Mason. "Blood and Treasure: Exiting the Great Depression and Lessons for Today." *Oxford Review of Economic Policy* 26, no. 3 (2010): 510–39.

Mumford, Lewis. *The Myth of the Machine*, vol. 2: *The Pentagon of Power*. New York: Harcourt Brace Jovanovich, 1970.

Nesvetailova, Anastasia. *Financial Alchemy in Crisis: The Great Liquidity Illusion*. London: Pluto Press, 2010.

Nietzsche, Friedrich. "Letter to Jakob Burckhardt, January 5, 1889." In *Selected Letters of Friedrich Nietzsche*, edited by Christopher Middleton, 347. Chicago: University of Chicago Press, 1969.

———. "On the Uses and Disadvantages of History for Life." In *Friedrich Nietzsche:*

Untimely Meditations, edited by Daniel Breazeale, 57–124. Cambridge: Cambridge University Press, 1997.

Nitzan, Jonathan, and Shimshon Bichler. *Capital as Power: A Study of Order and Creorder*. London: Routledge, 2009.

Noble, Gregory, and John Ravenhill, eds. *The Asian Financial Crisis and the Architecture of Global Finance*. Cambridge: Cambridge University Press, 2000.

Norman, Andrew. "Telling It Like It Was: Historical Narratives on Their Own Terms." *History and Theory* 30, no. 2 (1991): 119–35.

Norris, Frank. *The Pit: A Story of Chicago*. London: Penguin, 1994.

Novick, Peter. *That Noble Dream: The "Objectivity Question" and the American Historical Profession*. Cambridge: Cambridge University Press, 1988.

Nsouli, Saleh. "Lessons from the Recent Financial Crisis and the Role of the Fund." Paris, June 26, 2008. http://www.imf.org/external/np/speeches/2008/062608.htm.

Oakeshott, Michael. *On History and Other Essays*. Indianapolis, IN: Liberty Fund, 1999.

Oatley, Thomas. *A Political Economy of American Hegemony: Buildups, Booms, and Busts*. Cambridge: Cambridge University Press, 2015.

O'Connor, James. *The Meaning of Crisis: A Theoretical Introduction*. Oxford: Basil Blackwell, 1987.

Olick, Jeffrey. "Collective Memory: A Memoir and Prospect." *Memory Studies* 1, no. 1 (2008): 23–29.

Olick, Jeffrey, and Joyce Robbins. "Social Memory Studies: From 'Collective Memory' to the Historical Sociology of Mnemonic Practices." *Annual Review of Sociology* 24, no.1 (1998): 105–40.

Osborne, Peter. *The Politics of Time: Modernity and Avant-Garde*. London: Verso, 1995.

Osteen, Mark. "The Currency of DeLillo's *Cosmopolis*." *Critique: Studies in Contemporary Fiction* 55, no. 3 (2014): 291–304.

Overbeek, Henk. "Transnational Class Formation and Concepts of Control: Towards a Genealogy of the Amsterdam Project in International Political Economy." *Journal of International Relations and Development* 7, no. 2 (2004): 113–41.

Palan, Ronen. *The Offshore World: Sovereign Markets, Virtual Places and Nomad Millionaires*. Ithaca, NY: Cornell University Press, 2003.

———. "Is the Competition State the New, Post-Fordist, Mode of Regulation? Regulation Theory from an International Political Economic Perspective." *Competition and Change* 10, no. 2 (2006): 246–62.

———. "Transnational Theories of Order and Change: Heterodoxy in International Relations Scholarship." *Review of International Studies* 33, no. 1 (2007): 47–69.

Peel, Quentin. "Europe Writes a History of Crisis Management." *Financial Times*, October 9, 2008.

Perlberg, Steven. "We Saw 'Wolf of Wall Street' with a Bunch of Wall Street Dudes and It Was Disturbing." *Business Insider*, December 19, 2013. http://www.businessinsider.com/banker-pros-cheer-wolf-of-wall-street-2013–12?IR=T/.

Pocock, J. G. A. "The History of Political Thought: A Methodological Enquiry." In *Philosophy, Politics and Society*, edited by Peter Laslett and W. G. Runciman, 183–202. Oxford: Blackwell, 1962.

———. *The Machiavellian Moment: Florentine Political Thought and the Atlantic Republican Tradition*. Princeton, NJ: Princeton University Press, 1975.

Polanyi, Karl. *The Great Transformation: The Political and Economic Origins of Our Time*. Boston: Beacon Press, 2001.

Poovey, Mary. *Genres of the Credit Economy: Mediating Value in Eighteenth- and Nineteenth-Century Britain*. Chicago: University of Chicago Press, 2008.

Posner, Richard. *A Failure of Capitalism: The Crisis of '08 and the Descent into Depression*. Cambridge, MA: Harvard University Press, 2009.

Qlipoth. "Easier to Imagine the End of the World . . . " *Qlipoth* (blog). November 11, 2009. http://qlipoth.blogspot.com/2009/11/easier-to-imagine-end-of-world.html.

Ranke, Leopold von. "Preface to the First Edition of *Histories of the Latin and German Nations* (1824)." In *The Modern Historiography Reader: Western Sources*, edited by Adam Budd, 172–73. London: Routledge, 2009.

Rato, Rodrigo de. "Ten Years after the Asian Currency Crisis." Tokyo, January 22, 2007. http://www.imf.org/external/np/speeches/2007/012207.htm.

———. "Confronting the Future with Wisdom and Courage." Washington, DC, July 19, 2007. http://www.imf.org/external/np/speeches/2007/071907.htm.

Reinhart, Carmen, and Kenneth Rogoff. *This Time Is Different: Eight Centuries of Financial Folly*. Princeton, NJ: Princeton University Press, 2009.

Ricardo, David. *On the Principles of Political Economy and Taxation*. London: J. M. Dent, 1969.

Ricoeur, Paul. "History and Hermeneutics." *Journal of Philosophy* 73, no. 19 (1976): 683–95.

———. "Narrative Time." *Critical Inquiry* 7, no. 1 (1980): 169–90.

———. "The Narrative Function." In *Hermeneutics and the Human Sciences: Essays on Language, Action and Interpretation*, edited by John Thompson, 274–96. Cambridge: Cambridge University Press, 1981.

———. *Time and Narrative*, vol. 1. Translated by Kathleen McLaughlin and David Pellauer. Chicago: University of Chicago Press, 1984.

———. *Memory, History, Forgetting*. Translated by Kathleen Blamey and David Pellauer. Chicago: University of Chicago Press, 2004.

Rilke, Rainer Maria. *The Notebooks of Malte Laurids Brigge*. Translated by Burton Pike. London: Dalkey Archive Press, 2008.

Roberts, Geoffrey, ed. *The History and Narrative Reader*. London: Routledge, 2001.

Robinson, Joan. "What Are the Questions?" *Journal of Economic Literature* 15, no. 4 (1977): 1318–39.

———. *Collected Economic Papers*, vol. 2. Oxford: Basil Blackwell, 1979.

———. "Time in Economic Theory." *Kyklos* 33, no. 2 (1980): 219–29.

Roche, David. "Recession Is Inevitable." *Wall Street Journal*, March 14, 2008.

Roitman, Janet. *Anti-Crisis*. Durham, NC: Duke University Press, 2014.

Rosenfeld, Gavriel. "A Looming Crash or a Soft Landing? Forecasting the Future of the Memory Industry." *Journal of Modern History* 81, no. 1 (2009): 122–58.

Rothberg, Michael. *Traumatic Realism: The Demands of Holocaust Representation*. Minneapolis: University of Minnesota Press, 2000.

Ruggie, John Gerard. "International Regimes, Transactions, and Change: Embedded Liberalism in the Postwar Economic Order." *International Organization* 36, no. 2 (1982): 379–415.

Rushkoff, Douglas. *Throwing Rocks at the Google Bus: How Growth Became the Enemy of Prosperity*. London: Penguin, 2016.

Samman, Amin, Nathan Coombs, and Angus Cameron, "For a Post-Disciplinary Study of Finance and Society." *Finance and Society* 1, no. 1 (2015): 1–5.

Samuelson, Paul. *Economics*, 3rd ed. New York: McGraw-Hill, 1955.

Scheuermann, Christoph. "High Stakes: Making Sense of a Banking Intern's Death." *Spiegel Online*, October 11, 2013. http://www.spiegel.de/international/europe/ how-moritz-erhardt-worked-himself-to-the-top-a-927174.html.

Schonfeld, Zach. "Here Are the Absurd Instructions for Filming Donald Trump in Your Movie." *Newsweek*, October 14, 2016. http://www.newsweek.com/ here-are-absurd-instructions-putting-donald-trump-your-movie-509810.

Schumpeter, Joseph. *Business Cycles: A Theoretical, Historical, and Statistical Analysis of the Capitalist Process*. London: McGraw-Hill, 1939.

———. *Theory of Economic Development*. Brunswick, NJ: Transaction Publishers, 1980.

Schumpeter, Joseph, and Richard Clemence. *Essays on Entrepreneurs, Innovations, Business Cycles, and the Evolution of Capitalism*. Brunswick, NJ: Transaction Publishers, 1989.

Scorsese, Martin, dir. *The Wolf of Wall Street*. 2013.

Scott, Joan Wallach. "History in Crisis: The Others' Side of the Story." *American Historical Review* 94, no. 3 (1989): 680–92.

Seabrooke, Leonard. "The Everyday Social Sources of Economic Crises: From 'Great Frustrations' to 'Great Revelations' in Interwar Britain." *International Studies Quarterly* 51, no. 4 (2007): 795–810.

Secret Agent. "We Lived in Financial Times." *Financial Times*, February 10, 2012. https://www.ft.com/content/b879c584-517c-11e1-a99d-00144feabdco.

Sewell, William. "The Temporalities of Capitalism." *Socio-Economic Review* 6, no. 3 (2008): 517–37.

Sgambati, Stefano. "Rethinking Banking: Debt Discounting and the Making of Modern Money as Liquidity." *New Political Economy* 21, no. 3 (2016): 274–90.

Shackle, Gregory. *Time in Economics*. Amsterdam: North-Holland, 1958.

Shaikh, Anwar. "An Introduction to the History of Crisis Theories." In *U.S. Capitalism in Crisis*, edited by Anwar Shaikh, 219–41. New York: URPE, 1978.

———. "Political Economy and Capitalism: Notes on Dobb's Theory of Crisis." *Cambridge Journal of Economics* 2, no. 2 (1978): 233–51.

Sheppard, Eric, and Helga Leitner. "*Quo Vadis* Neoliberalism? The Remaking of

Global Capitalist Governance after the Washington Consensus." *Geoforum* 41, no. 2 (2010): 185–94.

Shilling, A. Gary. "Worse Is Yet to Come." *Forbes Magazine*, September 29, 2008.

Shlaes, Amity. "Ugly View from Below." *Forbes Magazine*, March 30, 2009.

———. "The New PC." *Forbes Magazine*, September 3, 2009.

Shonkwiler, Alison. "Don DeLillo's Financial Sublime." *Contemporary Literature* 51, no. 2 (2010): 246–82.

Siles-Brügge, Gabriel. "Explaining the Resilience of Free Trade: The 'Smoot-Hawley' Myth and the Crisis." *Review of International Political Economy* 21, no. 3 (2014): 535–74.

Skidelsky, Robert. *Keynes: The Return of the Master*. London: Allen Lane, 2009.

Skinner, Quentin. "Meaning and Understanding in the History of Ideas." *History and Theory* 8, no. 1 (1969): 3–53.

———. *The Foundations of Modern Political Thought*, vols. 1–3. Cambridge: Cambridge University Press, 1978.

Smaghi, Lorenzo. "From Tuscany's 19th Century Currency, the Fiorino, to the Euro." Florence, May 15, 2008. http://www.ecb.int/press/key/date/2008/html/sp080515_2.en.html.

———. "The Financial Crisis and Global Imbalances." Beijing, December 9, 2008. http://www.ecb.int/press/key/date/2008/html/sp081209.en.html.

———. "The Euro Area's Exchange Rate Policy and the Experience with International Monetary Coordination during the Crisis." Brussels, April 6, 2009. http://www.ecb.int/press/key/date/2009/html/sp090406.en.html.

Smith, Adam. *The Wealth of Nations*. Chicago: University of Chicago Press, 1976.

———. *The Theory of Moral Sentiments*. Indianapolis, IN: Liberty Fund, 1979.

Sobel, Mark. "Remarks on the Global Financial Crisis and the IMF's Response." US Treasury press release, December 2, 2008. http://www.treasury.gov/press-center/press-releases/Pages/hp1307.aspx.

Srinivasan, S. "Greed Is Back on Wall Street." *Forbes Magazine India*, October 4, 2010.

Srnicek, Nick, and Alex Williams. *Inventing the Future: Postcapitalism and a World without Work*. London: Verso, 2015.

Standing, Guy. *Basic Income: And How We Can Make It Happen*. London: Pelican, 2017.

Stark, Jürgen. "EMU: Weathering the Perfect Storm." London, June 25, 2009. http://www.ecb.int/press/key/date/2009/html/sp090625.en.html.

Starn, Randolph. "Historians and Crisis." *Past and Present* 52, no. 1 (1971): 3–22.

Stewart, James. "Retiree Hell Isn't as Bad As You Might Think It Is." *Wall Street Journal*, January 28, 2009.

———. "The Year of Investing Cautiously." *Wall Street Journal*, September 9, 2009.

Stockhammer, Engelbert. "Financialisation and the Slowdown of Accumulation." *Cambridge Journal of Economics* 28, no. 5 (2004): 719–41.

Stone, Oliver, dir. *Wall Street*. 1987.

Stone, Oliver, dir. *Wall Street: Money Never Sleeps*. 2010.

Strange, Susan. *Mad Money: When Markets Outgrow Governments*. Ann Arbor: University of Michigan Press, 1998.

Strauss, William, and Neil Howe. *The Fourth Turning: An American Prophecy—What the Cycles of History Tell Us about America's Next Rendezvous with Destiny*. New York: Broadway Books, 1997.

Strauss-Kahn, Dominique. "Remarks to the Board of Governors of the IMF." Washington, DC, October 13, 2008. http://www.imf.org/external/np/speeches/2008/101308.htm.

———. "Speech Delivered at the 44th SEACEN Governors' Conference." Kuala Lumpur, February 7, 2009. http://www.imf.org/external/np/speeches/2009/020709.htm.

———. "Multilateralism and the Role of the International Monetary Fund in the Global Financial Crisis." Washington, DC, April 23, 2009. http://www.imf.org/external/np/speeches/2009/042309.htm.

———. "Economic Stability, Economic Cooperation, and Peace." Oslo, October 23, 2009. http://www.imf.org/external/np/speeches/2009/102309.htm.

Sum, Ngai-Ling, and Bob Jessop. *Towards a Cultural Political Economy: Putting Culture in its Place in Political Economy*. Cheltenham: Edward Elgar, 2013.

Tarullo, Daniel. "International Cooperation to Modernize Financial Regulation." Washington, DC, September 30, 2009. http://www.federalreserve.gov/newsevents/testimony/tarullo20090930a.htm.

Taylor, Astra, dir. *Žižek!* 2005.

Taylor, Mark. *Confidence Games: Money and Markets in a World without Redemption*. Chicago: University of Chicago Press, 2008.

Temin, Peter. "The Great Recession and the Great Depression." *Daedalus* 139, no. 4 (2010): 115–24.

Tett, Gillian. "Wall Street's Crash Course." *Financial Times*, August 26, 2007. https://www.ft.com/content/f54fd878-5400-11dc-9a6e-0000779fd2ac.

Toporowski, Jan. *The End of Finance: Capital Market Inflation, Financial Derivatives and Pension Fund Capitalism*. London: Routledge, 2000.

———. *Theories of Financial Disturbance: An Examination of Critical Theories of Finance from Adam Smith to the Present Day*. Cheltenham: Edward Elgar, 2005.

Toscano, Alberto. "Seeing It Whole: Staging Totality in Social Theory and Art." *Sociological Review* 60, S1 (2012): 64–83.

Toscano, Alberto, and Jeff Kinkle. *Cartographies of the Absolute*. Winchester, UK: Zero Books, 2015.

Trachtenberg, Marc. "Keynes Triumphant: A Study in the Social History of Economic Ideas." *Knowledge and Society* 4 (1983): 17–86.

Trichet, Jean-Claude. "Reflections on the International Financial Architecture." Salzburg, September 29, 2007. http://www.ecb.int/press/key/date/2007/html/sp070929.en.html.

———. "Reflections on the Global Financial System." Washington, DC, October 20, 2007. http://www.ecb.int/press/key/date/2007/html/sp071020.en.html.

———. "Remarks on the Recent Turbulences in Global Financial Markets." New York, April 14, 2008. http://www.ecb.int/press/key/date/2008/html/sp080414_1.en.html.

———. "Lessons from the Financial Crisis." Frankfurt, October 15, 2009. http://www.ecb.int/press/key/date/2009/html/sp091015.en.html.

Turk, Michael. "The Arrow of Time in Economics: From Robinson's Critique to the New Historical Economics." *European Journal of the History of Economic Thought* 17, no. 3 (2010): 471–92.

US Federal Bureau of Investigation. "Financial Fraud Public Service Announcement." Video. Originally released on February 27, 2012. Accessed July 11, 2018. https://www.fbi.gov/video-repository/newss-financial-fraud-public-service-announcement/view.

Valéry, Paul. *Reflections on the World Today*. Translated by Francis Scarfe. London: Thames and Hudson, 1951.

Vardi, Liana. *The Physiocrats and the World of the Enlightenment*. Cambridge: Cambridge University Press, 2012.

Veblen, Thorstein. "Why Is Economics Not an Evolutionary Science?" *Quarterly Journal of Economics* 12, no. 4 (1898): 373–97.

———. *The Place of Science in Modern Civilization and Other Essays*. New York: Huebsch, 1919.

———. *The Theory of Business Enterprise*. New Brunswick, NJ: Transaction Publishers, 1978.

Vestergaard, Jakob. *Discipline in the Global Economy? International Finance and the End of Liberalism*. London: Routledge, 2009.

Vogl, Joseph. *The Specter of Capital*. Translated by Joachim Redner and Robert Savage. Stanford, CA: Stanford University Press, 2015.

———. "The End of an Illusion." *Finance and Society* 1, no. 2 (2015): 38–41.

———. *The Ascendancy of Finance*. Translated by Simon Garnett. Cambridge: Polity Press, 2017.

Wade, Robert, and Frank Veneroso. "The Asian Crisis: The High-Debt Model vs. the Wall Street-Treasury-IMF Complex." *New Left Review* (March–April 1998): 3–23.

Walras, Léon. *Elements of Pure Economics*. Translated by William Jaffé. London: Routledge, 2003.

Warsh, Kevin. "Market Liquidity: Definitions and Implications." Washington, DC, March 5, 2007. http://www.federalreserve.gov/newsevents/speech/warsh20070305a.htm.

Widmaier, Wesley, Mark Blyth, and Leonard Seabrooke. "Exogenous Shocks or Endogenous Constructions? The Meanings of Wars and Crises." *International Studies Quarterly* 51, no. 4 (2007): 747–59.

Wigan, Duncan. "Financialisation and Derivatives: Constructing an Artifice of Indifference." *Competition and Change* 13, no. 2 (2009): 157–72.

Williams, Raymond. *Marxism and Literature*. Oxford: Oxford University Press, 1977.

White, Hayden. "The Burden of History." *History and Theory* 5, no. 2 (1966): 111–34.

———. *Metahistory: The Historical Imagination in Nineteenth-Century Europe*. Baltimore, MD: John Hopkins University Press, 1973.

———. *Tropics of Discourse: Essays in Cultural Criticism*. Baltimore, MD: John Hopkins University Press, 1978.

———. *The Content of the Form: Narrative Discourse and Historical Representation*. Baltimore, MD: Johns Hopkins University Press, 1987.

———. *Figural Realism: Studies in the Mimesis Effect*. Baltimore, MD: Johns Hopkins University Press, 1999.

———. "The Historical Event." *Differences* 19, no. 2 (2008): 9–34.

———. "The Practical Past." *Historein* 10 (2010): 10–19.

———. *The Practical Past*. Evanston, IL: Northwestern University Press, 2014.

Wolf, Martin. "A Turning Point in Managing the World's Economy." *Financial Times*, April 22, 2008.

———. "Congress Decides It's Worth Risking Depression." *Financial Times*, September 30, 2008.

———. "It's Time for Comprehensive Rescues of Financial Systems." *Financial Times*, October 7, 2008.

———. "Why Fairly Valued Stock Markets Are an Opportunity." *Financial Times*, November 25, 2008

———. "Global Imbalances Threaten the Survival of Liberal Trade." *Financial Times*, December 2, 2008.

———. "How the Noughties Were a Hinge of History." *Financial Times*, December 23, 2009.

Yang, Andrew. *The War on Normal People: The Truth about America's Disappearing Jobs and Why Universal Basic Income Is Our Future*. New York: Hachette, 2018.

Yuran, Noam. *What Money Wants: An Economy of Desire*. Stanford, CA: Stanford University Press, 2014.

Zehfuss, Maja. *Wounds of Memory: The Politics of War in Germany*. Cambridge: Cambridge University Press, 2007.

Žižek, Slavoj. "The Spectre of Ideology." In *Mapping Ideology*, edited by Slavoj Žižek, 1–33. London: Verso, 1994.

Žižek, Slavoj, and Costas Douzinas, eds. *The Idea of Communism*. London: Verso, 2010.

Zola, Émile. *Money*. Oxford: Oxford University Press, 2014.

Index

in relation to, 71; memory in relation to, 92; narrative in relation to,
51–55; nature of, 5, 10; reflexive/
nonlinear character of, 3, 5; strange
loops as elements in, ix, 5, 15,
16–18, 41–43, 46, 59, 64, 87, 90,
111, 114, 119, 120, 135–36, 142;
subjectivity associated with, 8–10;
technology in relation to, 141;
theories of, vii–ix, 2–4, 15, 17–18.
See also Production of history
Hitler, Adolf, 78
Hofstadter, Douglas, ix, 16–17
Holmes, Brian, 113
Holocaust, 61, 94–95
Homer, 52
Homo economicus, 6–9, 132, 133,
146n19
Homo historia: characteristics of, 10,
11; heuristic value of, 11–12;
homo economicus in relation to, 9;
meaning-making as feature of, 10;
and names associated with economy, 132; in relation to time, 9–10;
as subject of historical discourse,
3, 8–10
Homo politicus, 8
Hoover, Herbert, 80, 82–83
Huizinga, Johan, 44, 51

IMF. *See* International Monetary Fund
Indeterminacy, in historical devel-
opment, 37, 39–41, 88. *See also*
Uncertainty, existential
Inside Job (film), 112
Insider trading, 113
International Monetary Fund (IMF),
73, 98–105, 109
Interventionism. *See* Government
interventionism
Irrealism, 92, 117, 130, 138

James, Harold, 13, 42–43

Jameson, Fredric, 14–15, 31, 115, 140,
178n7, 179n8
Jarecki, Nicholas, *Arbitrage*, 112
Jessop, Bob, 40
Jevons, William Stanley, 30
Joan of Arc, 113, 114, 119–22
Journalism: and history, 67; on sub-
prime crisis, 72–88, 163n28. *See
also* Media

Kennedy, John F., 61
Keynes, John Maynard, 4, 32–35,
144n8, 155n68; *The General
Theory*, 34
Keynesianism, 42, 67, 99
Kinkle, Jeff, 112, 115–16
Knight, Frank, 40, 155n68
Koselleck, Reinhart, 12, 18, 21–24,
27–28, 32, 41
Kristeva, Julia, 54
Kroker, Arthur, 142

Laissez-faire, 7, 29, 99
Lampert, Jay, 119–20
Landscape painting, 68, 86
Langenohl, Andreas, 143n5
Latin America, 78
Law, crisis concept in, 23–24
Left Keynesianism, 35
Left philosophy, 59, 139
Lehman Brothers, 2, 76, 127
L. F. Rothschild, 127
L'Herbier, Marcel, *L'Argent*, 115
Liberal economics, 13, 28–32
Linear progression, 90, 94
Lipietz, Alain, 35–37
Loops, historical, vii, ix, 5–6, 10,
16–18, 41–43, 46, 59, 64, 87, 114,
120, 135–36, 142
Lukács, György, 70
Lundy, Craig, 120
Luxemburg, Rosa, 33
Lyotard, Jean-François, 14, 54, 174n27

CURRENCIES

New Thinking for Financial Times
Melinda Cooper and Martijn Konings, Series Editors

In the wake of recent events such as the global financial crisis, the Occupy Wall Street Movement, and the rise of anti–student-debt activism, the need for a more sophisticated encounter between economic theory and social and political philosophy has become pressing. The growth of new forms of money and finance, which has only accelerated since the financial crisis, is recognized as one of the defining developments of our time. But even as finance continuously breaches limits and forces adjustments, much scholarly commentary remains focused on the limits of the market and the need to establish some prior state of political stability, thus succumbing to a nostalgia that blunts its critical edge. Not content to adopt a defensive posture, books in this series move beyond well-rehearsed denunciations of out-of-control markets and seek to rethink the core institutions and categories of financialized capitalism. *Currencies* will serve as a forum for work that is situated at the intersection of economics, the humanities, and the social sciences. It will include conceptually driven historical or empirical studies, genealogies of economic ideas and institutions, and work that employs new or unexplored theoretical resources to rethink key economic categories and themes.

Thomas Biebricher, *The Political Theory of Neoliberalism*

Lisa Adkins, *The Time of Money*

Martijn Konings, *Capital and Time: For a New Critique of Neoliberal Reason*